W9-CFI-910

# Path of Heroes

# PATH OF HEROES

# Birth of Enlightenment

## VOLUME II

Zhechen Gyaltsab
Padma Gyurmed Namgyal

with the Practice Instructions and Reflections

of Tarthang Tulku

Dharma Publishing

## TIBETAN TRANSLATION SERIES

Library of Congress Cataloging-in-Publication Data
Zhe-chen rgyal-tshab padma-'gyur-med-rnam-rgyal, 1871–1926
    [Theg pa chen po'i blo sbyoṅ gi man ṅag zab don sbraṅ rtsi'i bum bzaṅ.
English]
    Path of Heroes : birth of enlightenment / by Zhechen Gyaltsab Padma Gyur-
med Namgyal : with the practice instructions and reflections of Tarthang Tulku.
        p.    cm. -- (Tibetan translation series)
    Includes bibliographical references and index.
    ISBN 0-89800-274-5 (hardcover). — ISBN 0-89800-273-7 (pbk.)
    1. Spiritual life—Buddhism    2. Spiritual life—Rñiṅ-ma-pa (Sect) 3. Rñiṅ-
ma-pa (Sect)—Doctrines. 4. Bodhicitta (Buddhism) 5. Bka'-gdams-pa
(Sect)—Doctrines. 8. Chekhawa, Geshe, 1102–1176.
Blo spyoṅ don bdun ma.    I. Title.    II. Series.
BQ7805.Z4713      1995      294.3'444—dc20          95-150      CIP

Translated from the Tibetan by Deborah Black

No part of this book, including text, art, reproductions, and illustrations, may
be copied, reproduced, published, or stored electronically, photographically, or
optically in any form without the express written consent of Dharma
Publishing, 2425 Hillside Avenue, Berkeley, CA  94704 U.S.A.

Printed by Dharma Press, Oakland, U.S.A.
Copyright © 1995 by Dharma Publishing
A Division of Dharma Mudranalaya
All Rights Reserved

9 8 7 6 5 4 3 2

*Dedicated to all seekers of the Dharma*
*May all sentient beings attain Enlightenment*

# Contents

*Homage to*
*Buddha, Dharma, and Sangha*

ཇོ་བོ་རྗེ་དཔལ་ལྡན་ཨ་ཏི་ཤ་ལ་ན་མོ།

*Dīpaṃkaraśrījñāna Atīśa*

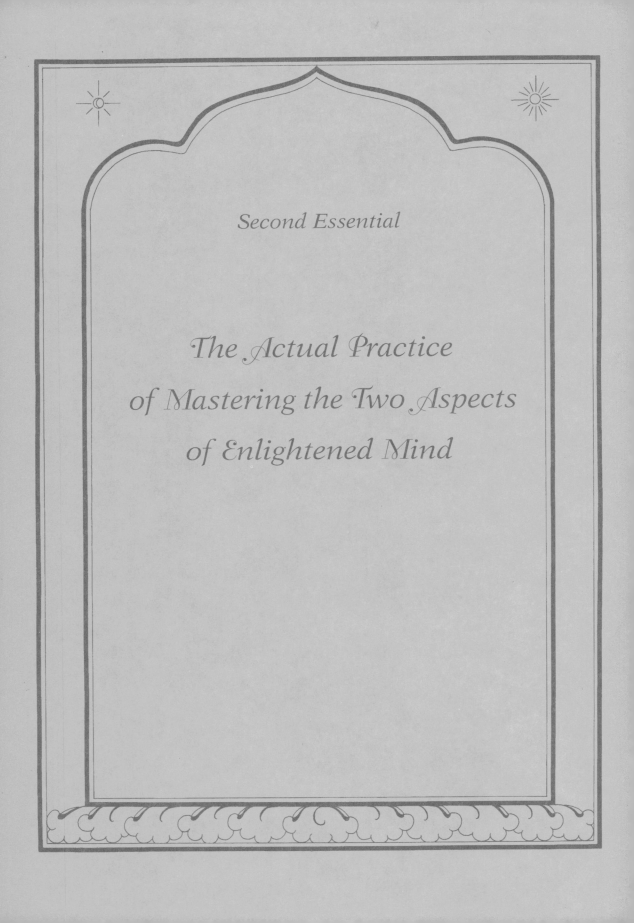

Second Essential

The Actual Practice
of Mastering the Two Aspects
of Enlightened Mind

## Practice of the Second Essential

*Consider everything to be like a dream.*

*Examine the nature of unborn awareness.*

*Let the antidote also liberate itself.*

*Rest in the stillness of the basis-of-all,*
*the ground of being.*

*Between sittings, act as a being of illusion.*

*Alternately practice unconditional giving*
*and taking on all suffering.*

*Mount them both upon the wind of the breath.*

*From three objects, the three poisons,*
*make three roots of virtue.*

*Tell yourself always: Remember only others.*

*Practice this principle in all you say or do.*

*Start the process of taking on suffering with yourself.*

# Reflections

## Enlightened Mind

*A*wakening to the nature of existence means quite simply that now is the time to act. Now is the time to conceive the inconceivable: It is possible to become a Buddha.

The path of self-mastery provides a structure for acting on this realization. Following in the footsteps of the Bodhisattva, practitioners learn to "give all gain and profit to others and take all troubles and difficulties upon yourself." At the outset, we develop understanding of the path by cultivating the spirit of inquiry and investigating our nature and the patterns that shape our lives.

As inquiry ripens into knowledge, we can extend our understanding to others, acknowledging and accepting that others experience and suffer as we do. In this way we sow the seeds for a genuine willingness to exchange our well-being and happiness for the suffering of others, confident that in so doing we prepare the way for the realization of universal enlightenment. In time, our hearts will open to the inspiration of the Enlightened Lineage of Buddhas, enabling us to fully engage the Bodhisattva's vision and vow.

This is the ideal. But our habits being what they are, we will likely tell ourselves that we will start practice soon, very soon, but first—just this cup of coffee, just this cozy afternoon reading a magazine, just

this next business deal. Perhaps the time is not right for meditation, or there is not enough time, or sitting on a pillow on the floor is too tedious or difficult. With thoughts such as these, we continue to feed illusion, supporting the self at the center of experience. The self conspires with samsara: It possesses, identifies, and manifests in innumerable guises, taking refuge in the restricted ways of knowing that samsara tolerates.

These patterns of the 'self' were the same over a thousand years ago, when Padmasambhava advised King Trisong Detsen:

If you put off practicing the Dharma, hoping
that your aspirations for future attainment are enough,
you are not a follower of the Dharma. If you put off
gaining familiarity with your own mind in expectation
of attainment in a future lifetime, you are not a follower
of the Dharma. Though you have established the root of virtue
in your actions, if you have not renounced the eight worldly
concerns, you are not a follower of the Dharma. . . .

As a weapon against the distortions of samsaric thinking, those who would follow the Path of Heroes take up practice of the six perfections or pāramitās. Practicing the perfections of giving, morality, patience, and effort, the Bodhisattva enacts a way of being that transcends the self and samsaric concerns. Practicing meditation and wisdom, the heroic being arrives at a new understanding of existence and sees for the first time that samsara is truly an illusion, having no substance whatsoever. This is the realization of śūnyatā, the radical emptiness or openness of all appearance.

Seeing the truth of śūnyatā and living this truth as an ongoing practice are essential to the path of heroes. Realizing the fundamental openness of everything enables us to break free from the crushing weight of samsara's gravitational pull and give ourselves wholly to selfless compassion. Guided by openness, embodying boundless compassion, the Bodhisattva becomes able to complete the path and fulfill the profound implications of the Bodhisattva vow.

From the moment of realizing śūnyatā, the Bodhisattva learns to take on and endure even the greatest suffering, for samsara holds no

fears. The weapon of śūnyatā cuts through all samsaric pretensions at once, freeing beings with each stroke.

When you practice compassion and develop insight into śūnyatā, the 'self' loses its hold; there are no obstacles, and you can succeed in your purpose. The ten stages of the Bodhisattva path unfold in turn, enabling you to practice with ever-increasing refinement. Even if this takes endless kalpas, the Bodhisattva never hesitates, for once compassion blossoms, the power of samsara and karma withers, and the prospect of endless kalpas of practice brings only joy. There is no enemy, no prisoner, and no need for a key to escape from bondage. The antidote itself vanishes: There is no need for conceptualization, for explanation, or for action directed at a goal. Samsara dissolves, revealing the realm of enlightenment as our true home.

# Overview:
# Enlightened Mind

*I* bow to the feet of the incomparable Lama
who views all dharmas as free from coming or going,
whose great mercy wholly embraces the world,
and whose pure activity destroys samsara's roots.

Chekhawa's root text, together with this commentary, presents the basic practices for mastering the two aspects of Bodhicitta, the enlightened mind. Bodhicitta is not only the basis of self-mastery; it is also the fundamental teaching of the Mahāyāna. Like a single vast ocean, Bodhicitta encompasses all the teaching of Sūtra and Mantra.

For those who have not yet generated the enlightened mind, I will explain ways to produce it. For those who have produced it, I will indicate the means or the path for increasing the enlightened mind and not letting it decline. For those who are practicing, I will show how to clear away obstacles to practice and ways to enhance practice. For those who are close to the culmination of practice, remember: As the practice of Bodhicitta determines the final result, Bodhicitta is the source, the root of everything.

If you have no desire to attain the highest state, to become a perfect Buddha, look elsewhere for teachings. But without adhering to

this path that goes beyond selfish desire, you will never gain any real success. As the Verse Summary of the Prajñāpāramitā states:

Without the mind of enlightenment,
the advent of a Jina in the world would be impossible.
How then could even an Indra or a Brahma
or the Śrāvaka disciples result? [5.5]

Again, we find in the Sūtra Assembling the Dharmas:

Bhagavan, perfect caring is the root of all the Dharma.
For those for whom there is no such caring, the whole
of the Buddhadharma remains far distant. Bhagavan,
when the highest caring is active, though the Buddha
may not presently be living, the Dharma continues
to speak softly from the sphere of space,
and even from walls and from trees.

Concerning the pure caring of the Bodhisattva,
all the instructions and precepts arise from self-analysis.
Therefore, I will practice this highest caring of the Bodhisattva.

Bhagavan, just as only those with feet can walk,
only those who proceed by caring attain the Buddhadharma.
Bhagavan, just as the head is the most important of the limbs,
allowing survival, whoever has pure caring also has
the enlightenment of the Buddha.

In the Secret Teachings of the Inconceivable Tathāgata, we find:

Guhyapati, the pristine awareness of the Omniscient One
comes forth from the root of compassion. It comes forth
with enlightened mind as cause, and through skillful means
it reaches the farthest limits.

And in the Bodhisattva-piṭaka, we find:

Śāriputra, Bodhisattva Mahāsattvas are endowed
with one dharma: the Buddhadharma. Moreover,
they grasp it perfectly and inconceivably.
What is this one dharma? It is the mind
of enlightenment: perfect caring.

Śāriputra, being endowed with that one dharma, the
Buddhadharma, Bodhisattvas completely grasp
the inconceivable aspects of the Buddhadharma.

Again, Orgyan Dusum Khyenpa has stated:

To obtain Buddhahood, you must generate
the ultimate mind of enlightenment.
To generate this ultimate mind of enlightenment
requires the relative mind of enlightenment,
and for the relative mind of enlightenment
there must be compassion. To generate compassion,
there must be love. Love is produced from knowing
that all sentient beings are our father and mother.
As the nature of the path of the Mahāyāna
is the enlightenment mind of love and compassion,
there is nothing other than this.

Concerning Bodhicitta, we find in Entering the Bodhisattva Path:

The Powerful Munis, reflecting for many kalpas,
see the benefit of the enlightened mind:
By means of it the immeasurable hosts of beings
quickly obtain the joy of supreme bliss.

Those who desire to overcome the hundreds of miseries
of existence; those who desire to clear away the unhappiness
of sentient beings; those who desire to enjoy multifold delights
must never give up the wondrous enlightenment mind. [1.7–8]

Again:

It is the most excellent elixir
that conquers the Lord of Death, ruler over beings;
it is the inexhaustible treasure
that ends all poverty.

It is the most excellent medicine
that cures the ills of humanity;
it is the shade-tree of welcome rest
for those weary from wandering the paths of samsara.

It is the bridge that leads all beings
to freedom from the lower realms;
it is the rising moon of the mind
that dispels the aching emotionality of beings.

It is the great sun that finally burns away
the gloom of ignorance for human beings;
it is the butter-essence
churned from the milk of the sacred teachings.

For travelers roaming the road of existence
who desire to experience the delights of total joy,
this great banquet will satisfy sentient beings
and place them near great bliss.

       —*Entering the Bodhisattva Path*, 3.28–32

By cultivating the enlightened mind, you will gain lasting benefit and complete happiness for both yourself and others. Though you may understand all the stages of the Nine Vehicles, without enlightened mind, that knowledge will not benefit you. Though you may listen to the teachings, contemplate, and meditate upon them; though you may practice the teachings of development and completion; though you may recite mantras, without cultivating the enlightened mind, you will not be traversing the right path, even though it may seem otherwise. Therefore, it is most important to focus on Bodhicitta, so that you will not be overwhelmed when dealing with the many extremely high and profound practices.

What, then, is this enlightened mind, this Bodhicitta? Bodhicitta is the essence of openness and compassion. In referring to enlightened mind, we speak of ultimate and relative Bodhicitta, as well as what are known as wisdom and skillful means. In the Sūtra Requested by Akṣayamati, we find:

What is the skillful means of the Bodhisattva?
What is manifestly established wisdom?
When you are in meditative absorption
and engage the mind in focusing on great compassion,
concentrating on all sentient beings, that is skillful means.
When your meditative absorption engages peace and great peace,
that is wisdom.

And again:

Skillful means is great compassion—the birthlessness
of that compassion is wisdom. At all times,
means and wisdom rule the pāramitās.

What we call the enlightened mind is the unity of skillful means
and wisdom. Thus it is said:

Openness and compassion, inseparable:
This is what is called enlightened mind.

Bodhicitta itself is the supreme practice:

It is that which is to be cultivated;
it is the non-abiding of nirvana.

Therefore, there is no practice that is ever separate from these two.
In The Teachings of Vimalakīrti, we find:

Wisdom detached from means is a shackle;
means detached from wisdom is a shackle as well.

And in The Manifestations of Mañjuśrī, we find:

Analyzing openness and ignoring sentient beings
is demonic activity. Not using the discriminating process
of wisdom and grasping at great compassion as the object
of your meditative focus is demonic activity as well.

In a śāstra commenting on The Jewel of Realization, we find:

Due to wisdom, the Bodhisattva does not abide in samsara;
due to compassion, the Bodhisattva does not abide in peace.

Concerning this, the Uttaratantra states:

With wisdom they sever all self-cherishing,
and because they cherish sentient beings,
those who are wise do not grasp at peace.
Relying upon the wisdom and compassion of enlightened mind,
the truly noble rest neither in samsara nor in nirvana. [1.39]

Nāgārjuna stated:

Should you or others of the world wish
to obtain unexcelled enlightenment,
its root is the enlightened mind.
Firm as Meru, the sovereign of mountains,
it is compassion that reaches everywhere
and wisdom that does not rely on duality.
　　　　　—*The Precious Garland, 175*

In a Dohā, we find:

Those who penetrate openness but lack compassion
do not find the supreme path.
But if you meditate only on compassion,
you will not obtain liberation, for you stay in samsara.
Those able to apply both
abide neither in samsara nor in nirvana.

This is taught in many places. In the Lamp of Enlightenment, we find:

Those with the power of proficiency in skillful means
who meditate on the aspects of wisdom
quickly obtain enlightenment.
Those who meditate only on the lack of a self, do not.

The wise practice in this way. Just as a bird must use both wings to fly into the sky, both openness and compassion must be active to gain the non-abiding nirvana. If both openness and compassion are not present, you are like a fool attempting to get someplace by hopping along on one foot. As the Great One of Oḍḍiyāna stated:

If you do not know the unity of skillful means and wisdom,
you are being foolish, like someone trying to walk on one foot.

Here, then, is the practice of the two aspects of enlightened mind: a path of little difficulty and great benefit, flawless and nearly foolproof. What does this practice entail? Helping others. And to truly help others, you will need various practices to assist you. To do these practices, whether you are of high, low, or middling ability, you will need humility to carry them through.

This teaching is based on one axiom: that you must give every gain and victory to others and take upon yourself all their troubles and difficulties. If you study and practice this teaching and other definitive guides for developing the ultimate mind of enlightenment, those of you who have not developed Bodhicitta will gain the means to develop it, and those who have developed it will increase it until it is fully developed, never letting it subside.

For those of you who have already done this, I have nothing else to offer except the few supplementary teachings collected here. However, for others, particularly for intelligent new students, it is very important to meditate on developing the enlightened mind and to generate the experience of it. As will be explained, this is done in two ways: by using meditation to generate ultimate Bodhicitta and by using self-mastery to develop relative Bodhicitta.

Concerning the first of these, there are preliminary practices, actual practices, and practices to follow meditation.

*Section One*

*Ultimate Enlightened Mind*

# Reflections

## Penetrating Dualism

While compassion for others is the basis of the mind of enlightenment, the enlightened mind expresses the unity of compassion and wisdom. As compassion deepens into the contemplations of samādhi, the wisdom gained through meditation sees all existence as being open in nature. Seeing all existence to be like a dream, the Bodhisattva generates great compassion for beings caught in the illusory realm of samsara. Thus Guru Chekhawa's root text advises us to

*Consider everything to be like a dream.*

Experiencing the unity of compassion and wisdom frees the Bodhisattva from the kleśas and from the operation of karma: from the destructive emotionality based on ignorance and the actions and reactions that arise from these emotions. Whether focusing on the objective world as apparitional or on the mind as the source of meaning, the result is the same: Samsara loses its hold.

Cause and effect themselves are discovered to be productions of the mind. But this realization cannot come about through the ordinary operations of mind; a far more fundamental shift is required. Through meditation and analysis, the mind itself can be seen as having no specific location. Lacking form, it cannot be found either

inside the body or outside it. And yet objects cannot be seen as having any true existence apart from the mind. The Bodhisattva sees how isolated entities appear to arise and how, though they lack any substance whatsoever, they arouse attachment and engage the emotions. From this, the Bodhisattva realizes that all samsaric suffering arises from our tendencies to mistake appearance for reality. A new way of seeing self and the world takes form, based on understanding of nisvabhāva—the illusion of self identity.

The schools of Buddhist philosophy use precise methods to penetrate and explore the illusion of self, for unless dissipated by clear and convincing inquiry, the illusion will perpetuate itself. Analysis and examination serve as tools that clear the way for practice that extends experience beyond the confines of the self and its constructed world. Compassion is the natural response to this new realization. To emphasize this, Zhechen Gyaltsab quotes from the Uttaratantra:

Due to wisdom, Bodhisattvas sever all self-cherishing,
and because they cherish sentient beings,
those who are wise do not grasp at peace.
Relying upon the wisdom and compassion of enlightened mind,
the truly noble rest neither in samsara nor in nirvana. [1.39]

Our minds, by nature, have the potential to develop into the perfect mind of enlightenment. This enlightened potential is never lost and is always accessible. Though at any moment our minds may be full of suffering and destructive emotions, the mind itself remains pure in the same way that the water of a muddy pond is pure. And just as mud nourishes the growth of the lotus, the emotions act like fertile soil to stimulate the aspiration for enlightenment, for without suffering, we would have no motivation to change. The seeds of compassion and wisdom—the two aspects of enlightened mind—are intrinsic to our nature. In studying self-mastery, we encourage these seeds to grow so that enlightened qualities can blossom.

In this way, the mind of enlightenment can arise in ordinary beings who are attached to samsara and completely enmeshed in confusion and emotional pain. From the depth of personal anguish, compassion is born for other sentient beings.

Generating the twin aspects of enlightened mind—the relative enlightened mind of great compassion for all beings and the ultimate enlightened mind of openness (śūnyatā)—dissolves the final obstacles to realization. Bodhicitta is born from insight into openness and the awakening of compassion, which are brought to fruition through wisdom and skillful means. The Sūtra Requested by Akṣayamati, as quoted by Zhechen Gyaltsab, gives a clear picture of how these four elements relate to one another:

What is the skillful means of the Bodhisattva?
What is manifestly established wisdom?
When you are in meditative absorption
and engage the mind in focusing on great compassion,
concentrating on all sentient beings, that is skillful means.
When your meditative absorption engages
peace and great peace, that is wisdom.

Thus the Bodhisattva acts with skillful means and wisdom, with knowledge of both compassion and openness. Because Bodhisattvas see clearly the illusory nature of samsara, its terrors cannot alter their resolve. Their seeing is not just a compassionate gaze, but a manifesting of heroic energy and unshakable confidence. In the battle with samsara, Bodhisattvas will settle for nothing less than unconditional victory.

# Preparation:
# Penetrating Dualism

*B*efore the main practice, generate tranquility by concentrating on the antidote to the stream of intrusive thoughts. As the Buddha taught, "When there is thinking, count each breath."

First complete the preparatory practices[1] as indicated previously. Then sit in the meditation posture.[2] Sit very straight and count each breath as it goes in and out of your lungs. Do this twenty-one times and then start the counting over again. After practicing in this way for a while, you will definitely gain some experience of meditation and become a vessel for meditation.

The main practice involves determining the nature of existence in order to generate awakened awareness, and then generating the unity of tranquility and awakened awareness by setting the mind in a non-conceptual state, free from any sort of intellectualizing.

To prepare for the main practice, you must initially see what is to be abandoned and then determine the antidote. Here you need to do a penetrating analysis of the dualistic mind: subject as it relates to object.

## *Examining the Apprehending Object*

Analyze any object that comes to mind. Reflect that all aspects of the environment—animate and inanimate—that appear in the mind as objects do not truly exist as external objects. Evidence of this is found when contemplating the following:

*Consider everything to be like a dream.*

All appearances are similar to dream images: like what appears to the mind when it is dulled by sleep. The various images that the mind perceives are imperfect mental impressions, appearing because of mistaken residual patterns. In the Laṅkāvatāra Sūtra, we find:

Stirred up by residual patterns, the mind
emerges, appearing as objects.
Objects do not exist—just the mind itself.
Seeing objects as being external is erroneous.

Regarding this, Śāntideva has said:

Who made the burning iron pavements of hell?
What is the source of hell's infernal weapons?
All such things, the Muni has stated,
proceed from the harmful mind.
—*Entering the Bodhisattva Path*, 5.7

It is also said in the Sūtra on the Ten Stages: "O children of the Jina! The three realms are but the mind."

In The King of Samādhis, we find:

When a young maiden dreams
of giving birth to a baby boy that she then sees die,
she feels joy at the birth and misery at the death.
Know all phenomena to be like this.

There is but one underlying basis to existence, but because different types of beings accumulate different karma, different realities appear to exist. However, these are but appearances of the mind. Thus we find in the Review of the Great Vehicle:

Each object is seen differently
by each kind of being—

hungry ghosts, animals, men, and gods.
Thus it is asserted that objects
cannot be established as being real.

Even if you have the ability, or command a power able to change one thing into another, these things are still the appearance of mind. Thus we find again in the Review of the Great Vehicle:

For Bodhisattvas who have attained the powers,
as well as for yogins, everything on earth
appears as whatever they wish it to be.

This can be proven experientially as well. A great meditator of the Lam-'bras teachings, the teachings of Path and Result, while doing rtsa-rlung practices, began to think that he was thirsty. So he went for a drink of water. He went first to his water pitcher. Finding it empty, he went to a spring, and then to a large river, but he could find no water. Perplexed, he decided to rest a bit in a mountain cave, where he took off his Dharma robes and went to sleep. Then, while still asleep, he returned home. Upon waking, even the thought of thirst had disappeared. Inside the water pitcher there was water. But his Dharma robes were still across the river, and he had to send someone to fetch them.

Water may appear to exist, without this being the truth; it may appear not to exist, without this being false. Whatever appears is decided in your own mind. Appearances are not external objects. Although they appear to be solid, such thinking is not correct: Appearances seem solid because we have accustomed ourselves to such a way of thinking based on residual patterns established from beginningless time. We find in the Celebrations of Mañjuśrī:

The devaputra Vikrīḍita spoke thus to Mañjuśrī:
"Mañjuśrī, how should one look upon external objects?"
Mañjuśrī replied, "External objects appear
through the sense of vision, due to the residual pattern
of seeing things with the conceptual mind."

The devaputra asked again: "How is it that the things we see
due to our residual thought patterns appear to be solid?'
Mañjuśrī replied, "This is the way of appearance.
Once a woman who dwelled in Vārāṇasī saw herself

in meditation as having the body of a tiger.
Many people in the city saw her as actually being a tiger,
and everyone ran away in terror, leaving the city deserted.

"Another time, a bhikṣu, having meditated
that his body was unclean, was seen by everyone
as being a skeleton. If things can appear like that
in such a short time, no wonder they appear real
when viewed through residual thought patterns
imprinted from beginningless time."

Therefore, it is said: "The mind is full of the various things that appear." The Crown of Sūtras states:

Though there is nothing other than mind,
the mind perceives things. [7.8]

All that appears is an illusory vision of our own mind. Do not misinterpret such appearances as existing in any way at all apart from the mind.

## Examining the Apprehending Mind

In analyzing the apprehending mind, consider: Outer appearances are subjective; they have the very nature of the mind. The root text thus states:

*Examine the nature of unborn awareness.*

In determining the nature of the mind, three crucial points show that mind itself is open: production, cessation, and location. The mind is without color or form or the like. The mind is not located either inside the body or outside the body. No nature for mind can be established. It is the Dharmakāya, present from the beginningless beginning as the very ground of being. The Crown of Sūtras states:

Thus, even the mind is intrinsically perceived as an absence. [7.8]

In the Heap of Jewels, we find:

Śāriputra, the mind does not exist within, nor does it
exist without, nor does it exist both within and without.
It cannot be observed. The mind is without form,

invisible, and without boundaries. It is not seen,
not seeable, and not to be seen—even by all the Buddhas.

Śāntideva has stated:

The mind is not located in the senses,
nor is it in form nor is it in between.
It is not within nor is it without,
nor is it to be found anywhere else.

Being neither the body nor other than the body,
not mixed with the body, not separate, not anywhere at all,
it has no existence whatsoever.
Therefore the nature of sentient beings is nirvana.
                              —*Entering the Bodhisattva Path, 9:103–4*

All these beings are never produced and never cease.
Beings are like a dream: Upon examination,
they are like a hollow reed. [9.150]

In the Crown of Sūtras, we find:

Peace comes from the patient acceptance
of non-arising and non-cessation.
Its nature: nirvana. [12.51]

The Perfection of Wisdom in Eight Thousand Lines states: "As for
the mind, there is no mind: The nature of mind is light."

And in the Sūtra of Pristine Awareness, we find:

As all dharmas are by nature totally pure,
meditate on the perception of their lack of substantiality.
As intrinsically they have the nature of light,
meditate on the perception of their being non-observable.
The mind itself is the Buddha—
no other Buddha should be sought.

Having concluded that the way the mind abides is neither more
nor less than this, let this specific knowledge free you from uncertainty. Strive by whatever means to make this understanding a part
of your being. Śāntideva states:

Those who do not know this secret of the mind,
the foremost principle of the Dharma,
though they desire to obtain happiness and to conquer suffering,
wander continuously and aimlessly.

—*Entering the Bodhisattva Path*, 5.17

If you know this, you know the nature of existence of all dharmas.
Thus it is said in a Pāramitā Sūtra:

The very nature of one thing is all things;
the very nature of all things is one thing.
Whoever sees one thing just as it is
sees the nature of everything as well.

In the Cloud of Jewels, we find:

The mind precedes all things;
if you completely understand the mind,
you will truly understand all things.

And in the Verse Summary of the Prajñāpāramitā, we find:

Bodhisattvas know that they share the same properties
with all sentient beings and know that all things
have the same properties as sentient beings as well.
Birth and birthlessness are not to be understood as two things:
This is the paramount activity of the pāramitā of wisdom. [1.26]

## *The Antidote*

In determining the antidote itself—pristine awareness or the mind
that knows subject and object as non-produced—do not think of the
antidote as either existing or non-existing:

> *Let the antidote also liberate itself.*

If you start thinking of the antidote as, "Objects and mind are
empty," look at the nature of the antidote. Ultimately you will
understand that the antidote itself is without self-nature, and you
will rest in this state.

Śāntideva stated:

Passing beyond sorrow (nirvana)
and not passing beyond sorrow (samsara)
do not essentially differ.
　　—*Entering the Bodhisattva Path, 9.151*

And again:

All is like the sky!
Understand this completely, as I have done. [9.155]

The Crown of Sūtras states:

In ultimate terms, there is no difference at all
between production and peace. [7.5]

In the Prajñāpāramitā, we find:

All things in their very equality
share the very equality of the pāramitā of wisdom.

And the Verse Summary of the Prajñāpāramitā states:

Bodhisattvas who formulate the realization:
"The skandhas are empty" are acting
in conformity with conventional designations.
They do not truly abide in non-production. [1.9]

And again it states: "The openness of openness . . . ."

　　When you realize all things as being open, you realize true meaning. In the Crown of Sūtras, we find:

All forms are unobservable:
This is the supreme observation. [10.78]

In the Verse Summary of the Prajñāpāramitā, we find:

Forms are not seen; feelings are not seen;
since perceptions are not seen,
the mind's activities are not seen.
This way as taught by the Tathāgatas
is called "seeing Dharma."

Expressed in the words of ordinary beings,
it is called "seeing the sky."
Examine the meaning
of this "seeing that is like the sky."
The Tathāgatas taught that existence
is to be seen in such a way:
Such seeing can not be demonstrated
by any other illustrations. [12.9–10]

And again:

To understand all dharmas in the way
of their being non-produced and open
is the supreme practice of the pāramitā of wisdom. [5.2]

And the 'Gyod-bsal states: "Great King! Not seeing anything, you see the true meaning."

Atīśa has said:

By way of non-realization comes the realization
that what is called "realizing the absolute"
is a conventional designation.

# Reflections

# Unity of Tranquility and Awakened Awareness

While only the path of the Bodhisattva centers on developing great compassion, all paths to enlightenment followed by the Buddhist traditions focus on negating the power of karma and the destructive emotions by learning to control the mind through meditation. Gaining control of the mind involves uniting two forms of meditation: śamatha, the meditation for developing tranquility; and vipaśyanā, the meditation for developing awakened awareness.

With the generation of tranquility, the mental state of inner calm and balance, the emotional reactions that shape our ordinary experience subside in a serene and nourishing silence. In this silence, meditation deepens into samādhi, the foundation for awakened awareness: a clarity without conceptuality, free from the distinction between subject and object.

Calming the mind is essential for the process of developing awakeneed awareness, for without a calm mind, whatever insights may arise in meditation will be lost in distraction, turmoil, and confusion. When the mind becomes calm and steady, obscurations settle down like silt in a still pool, and we experience the luminescent clarity of awareness. As tranquility deepens and awareness shines in the mind more brightly, compassion and wisdom, the two aspects of enlightened mind, can develop as well.

Armed with the powerful weapons of inner calm and awakened awareness, we are well prepared to trace the arising of experience and see its nature as open and empty. Through tranquility the emotions are controlled, and through awakened awareness they are uprooted. Gradually the mind is transformed into a vehicle for ultimate Bodhicitta.

The Buddha also taught that the unwavering mind is the path of the Buddhas of the Three Times. If you abide serenely even when you are not in meditation, all will be well. If you do not, alertness and mindfulness will be disrupted, and again and again you will have to restore them. Both śamatha and vipaśyanā work together and build upon one another. With the joining of the two, the Path of Heroes reaches its culmination.

# Practice: Unity of Tranquility and Awakened Awareness

While an abiding reality is nowhere established, it is important to be well-versed in how existence manifests. Meditating on this, it suddenly strikes home that as existence does not exist anywhere, there is nothing to take hold of. The root text suggests the way to meditate:

*Rest in the stillness*
*of the basis-of-all, the ground of being.*

When you thoroughly investigate the seven consciousnesses, both individually and collectively, no 'natural mode of existence' can be found anywhere. The mind in its non-discursive nature does not hold anything; it has no subjective thrust and is settled in pristine clarity. Thus it is difficult to even recognize the basis-of-all. Therefore, we find in the Laṅkāvatāra Sūtra:

The basis-of-all, which is like the ocean,
is always agitated by the wind of objects.
Calming the dancing waves of the different consciousnesses
leads to emergence from cyclic existence.

The mind, in just gently being, acts as the basis-of-all. Thus, no basis-of-all is established anywhere other than simply resting in this nature.

Atīśa states:

Since the nature of truth cannot be intellectualized,
understanding also remains non-intellectualized.

This is the finest of meditations. Thus the Crown of Sūtras states:

Not seeing any meditation
is accepted as the ideal meditation. [10.79]

Śāntideva states:

When neither existence nor non-existence
rests before the mind,
no other form being possible, the mind,
being without an object, is completely at peace.
                —*Entering the Bodhisattva Path, 9.34*

In the Jewel of Realization, we find:

Concerning this, there is nothing to be cleared away
and nothing at all to be established.
As the essence of reality is right view,
in seeing the right way, you are liberated.

We find in the Verse Summary of the Prajñāpāramitā:

Perceptions that are drawn forth and sounded out
are said to be "on this side."
When perceptions are annihilated
and you have abandoned them,
you go to the other side. [2.11]

Again, the Prajñāpāramitā states:

No activity in the mind: This is what is known as
"being mindful of the Buddha, Dharma, and Sangha."

   Not meditating on anything, not thinking about anything, settle
your gaze nakedly, firmly, and clearly, in the state where there is no
mental activity. By doing so, by gazing on just that itself, the nature
of existence becomes very clear, just as it is. In unsullied water there
is sparkling clearness; in the still mind there is bliss; in the unob-
structed sky there is what is called clarity. It is said:

In the great ignorance of disturbed thought-formations,
we fall into the ocean of samsara.
Abiding in conceptless samādhi,
we manifest without activity, like the sky.

It is most important not to let the essence of this practice waver.
We find in the Prajñāpāramitā:

The agitated mind cannot achieve even its own purpose—
what need to speak of the purpose of others?

Śāntideva states:

A person whose mind is agitated
is caught between the teeth of emotionality;
but when body and mind abide in solitude
agitation does not arise.
In peace I will abandon the world,
giving up all discursive thinking.
     —*Entering the Bodhisattva Path, 8.1–2*

And further:

Austerities and all holy recitations,
though they be practiced for a long duration,
are said by the Wise One to be useless
as long as the mind is stirred up by many things. [5.16]

And so it is said: "This is the supreme import of mind."

All other thoughts given up,
my mind fixed on one thing alone,
I will strive for inner discipline
and bring my mind into balance. [8.39]

In the Instructions from a Spiritual Friend, we find:

The Bhagavan has said: "You must subdue your mind!"
He taught that mind is the root of the Dharma. [117]

The Buddha also taught that the unwavering mind is the path of
the Buddhas of the three times. If you abide serenely even when you
are not in meditation, all will be well. If you do not, alertness and

mindfulness will be disrupted, and again and again you will have to restore them. Thus the Crown of Sūtras states:

Fixing the mind on the object of meditation,
do not let the stream of consciousness waver.
Realize quickly when it is wavering;
catch it, and start over again. [15.11]

When meditating, if any of the five defects of samādhi should arise, concentrate on the eight activating antidotes.

Of the five defects, the two main ones to correct are lethargy and excitement. When you are feeling lethargic, tense your body until it shakes and trembles. Loudly recite various prayers and make fierce mental effort as you chant. Clear your mind with prayers to the Buddhas and Bodhisattvas.

When you are too excited or tense, quiet yourself, regulate your voice, calm your mind, and generate a feeling of heartfelt concern. Doing this will clear the mind.

Along with these methods, there are other effective means for identifying and dealing with both of these problems, such as being careful of what and how much you eat. In the Crown of Sūtras, we find:

A lethargic mind must be thoroughly brought under control;
the excited mind must be calmed. [15.9]

When you are free from both lethargy and excitement, everything falls into place. In the Crown of Sūtras we find:

When all becomes balanced, you rest in equanimity. [15.8]

When your meditation is thus stabilized, there is mental acuity and ease of mind, nothing else. Concerning this, Saraha stated:

When you sharpen the mind,
you gain mental acuteness;
through relaxing, you gain ease.
This is the mind's resting place.

If you find yourself unable to meditate, make sure that you are relaxed as you proceed and that you are alert to when your attention may begin to slip away. When dealing with any degree of mental

lethargy or excitement, the teachings of blo-rigs (teachings concerning the mind); khams-rigs (teachings concerning the elements); and dus-tshod (teachings concerning time) can be very effective when applied in a sustained fashion, each in turn.[3] Through such application, the mind will come to rest in the samādhi that is one-pointed in its focus: the state of tranquility. Thus, in the Cloud of Jewels, we find:

Tranquility is one-pointed mind.

And again in the Crown of Sūtras, we find:

As for the names of dharmas, "to be engaged"
is understood as the path of tranquility. [15.8]

Through the potent force of meditative balance, you can see the two truths as well as the way the mind abides, just as it is. Such realization is the state of awakened awareness. Thus, in the Cloud of Jewels, we find:

What is awakened awareness?
It is the state of individual investigation
functioning properly.

Concerning this, the Crown of Sūtras states:

Understand awakened awareness as being
the analysis of phenomena. [15.8]

And again:

In applying mind to the mind
and analyzing phenomena,
there is tranquility and awakened awareness. [15.10]

These two are completely interconnected and partless. The Crown of Sūtras states:

The path of unification
is to be understood as being engaged. [15.9]

This is the foremost of samādhis. We find in Entering the Bodhisattva Path:

Through awakened awareness endowed with tranquility
one knows how to conquer the kleśas. [8.4]

It is crucial to apply yourself to this meditation continually and humbly. Again the Crown of Sūtras states:

You must apply yourself continually
and proceed with humility. [15.11]

We find an example of this in the story where Lord Milarepa lights a fire to teach Rechungpa humility, and again when he shows Rechungpa the callouses he has acquired from long hours of meditation. If you practice in a similar way, you will effortlessly generate many wonderful qualities of spiritual understanding and quickly obtain supreme spiritual powers. Thus, in the Sūtra of Pure Intent, we find:

Maitreya, know that all mundane and supramundane
virtuous qualities, whether those of Śrāvakas,
of Bodhisattvas, or of Buddhas, are the result
of tranquility and awakened awareness. [ch.8]

Atīśa has stated:

Having contemplated the nature of existence
and having obtained spiritual warmth by stages,[4]
you obtain supreme delight,
and the enlightenment of a Buddha is not far distant.

Śāntideva has stated:

Openness is the antidote for the darkness
of the obscurations of the kleśas
and the obscurations of the knowable.
For those of us who desire all-knowingness quickly,
should we not meditate to achieve this?
                    —*Entering the Bodhisattva Path,* 9.55

In the Verse Summary of the Prajñāpāramitā, we find:

Whoever takes in hand the pāramitā of wisdom
touches the enlightenment of the Jina without delay. [11.7]

# Reflections

## Play of Illusion

*M*editation is much more than a process of deep reflection, being linked to the transformation of view that is ultimately translated into virtuous action. In preparing to meditate on the unity of tranquility and awakened awareness, everything should be considered to be like a dream. This dreamlike quality is seen as intrinsic to the nature of the mind, and indeed, to all existence. In carrying awareness of dreamlike existence into all other aspects of life, everything will naturally come to have a magical and lustrous quality.

After meditation, while continuing to contemplate that everything is like an illusion, bring this contemplation to bear on all activities, remembering at every moment that all appearance is illusory. For those who have this realization and have gained control over the mind, the world erects no barriers to accomplishment.

Practitioners who thoroughly understand that appearances do not truly exist, but are like an illusion, may spontaneously gain various seemingly miraculous powers. People tend to be fascinated by 'magical' powers, not realizing that unless accompanied by compassion, these abilities only emphasize worldly concerns and entrap us further in self-centered views. In the Kaliyuga, our present age, this basic point is often misunderstood. Teachers with such powers attract numerous students who wish to develop the same powers but

lack the proper orientation and training. With both teachers and students propelled by selfish motivations, the true teachings are lost.

There are also charlatans and tricksters who use various ploys to convince others that they have magical powers in order to gain influence. Since their audiences often want to believe in such magic, it is not difficult to trick them. As the Buddha said in the Prophecy of the Magician Bhadra's Attainment of Buddhahood:

Thus do the masters of illusion act.
The things of the world
are like the illusions made by Bhadra—
foolish people do not know this.

For those who are fascinated by Vajrayāna but have little actual knowledge of the texts or practices, it may seem that the Vajrayāna teachings provide a shortcut that bypasses study and preparation and allows one to escape the operation of karma. After all, "we are all already enlightened." This partial understanding is both seductive and deeply dangerous, for once someone has set out on this "shortcut," it can be difficult to find the way back to the crossroads where wisdom and compassion meet. The story of Bhadra the magician illustrates the problems that come from gaining power to manipulate the objective world without the foundation of selfless compassion.

The powers that fascinate worldly people, however, are trivial when compared to the powers of one who sees all existence as empty. Insight into śūnyatā reveals the open-ended aspect of experience, so that the solidity of what we consider reality is no longer a limiting factor. With the practice of meditation, certain powers do naturally arise. The truly adept, however, generally conceal their abilities, manifesting them only for spiritual purposes.

When the view that all appearance is like a dream is combined with compassion, action is performed only for the welfare of others. Such virtuous action leads to the ever-greater accumulation of wisdom and merit, which the Bodhisattva dedicates to all sentient beings, that they might obtain perfect enlightenment.

# After Meditation:
# Play of Illusion

*I*n the aftermath of meditation, flowing from the experience of meditative balance, comes a way to continue your meditation. The next line of the root text indicates how to proceed.

*Between sittings, act as a being of illusion.*

Consider all appearance, self and other, the universe and all that it contains, as being unreal, like an illusion. If your meditation experience has been good, everything will naturally come to have the magical quality and luster of this dream-like illusion. If your experience has not been good, it is important to recall firmly that all appearance is not truly existent, like an illusion. If your meditation is not like this, it is not meditation. Once you have generated certain knowledge of what meditation is, continue to practice and visualize in this way.

In the Heap of Jewels is found the story of how a magician named Bhadra, in order to test the Buddha, invited the Buddha and his attendants to visit at noon the next day, at which time he planned to present magical offerings. The Buddha accepted the invitation, knowing what would come to pass.

The next day Bhadra called together all the principal citizens of Rājagṛha, and in their presence magically caused an elaborate gallery to appear, lined with a row of cushioned thrones, as well as a

magnificent feast. The Four Great Kings and Indra with a retinue of thirty thousand then approached Bhadra and said to him, "For the sake of the Buddha, you have set forth this fine array of offerings and have displayed it well. All of the rest of us, for the sake of honoring the Buddha, must also present at least a small array of offerings." So saying, they each prepared a fine display, with Indra's being so fine that the previous presentations appeared to be made of darkness. Chagrined, Bhadra prepared to destroy his own creation, but was unable to do so.

Indra, knowing his thoughts, said, "You cannot destroy your presentation, for having focused your mind on making offerings to the Buddha, they cannot be destroyed. Though you put forth but the smallest of good thoughts, they have become the cause of your enlightenment."

At midday, Bhadra joyfully went to greet the Buddha as he approached with his assembly. Having confessed his faults to the Buddha, Bhadra then asked, "Why was I unable to destroy these things that I wished to destroy?"

The Buddha replied, "This display of yours manifests through illusion. Sentient beings manifest through karma; the bhikṣus manifest through the Dharma; and I manifest through the illusion of wisdom. If you understand this, present your offerings!" And even as the Buddha said this, Bhadra presented his offerings. The Buddha and his assembly then accepted the offerings, with the Buddha indicating his acceptance in verse, followed by the rest of the assembly:

Thus do the masters of illusion act.
The things of the world
are like the illusions made by Bhadra—
foolish people do not know this.

The Bhagavan then manifested three householders and Indra, one after the other, who appeared before Bhadra. Each of them asked, "Bhadra, what are you doing?" Bhadra replied to each, "I am inviting the Bhagavan to partake of the midday meal."

At that, each said in turn to Bhadra, "Bhadra, how can you be doing this? Look: The Bhagavan is teaching the Dharma in the household of Ajātaśatru." "The Bhagavan is seeking alms on the

Street of the Wanderers." "The Bhagavan is teaching the Dharma to the assembly in the garden of Jīvaka." "The Bhagavan is teaching the Dharma to the gods in the tree-lined walkway of the Gods of the Thirty-three." And Bhadra, in turn, saw each of these statements to be true.

Moreover, throughout Rājagṛha, in all the homes, at every city wall and all the streets and passages, the Buddha and his assembly appeared on magnificent thrones. Simultaneously they appeared on every tree and flower, and everywhere else as well. And in front of each and every one of the manifestations of the Buddha, Bhadra saw himself confessing his faults. Then Bhadra said:

I see all this with the ordinary eyes of flesh;
all the holy bodies I see
are ornamented with the auspicious signs.
As I wish to make offerings, pray tell me!
Which of these is the actual Buddha?
Which offering will lead to the greatest benefit?

The Buddha replied:

All are the essence of illusion—wholly liberated.
They are undifferentiated and indistinguishable.

The text goes on:

Giving gifts without discrimination
as to gift, giver, and recipient:
May Bhadra bring to perfection
such equality of giving!

The Buddha having spoken, Bhadra gained great faith and produced the most excellent mind of enlightenment. He then asked the Buddha, "Through learning what teachings can one obtain unexcelled enlightenment?"

At which the Buddha replied, "Enlightenment is obtained from practicing four dharmas. What are these four? Never rejecting the mind of enlightenment. Never mentally forsaking sentient beings. Never being satisfied with the virtuous acts you have done. Continually striving to protect the Dharma."

Through these and other teachings of the Buddha, Bhadra gained patient acceptance of the teaching of non-arising. The Bhagavan then made the prediction that when ninety-nine thousand kalpas had passed, Bhadra would become a Buddha called King of Manifest- tion in the universe called Sovereign Array.

In the King of Samādhis, we find:

A master of illusion manifests various forms
such as horses, oxen, and chariots
that appear to exist but in truth do not.
Know all dharmas to be the same.

And Śāntideva states:

Whatever manifests through illusion
and whatever manifests through causes:
Examine them both! Where do they come from?
Where do they go?
          *—Entering the Bodhisattva Path, 9.144*

And again:

The dull-witted take these things to truly exist:
But how do they differ from illusion? [9.143]

Meditate and pray accordingly. When you thoroughly understand that appearances do not truly exist, but are like an illusion, and med- itate accordingly, you will accumulate merit and wisdom for many lifetimes. In the Verse Summary of the Prajñāpāramitā, we find:

Know that those who hear that this existence
is like an apparition or illusion and do not doubt this,
and having learned this teaching apply it,
are beings who have practiced the Great Vehicle
starting from long ago. They have practiced
under many hundreds of billions of ten millions of Buddhas. [10.2]

And so:

View that recognizes whatever arises as luminous and open,
meditation that frees the mind,
activity that carries whatever is met into meditative action—
These are the practice of ultimate enlightened mind.

The stages of meditation for producing ultimate Bodhicitta as just indicated can be found in the Zin-bris of Drogon Palden Yeshe, a guide to the teachings of the oral lineage of Gyalsay Rinpoche Ngulchu Togmed, whose precepts are the source of this precious lineage. The majestic and shining waves of his instructions are a lineage that the winds of argument cannot bring into disarray. More noble than other teachings, these precepts have been set forth in such a way that not even a single word is false. In their joyful spiritual effect on others, they are most like the fundamental texts on meditation and the scriptures of the Middle Way.

The practice for contemplating the selflessness of persons entails analyzing the partless particles of the apprehended object and the partless instants of consciousness. By using the many aids of logic for distinguishing such things as the aspects of the three times in instants of consciousness and the directionality of particles, you will discover the selflessness of dharmas. Finally, by means of both scripture and correct perception, you will determine the true nature of existence: the unification of the appearance of dependent origination and openness, free from all words, thoughts, expressions—the view of the Great Madhyamaka, free from all assertions.

Connected with this experiential contemplation of the nature of existence is the way of practice free from acceptance and rejection, free of positions and beyond clearing anything away: pristine awareness, unimpeded, luminous, and open.

After this meditation, practice the appropriate way of unifying merit and wisdom, never breaking off the contemplation that all is like an illusion. In a timely fashion follow the precepts of the Lama and the scriptures. With humility and total admiration for your principal Lama, strive in every way for purification and accumulation of merit, for example, by offering the mandala. We find in the Prājñāpāramitā:

The ultimate is to be realized by way of conviction.

And further, Maitreyanātha has said:

Having delighted the perfect Buddha,
garner the accumulations of merit and wisdom

to activate non-conceptual pristine awareness regarding all things. Accept this as supreme.

Again, in the Sūtra of the Play of the River of Tranquility, we find:

Know that it is foolish to seek the ultimate—
spontaneously-arising pristine awareness—
through means other than these:
the blessings of the realized Lama,
successfully purifying the defilements,
and amassing the accumulations of merit and wisdom.

A Dohā states:

Penetrating to the heart of what the Lama expresses
is like finding a precious object in the palm of your hand.

And again, the Great Teacher states:

When yearning for the Lama arises,
experience and realization are sure to shine.

Accordingly, recite the teachings of the Great Vehicle periodically throughout the day, and also explain these teachings to others. In this way, learn to practice the ten virtuous actions of the Dharma without interruption. Then, through dedicating your merit to obtain perfect enlightenment for the benefit of all sentient beings, you will obtain and extend the Dharma. Thus the Verse Summary of the Prajñāpāramitā states:

Bodhisattvas who have contemplated supreme wisdom
when arising from that meditation express the immaculate Dharma,
dedicating it to the cause of enlightenment for the benefit of beings.
Their virtue has no equal in the three worlds. [18.5]

Section Two

Relative Enlightened Mind

# Reflections

## Exchanging Self for Others

Grounded in the openness of śūnyatā, the meditator can enter samsara with open eyes and an open heart. The willingness to look creates a willingness to care; the willingness to care creates a willingness to respond and then to take responsibility. Taking responsibility fosters awareness that guides the mind toward greater insight and more skillful action. Life becomes more balanced and healthy, and we gain the ability to achieve all our highest goals. From this first step, the flower of compassion can grow until it blossoms into Bodhicitta.

In this dark age, when ignorance and the rule of the ego sometimes seem total in their domination, there can be no greater treasure than following the Path of Heroes. We can cherish our compassionate thoughts and caring actions, cultivating a humility that takes the place of ego-domination and relationships based on power and control. Following this humble path, the Buddha conquered the Marayas: the inhuman forces of ignorance, destruction, hatred, and self-interest.

If we want to put an end to samsara, we must transform our understanding so that it centers on Bodhicitta. Love, compassion, and the precious enlightened mind are the essence of all the paths of the Great Vehicle. The essence of love is the motivation to benefit all sentient beings and the desire for all beings to be happy. The essence

of compassion is the desire for all sentient beings to be free from misery and its causes. The mind of enlightenment is the desire for all beings to obtain the awakening of a Buddha, and the desire to obtain the omniscience of a Buddha in order to free all sentient beings from samsara. Learning to draw on the riches of our human nature, allowing our hearts to open, we too can walk this path. The practical impact and benefit for all humanity are beyond calculation.

If we could exchange for just one moment the feelings going through our mind and heart with the full weight of suffering endured by all beings everywhere, we could never again return to the close-minded, self-centered understanding that we have adopted as our method for dealing with samsara. From there, it is not so great a step to the revolutionary thought: "All beings are my parents." Now we have a way to begin to comprehend, at least in our mind's eye, the full scope of samsara.

Even if we cannot easily develop compassion for all the beings trapped in samsara, we can at least observe ourselves, refusing to ignore the chains of suffering that renew themselves every day. When we know our own frustration and pain, we can recognize how we fabricate samsara by enslaving ourselves to habits and negative patterns.

An ancient image likens sentient beings to bees trapped in a giant vase: Some fly to the top, some to the bottom, some circle in the middle, but none escape. Trapped like this, we can only fight endless battles in a war we are doomed to lose; what is more, our defeat will be repeated again and again. There is nowhere to turn for relief; there is no end to suffering.

When we give up the last vestige of hope for finding freedom or happiness within the samsaric realms, we can accept the truth of suffering. Its power hits like a slap in the face or a stinging rain of fire. Now there is no choice: "These are my relatives and friends, my companions in destiny. I must find the way for all of us—the path that leads beyond samsara." With such thoughts, based on the true practice of compassion, we begin to cultivate Bodhicitta.

# Exchanging Self
# for Others

*T*he relative mind of enlightenment centers around the meditation on exchanging self for others. As this process is pivotal for gaining enlightenment, many of the Buddha's teachings of his past lives, such as the story of Dzawo's 'daughter', illustrate this point.

The story goes like this: There once was a seafarer by the name of Dzawo whose sons had all died at birth. At last another son was born. Hoping to keep him alive, Dzawo gave the child the name Bumo, which means daughter. The seafarer then went off to sea and died in a storm.

When Bumo grew to adulthood, he questioned his mother about his father's occupation and station in life. She told him a series of lies, fearing that if she told him the truth he would also travel the seas and meet an untimely end.

First she told him that his father was a merchant who sold grain, so Bumo became a grain merchant. But soon the head of the guild put a stop to his activity. She then told him that his father had sold incense, then clothes, and then gems. Selling these goods in turn, Bumo successively earned his mother four, then eight, then sixteen, and then thirty-two gold coins. But each time the head of the guild put a halt to Bumo's work. Finally his mother reluctantly said to him:

"Your hereditary calling is that of seafarer: those who go to sea to find gems. But all who follow this occupation meet an early death!"

Not listening to his mother, Bumo at once prepared to become a seafarer. Although his mother again and again attempted to dissuade him, she could not make him listen to her. Knowing he was making arrangements to leave, she decided to sleep in front of the door to bar it. That night, while she was sleeping, Bumo left, kicking her in the head to render her unconscious so he could run away.

The ship on which he took passage was wrecked in a storm and most of those on board perished, but Bumo held onto a large plank and drifted to an island. There he came upon a house of jewels, from which four most beautiful maidens came forth. Beckoning to Bumo to enter, they served him fine food and provided him entertainment suitable for the gods. From there Bumo traveled on, visiting a series of magnificent jeweled castles that respectively housed eight maidens, then sixteen, and then thirty-two. All the maidens offered to serve him, and entertained him as before.

The last group of maidens begged Bumo to remain and not to travel south, but he turned a deaf ear to them. Traveling south, he happened upon a fearsome castle of iron. Entering the castle, he met with a man with an iron wheel turning around on his head, its axle attached to a hole in the middle of his skull.

"What did you do to deserve this?" Bumo asked.

"It is the ripening of karma from kicking my mother in the head!" the man howled.

"Oh!" thought Bumo, "Perhaps I was led here by my karma!"

At once a voice boomed forth: "May he who is bound be freed! May he who is free be bound!" Immediately the wheel attached itself to the top of Bumo's head, and as it turned, he experienced unbearable suffering.

Due to his suffering, Bumo generated fierce compassion for sentient beings in similar circumstances. And he thought: "There are many who suffer like this in the world of sentient beings. May their wrongdoing and suffering descend upon me alone!" As soon as he thought

this, the wheel lifted and vanished into the sky and his suffering ended. This account is said to concern the Victorious One himself.

Again, the Buddha was once born in the hell called "Pulling Chariots." He and another hell-being were forced to pull an iron ox-cart over a plain of burning embers while being beaten by a servant of the Lord of Death. Even with the two of them straining as hard as they could, they could hardly make it move, and so the guardians of the hell, with burning weapons, beat them again and again, until their suffering was so great their hearts were breaking.

Then the Victorious One considered: "When two of us draw this cart, the suffering is the same as if it were drawn by only one. I will therefore draw the cart alone and free my companion."

Knowing his thoughts, the guardian of hell howled: "You have such great compassion, do you?" And saying this, he hit him on the head with an iron hammer. Thus the Victorious One left that life and was born among the gods. It is said that this was the first time the Buddha aided others.

For the above teachings, Lord Atīśa is said to have had three lineages. The first, which follows the Śrāvaka Vaibhāṣika philosophical system, he heard from Dharmarakṣita. This is the oral lineage of the dByug-pa-gsum-gyi-phreng-ba, said not to have been translated into Tibetan. Its teachings are similar to the Sautrāntika Jātaka as recorded by Aśvaghoṣa.

The second Atīśa heard from Maitriyogin or Kusulu the younger: This is the oral lineage of Namkay Nyingpo. The philosophical system is not established, but it follows the teachings of Śāntideva.

The third he heard from Lama Serlingpa, who studied the systems of the Tīrthikas. It is the oral lineage of the Dri-ma-med-par-grags-pas-zhus-pa, and follows the teachings of Śāntideva's Entering the Bodhisattva Path.

The teaching of this last system is similar in many ways to the Tīrthika view. Though it does not accept an eternal single, independent self such as the Tīrthikas believe in, it does accept, as part of the individual, something that holds to 'I' and 'mine' in the five skandhas and takes up birth as an individual entity. This is the individual 'self'

taught in the context of the practice of seeing the happiness and suffering of both self and others as being true in application. The oral lineage is said to be based on the Sūtra of Purity. Thus the Dri-ma-med-par-zhus-pa'i-mdo states:

The self and the conception 'mine' are the progenitors
of the Tathāgata.

And The Heap of Jewels states:

Just as human waste gathered in the cities
benefits the sugar-cane fields,
so do the excretions of the kleśas of the Bodhisattvas
help the field of Buddhadharma grow.

Again, the Chapter of Kāśyapa states:

Just as the lotus grows quickly
in swampy water full of excrement,
the Buddhas cause the sprout of the Jina to grow
in beings full of wrong views and the emotions.

The flower of the lotus does not grow on solid ground or in a desert; it grows in swampy water. Likewise, the mind of enlightenment does not grow in the personality of the Śrāvakas and Pratyekabuddhas, those free from the moisture of desire. Rather, Bodhicitta arises in the personality of ordinary beings who are completely attached to samsara. The reason? Such beings constantly grasp at a 'self' and thus experience intense feelings of suffering. From the depth of that personal suffering compassion is born for other sentient beings. This process is the extraordinary cause for becoming a Buddha. Also, because the self makes it possible for us to cultivate the precious mind of enlightenment that exchanges self for others, it is the progenitor of the Buddha. This is called following the spiritual practice set forth in Entering the Bodhisattva path:

If you harm others for your own sake,
you will experience the suffering of the myriad hells.
If you undergo harm to benefit others,
you will obtain all the perfections.

By desiring happiness for yourself
you become a fool among the worst of the lower creatures.

If you bring delight to others,
you will obtain an exalted position in the states of bliss.

If you employ others for your own benefit,
you will experience servitude.
In devoting yourself to the purpose of others,
you will obtain the exalted state of a lord.

Whatever joys there may be in the world
all come from desiring the happiness of others.
Whatever sufferings there are in the world
all come from desiring your own happiness.

What need to state this many times?
Foolish people act for their own benefit;
the Victorious One acts for the benefit of others.
Look at the difference!

If you do not actually exchange
your own happiness for the suffering of others,
you will never attain Buddhahood,
or ever be truly happy in the world. [8.126–31]

Having followed the many wise teachings presented above, concentrate on developing the mind of enlightenment that exchanges self for others. This is the real heart of the doctrine.

The practice of exchanging self for others has three parts. First are the various preliminary practices that include cultivating love and compassion. Then comes the actual practice of meditating on the exchange of self for others. Finally, there is the after-meditation practice for transforming the three poisons of desire, hatred, and ignorance into virtuous actions.

# Reflections

## Love and Compassion

*U*sually we seek to distance ourselves from suffering. We are uncomfortable in its presence, for seeing the suffering of others reminds us of our own vulnerability. There are times, however, when we come face to face with its horror and are unable to ignore it. When the anguish of others truly touches our hearts, we feel impelled to do something, however small, to relieve it. In setting aside reluctance and directly engaging the pain of others, we nourish the seeds of compassion, which take root in our hearts and grow.

Compassion creates a connection with others that allows love to flow through our being and outward. Thus compassion leads to experiencing the other side of suffering: a deepening sympathy that develops into a true rapport with others that gradually extends to all living beings. Not all forms of life think or act alike or have the same sense faculties, but all are part of the same cycle of birth and death; all have a consciousness that responds to the world around them; and all share the same needs for nourishment, propagation, and survival. As we reflect on other people and observe them with the eyes of compassion, we begin to see that those who at one time seemed alien to us are not alien after all; they are literally our relatives, born from the same genetic constituents as we are, with the same feelings, the same form of mind, and the same senses.

Once we extend this sense of interconnectedness to all living beings, we realize that their sufferings are not essentially different from our own, for all life forms participate in the same cycle of existence. This insight alone can be a powerful impetus for compassion, as the enormity of pain in the world becomes increasingly obvious. If we wish to further expand our capacities for compassion, we can imagine that all beings are identical to the mother who gave us birth and cared for us with selfless devotion in the earliest, most vulnerable years of our life. Perhaps other beings have not sheltered or cared for us in this life, but in essence they are no different from our parents and loved ones.

Thus, most practices for developing the relative mind of enlightenment—the mind of compassion—focus first on the kindness of our own mothers. For those who have trouble with their family relationships, however, it may be helpful to begin by looking at the earth as the mother, cultivating a way of understanding that heightens responsibility and caring for the whole environment.

If we truly wish to empathize with the suffering of others, so that understanding works within us and motivates our practice, we must accept others' suffering as our own. The more we can take on the pain of others, the more our knowledge of samsara will grow, and the closer we come to the day when we can act with confidence to benefit all beings.

# Preparation: Cultivating Love and Compassion

*F*irst of all, keep in mind that love, compassion, and the precious enlightened mind are the essence of all the paths of the Great Vehicle. There is no other. Thus, the Great One of Oḍḍiyāna states:

Truly, these three—love, compassion, and the mind
of enlightenment—are the essence of the path
of the Great Vehicle: nothing else.

The Master Jampel Dragpa also stated:

As a follower of the Mahāyāna, never distance yourself
even for an instant from love and compassion.

And again:

The welfare of others follows from love and compassion.
It never follows from hatred.

Reflect upon the special qualities of love, compassion, and the mind of enlightenment. The essence of love is the motivation to benefit all sentient beings and the desire for all beings to be happy. The essence of compassion is the desire for all sentient beings to be free from misery and its causes. The mind of enlightenment is the desire for all beings to obtain the Awakening of a Buddha and the

desire to obtain the omniscience of a Buddha in order to free all sentient beings from the ocean of samsara. Concerning these three, the Great One of Oḍḍiyāna states:

All sentient beings, their numbers vast as space itself,
have been our parents and have shown us inconceivable kindness.
Thus, concentrate on the thought: "May all beings be filled with
happiness!" This is the mind of love.

These beings are all our dear mothers.
Caught up in so much suffering, how pitiful they are!
Concentrate on the thought: "I must free them all
from this suffering!" This is the mind of compassion.

Concentrate on the thought: "May these beings,
who are all my dear mothers, be filled with happiness.
May they be free from suffering and quickly obtain
precious and unexcelled enlightenment!"
This is the mind of enlightenment.

Concentrate on all of these thoughts constantly
and with total impartiality.

Again, love is the mind free from hatred.
Compassion is the mind free from attachment.
Enlightened mind is the mind free from ignorance.

If you do not first purify your mind through love and compassion, you will not be able to generate the actual practice of Bodhicitta. So first, it is vital to train the mind in love and compassion. There are three specific ways of meditating to accomplish this: focusing on sentient beings, focusing on 'truth', and meditating on love and compassion without a focus. Regarding these, we find in the *Sūtra Requested by Akṣayamati*:

Meditation that focuses on sentient beings is for Bodhisattvas
who have generated the mind of enlightenment.
Meditation that focuses on 'truth' is for Bodhisattvas
who have engaged in Bodhisattva activity.
Meditation without a focus is for Bodhisattvas who have learned
to patiently accept the non-arising of all dharmas.

The Great One of Oḍḍiyāna described the characteristics of these three:

Love that focuses on all sentient beings arises when the mind reflects: "I know that all sentient beings are my parents; therefore may they all be filled with happiness!"

Love that focuses on 'truth' arises when the mind reflects: "Though nothing ultimately exists, beings do exist in a relative sense. They are merely an illusion, a dream, but in their relative existence they suffer. As all these beings are my mother, may they all be filled with happiness!"

Love without a focus arises when, in the course of your meditation, you see that all beings, both self and others, have the nature of openness; free from intellectualization, they are like the sky. From that knowledge love grows continuously like a ceaseless melody. Love projects itself as open-ended, with no set nature. With no limited focus and being non-conceptual in its being, it exhibits the threefold purity. Thus love is transformed into compassion.

While the above practices are very effective for laying the foundation and thus evoking the experience of the ultimate mind of enlightenment, here I draw on the celebrated hearing lineage of the Seven Essentials of Self-Mastery. Although there are many different guides to meditation, within this particular system, the first meditations taught are those easiest to generate. These are followed by those more difficult meditations, and lastly by the comprehensive meditations. The first is the meditation on great kindness; the second, the meditation on great suffering; and the last, the meditation on great wrongdoing.

## Meditation on Great Kindness

To meditate on great kindness, consider: In your present lifetime, the person who has shown you the greatest kindness is your mother who gave you birth. Thus, begin your meditation by visualizing your mother in front of you. Concentrate on her great kindness, and only

on her kindness: kindness in producing your body, kindness in going through great hardships for you, kindness in giving you life, and kindness in teaching you about the world. Regarding this, The Perfection of Wisdom in Eight Thousand Lines states:

In what way is your mother so kind? Your mother has thought
only of you. She underwent great hardships for you;
she gave you life; she taught you about the world.

Consider your mother's kindness in providing you with a body: To begin with, she carried you for ten lunar months in her womb, and during that time she produced your body from her own flesh and blood and vital fluids. You grew in her womb due to the wholesome food she consumed. She underwent many forms of mortification, sickness, and suffering as she bore you. After your birth, she contributed to what you are now, training you when you were young and weak so that you could become strong.

Consider her kindness in undergoing hardships for you: At first your mother had to feed you one mouthful at a time. You had nothing at all. Friendless, empty-handed and naked, you arrived alone in a land where you knew no one. Your mother gave you food when you were hungry and drink when you were thirsty. She clothed you when you were cold.

A mother naturally gives her child whatever she can to ward off privation. She keeps nothing for herself; she considers all she has earned—food and drink, clothes, and material goods—to be too dear for her own use, and so she gives everything to her child. Not thinking of her own good in either this life or the next, she has little time for happiness or rest. She thinks nothing of doing the most dangerous and terrible actions for her child, thus hindering her own good. To protect her child she will commit any number of harmful acts. She will kill, rob, and steal for her child—actions that will lead her to be born in hell and the other lower states of being in later lifetimes.

A mother works extremely hard for her child: Day and night she must labor for her child's livelihood by selling things or by farming and the like. With the stars as her hat, the soil as her shoes, her legs as her horse, woolen thread as a whip, she presents the flesh of her legs for dogs to bite and offers her face for men to gaze upon. In

short, her sad lot means that she will never be able to live easily or happily, for even a single day, all the rest of her life.

Who is kinder: your parents who have shown you such great kindness in this life or the Lama who teaches you the path for the next? Who gives to her child without holding back, considering her child to be unequaled? She gazes upon you with loving eyes; she nurtures you with the sweetness of her warmth. She wipes away your filth with her hands; she mixes your food with her fingers. She gives you milk from her own body and showers you with words of joy; she protects you from the inroads of many hardships.

Consider her kindness in giving you life: At birth, you have the strength of a worm, and your thoughts are as lost and unformed as those of a worm as well. But your mother cares for you and constantly serves you. She takes you upon her lap; she protects you from places where you might fall, from fire, and from water. Trying to protect you from sickness or death, she does many strange things—she casts auguries, consults astrologers, has rituals performed. All in all, she gives up her life for you. To keep you healthy and alive, she herself undergoes such hardships and worry that she becomes easy prey for sickness and death.

Consider her kindness in teaching you about the world: When you first come into the world, you know nothing, having no experience upon which to base any knowledge. You scream at those who care for you, knowing only how to cry and how to wave your arms and legs. Later, your mother has to train you to eat, as you do not know how to eat; she must teach you to clothe yourself, as you do not know how to dress. When the time comes, she teaches you how to walk; she teaches you how to talk. She teaches you all she knows: how to act and how to make things, and she also arranges for you to learn what she herself does not know.

Even when you simply learn to crawl, she finds you exceptional. She bursts with joy when you have learned only a few short words. Though there is no cause to praise you, she sings your praises. Even if you have no exceptional qualities she praises you. She thinks, "How clever my child is! My child will be respected and honored!"

No one else has thought about you so, keeping you constantly in mind. Such is her great kindness! Moreover, she has done all this not

just one time, but innumerable times: She has shown you the greatest kindness and protected you through all your beginningless lives in samsara.

A Sūtra states:

Should someone turn all the stones of the earth and all the fruit trees and forests into kernels of juniper berries, another person could conceivably have time to count them, but no one could possibly count what a mother has done for her child.

In such a way, lay out your mother's kindness. Since her kindness is immeasurable, concentrate on the thought: "May I obtain the perfection of Buddhahood quickly, so that my mother may be filled with happiness and freed from suffering! May I do whatever is necessary to make this happen!"

As you are thinking this, concentrate strongly on love, compassion, and Bodhicitta. During your practice, whether you are praying to the Lama and Three Jewels, taking refuge, or meditating, this practice is easy to generate and has great strength.

## Meditation on Suffering

While you are going for refuge, fill your heart with feelings of equanimity. Pray to be able to help your dear mother. With your mother as the object of your focus, think of all she has suffered and all the wrongs she has committed for you. From the depth of your heart, pray for her protection and refuge, and pray that she meet with no harm from others. Whenever you chant prayers or mantras, keep this strongly in mind. When feelings of love and compassion arise, protect these feelings just as a king protects his subjects, never forsaking them.

Still, though you may greatly desire to provide true happiness for your dear mother, you are powerless to clear away her sins and sufferings. Nor can others: not Brahma or Indra, or the Guardians of the World. What refuge then does your mother have? Only the Lama and the Three Jewels have power to give refuge. If the child of a crippled mother is carried away by a flood or trapped in a raging fire, the mother seeks the help of other hands. In the same way, you must take

refuge in the Lama and the Three Jewels, praying intensely for them to help her.

Having meditated in this way on your mother, use the same pattern of meditation to contemplate your father, uncles, and other relatives. Picture their great kindness and compassion in your mind.

Secondly, meditate on all the great suffering in the world. Sentient beings desire happiness. No one wishes to suffer, but in ignorance, people do not practice what would bring them true happiness. They strive instead for those things that cause suffering. And so their existence is comprised of suffering and not happiness.

For the hell beings there is heat and cold; for hungry ghosts, hunger and thirst. Animals eat one another. Even for beings in the higher realms, life is short, and sickness abounds. Their senses are weak; they are hungry and destitute; they are enslaved by their work; they are punished for various transgressions, and so on. There is no action through which they do not experience suffering. Meditate with the thought of their total suffering in mind.

When you first do this meditation, evoke the tragedy of suffering by picturing the actual torment of poverty, the decrepitude of old age, the suffering of illness. Visualize how people are like animals bound in front of a butcher, tormented, without any protection.

Then picture yourself as the animal being tortured. If you visualize yourself or the mother who gave you birth in that situation, you will be unable to bear the thoughts of suffering that arise. If just imagining such a frightful condition causes you to feel terror-stricken—though nothing is actually happening to you—how could anyone actually bear to experience such pain? Although a suffering creature is not your mother in this life, it has been your mother in a previous lifetime. So how can you consider this being as any different from your actual mother?

Think: When you could not bear even a little heat, she did what she could to make you cool. When she feared that you might burn your mouth, she blew on your food to cool it. When she feared you would freeze, she heated you with the warmth of her body. Attuned to your hunger and thirst, she offered her breast, just as did your present mother.

As you think of how greatly these beings have suffered, tormented by worries, concentrate very strongly on compassion. Having accustomed yourself to that meditation, meditate on all sentient beings who suffer in hell and in similar agony. Generating compassion, pray that you will be able to take responsibility for freeing all beings from suffering and that you will be able to establish them all in a state of happiness.

## Meditation on Great Wrongdoing

On wrongdoing, Śāntideva states:

Although in your mind you desire to cast off suffering,
you run after that same suffering.
Although you desire happiness,
your ignorance defeats happiness as if it were its enemy.
—*Entering the Bodhisattva Path*, 1.28

Many of the things people desire in their lives put them in grave danger but provide them little profit. Yet to get these inconsequential things, people have been known to cruelly murder their own parents, to destroy religious assemblies, to kill holy people, to take away the Sangha's place of assembly: in other words, to commit all the terrible acts for which there can be no forgiveness, or for which forgiveness is all but impossible. With the accumulation of these very terrible sins, they are certain to fall into the Avīci Hell as soon as their breath ceases.

Great Beings, on the other hand, always feel compassion for everyone, even holding in their hearts the fierce and heartless armies of this present eon and the vicious hordes who seem to have the strength of demons. They also keep in mind the beings of the lower realms, and continually reflect on their pitiful state.

Should you not be feeling such compassion as well? In not concentrating on compassion, are you not inviting into your innermost heart the demon-mind that desires worldly enjoyments? In letting yourself be satisfied with what you are presently accomplishing to spiritually benefit either yourself or others, are you not leaving yourself room to hope for just a little more time to enjoy worldly

activities? And then your actions lead to wrongdoing. In the process of convincing yourself there is nothing more you can do, you actually bring ruin upon both yourself and others.

When you give in to temptation, as by becoming intoxicated, you are dealing with substances that are little different than virulent poisons and that can cause you to become crazy and vicious. By taking such poison, people not only cut short their lives, they also ruin their chances for happiness in innumerable future births. They ensure that they will experience the great suffering of hell without any chance of liberation for the whole of this great kalpa. Thus, meditate strongly on compassion. Concentrate on the thought: "All beings have been my parents in previous lives and have shown me extreme kindness." Visualize with great intensity the terrible things done by fishermen and butchers and the like. Finally, meditate as before on all beings.

## Expanding the Practice

Now, concentrate on all those who have ever caused you difficulties or harm. Think about a time when someone treated you very badly in return for your help. You may not have done anything to deserve such treatment, and actually have shown that person only the greatest kindness. In such a way, from beginningless time, due to karma, we experience immeasurable suffering. Again and again, we meet with people who return evil for good. These people accumulate much bad karma and later will experience immeasurable suffering.

Contemplate as before, thinking: "Whoever is now harming me was my mother in past lives and showered me with kindness. How pitiful that this person is now acting like this; it is due to the influence of ignorance and the destructive emotions."

When demonic beings, both human and nonhuman, cause you harm, this does not mean that your good karma has been exhausted. Rather, such difficulties help your good karma to grow greater. If it were not for the harm you endure at the hands of others, merit from meditating on patience would not arise. Because you gain patience from such situations, take delight when people harm you, and look at harmful beings as having the kindness of your parents. See them

as showing the kindness of a spiritual teacher to a student—and thus
as suitable to honor. Regarding this, Śāntideva states:

Should a beggar appear when you are giving alms,
he presents no hindrance to your generosity.
The one who causes you to renounce the world
could never be an obstacle to moral practice.
> —*Entering the Bodhisattva Path 6.105*

How could I achieve patience if all were like
the physician, who always seeks to help me?
No, it is by depending on those whose minds are
full of fierce hatred that I generate patience.
They are the ones as worthy to be honored
as the sacred Dharma. [6.110]

There is no challenge like patience. [6.2]

Just as if a treasure had appeared in my house
without my making any effort to obtain it,
I must rejoice in my enemies,
who help me to perform enlightened actions. [6.107]

Then, as before, think to yourself: "How sad it is that those who
have shown me such great kindness should experience so much suffering." Again, Śāntideva states:

I once harmed sentient beings in ways like these.
Therefore how fitting that
the injury I have done to sentient beings
should return now to harm me. [6.42]

Urged on by my own karma
those who cause me harm appear;
if such harm should lead these beings to hell
am I not the one destroying them?

I depend on these very beings to give me patience
so I might purify my many harmful acts.
Yet the sentient beings who depend on me
abide at length in hell.

Since I am harming them in such a way
and they are benefiting me—
why grow angry, O misguided mind?
You have it all wrong!
—*Entering the Bodhisattva Path,* 6.47–49

Many times in the past we have harmed each and every sentient being, and with the ripening of our harmful acts, we have experienced great suffering in terrible states of being. But it is important to wish earnestly for such retribution, for later, when the burden of this retribution is removed, ah! What joy! Thus, concentrate strongly on the thought: "How kind these beings are! They have only helped me, while I have only harmed them. The harmful things they do to me, though brought on by my own bad karma, will cause them to suffer for a very long time."

## Repaying Kindness

Next, concentrate on all beings: Just as you cannot comprehend the extent of space, likewise you cannot assess the number of the worlds of sentient beings. Examine the magnitude of various aspects of existence: Consider the world with its four continents, with Mount Meru and the four lesser continents, surrounded by a wall of iron. Thousands upon thousands of worlds like these make up one universe. The universe of Cūḍika contains this world of human beings, but there are thousands upon thousands of similar universes. Of those world-systems called 'Great Trichiliocosms' there are tens of hundreds of millions that include worlds like this one, with its four continents.[5]

All those worlds were once filled to overflowing with manna: From one seed, manna replicated itself, establishing itself in the eastern trichiliocosm. Spreading to each of the world-systems, each seed replicated itself abundantly, so that in all of the world-systems, this manna, even when consumed, was never depleted. As it continued to replicate, there was no end to its availability for consumption.

In all directions, it is the same: There is no limit to the number of earth-like realms. Sentient beings exist in each one, and of all these sentient beings, not a single one has not been your father and also

your mother, and as father and mother shown you only great kindness. Moreover, each one has shown you such kindness an inconceivable number of times.

Even in your present lifetime, you cannot begin to measure the benefit these beings have brought you. Should you place a value on their attempts to protect you from harm, only the great kindness of the Protector can compare. Concerning this, Nāgārjuna wrote in The Wish-Granting Gem of Dreams:

Not just once have I been in someone's womb:
There is no sentient being
who has not been in my womb
or I in theirs. Therefore, all are my relatives.

And we find in his Instructions from a Spiritual Friend:

If all the mothers we have had were round juniper kernels,
the earth could not hold such a great number of berries. [68]

Regarding this point Aśvaghoṣa tells us:

If all the friends and relatives you have had
were gathered together in the world,
the sands of the Ganges River
would not even partially equal their number.

The master Candragomin wrote:

You who were a helpless infant held on the lap
and given a breast to suckle through the power of love:
How could you abandon one who showed such unconditional love,
even if that one were the lowest of the low?
How could you cause that being ruin?

You rested so long inside the body of one
who treated you with loving kindness and care.
How could you desert one now so torn by emotions,
suffering, with no protection, even if that one were
the lowest of the low? How could you desert such a being?
                                        —*Letter to a Disciple, 97–98*

Again, we find:

The milk I have drunk from the breast
of those who have been my mother
exceeds by far the waters of the four oceans.
The gifts of horses and elephants
from those who have been my father
would fill more than the world of Brahma.

The good our fathers have done for us also cannot be measured. As for those who have been our friends and relatives, their tears of misery when separated from us would more than fill the boundless ocean. You need to grasp what they have done for you, and return their kindness. Thus the Treatise on Wise Conduct states:

The helpless are the finest burden, deserving honor:
They deserve the warmest love.
Do not forget the kindness they have done
in awakening the virtuous actions of the holy.

And again it is said:

In acknowledging what has been done for you
and returning such kindness,
you serve as a protector for those who
have not brought an end to their worldly actions.

From beginningless time, these beings who have shown such great kindness have done nothing but wander in samsara: here, there, everywhere. As Letter to a Disciple[6] states:

What beings have not traveled this route
hundreds of times in the past?
There is no suffering that has not existed
many times before. [91–93]

It is impossible to count the number of times each person has been born in the Avīci Hell. There is nothing we have not done. We cannot even begin to count the number of times we have killed our parents. With no food to eat and no clothes to wear, we have eaten excrement, drunk filth, and donned burning iron garments. Though we have accumulated more possessions than could be contained in

the world, we always find fault and are never satisfied with what we have. As the Buddha taught:

All beings desire satisfaction, but none ever truly find it.

In the past we have been like all the rest. Those of us who have not gained liberation from samsara and who even now do not practice to attain the path will naturally be burdened with a life full of many difficulties. The great master Togmed has said:

Seeing the faults of samsara, we have few misgivings.
Hearing of the qualities of the Buddha, we have little faith.
We have no conscience or restraint;
we lack the slightest compassion.
We do great wickedness and lack the slightest contrition.
When these six factors come together,
there is no chance to become a Buddha.

Alas, how wretched!

Each and every sentient being is my dear, aged mother who has been so very kind to me. Alas, their eyes are blinded by the film of ignorance. They cannot see what to accept and what to reject. They have no spiritual friend—no guide to the blind—and lack the sturdy staff of good friends. Their two feet, method and wisdom, have become lame, yet still they must wander in the wilderness of samsara, unfamiliar with the path of liberation. They are afflicted by the disease of the fettering passions and weighed down by the burden of bad karma. They are burned by the heat of suffering and tormented by the thirst of desire. Wherever they go, they are raped and violated. They do not know what to do. With no help and no refuge, they are oppressed by many frightful and harmful things.

Intensely meditate on love and compassion as before, concentrating on how pitiful these beings are who have lost their footing and will fall from the higher to the lower states of being. This meditation is easy to carry out, and the merit from it is great. It is said in The Precious Garland:

The expanse of sentient beings is immeasurable;
likewise the desire to benefit them. [219]

## Love and Compassion

Nothing is more important than to cultivate love and compassion. In the Sūtra Assembling the Dharmas, we find:

Avalokiteśvara said: "For those who desire to become a Buddha, there is no need to learn many dharmas, but only one dharma. What is this dharma? It is great compassion. Those who have great compassion have the complete Buddhadharma in the palms of their hands. Bhagavan, just as a chakravartin king, traveling with his precious wheel,[7] is joined by all the divisions of his army, so does the Bodhisattva travel everywhere with great compassion, which contains within it the complete Buddhadharma."

In the Sūtra of the Questions of Sāgaramati, we find:

The Buddha obtains but one dharma: great compassion, which means never to be concerned with your own happiness.

And again, the Verse Summary of the Prajñāpāramitā states:

Those who desire to go forth in this vehicle of the Buddha
must proceed with equality of mind towards all beings,
with the perception of all beings as their parents, with the
mind of love and benevolence. They must speak gentle words
honestly and without artifice. [16.6]

In the Sūtra of the Ornamental Array, we find:

The night goddess Vasantī said to Sudhana:
"Measureless is the ocean of my compassion:
From this the Jinas of the three times come into the world,
and with this they clear away the suffering of beings.
Know this way, O Sudhana, steadfast one."

The merit resulting from such compassion is very great. In The Precious Garland, we find:

Giving food to three hundred men,
though you give it three times each day,
could not give rise to the merit
of one instant of loving-kindness. [283]

Even before you obtain enlightenment, you will obtain eight great qualities as indicated in the same text:

Even if love does not gain you liberation,
you will obtain the eight qualities that love produces.
Gods and men will be your protectors;
your life will be full of delight.

You will become most happy,
neither weapons nor poison will harm you;
you will effortlessly attain your goals,
and you will be reborn in the realm of Brahma. [284–85]

Thus you become the finest of protectors for both yourself and others. This is also the best way of honoring the Buddhas. As is stated in a Sūtra:

There are three unexcelled offerings: generating the mind
of enlightenment, upholding the Dharma, and the meditation
of compassion.

We find in The Lantern of the Moon Sūtra:

However many marvelous and varied offerings you make
to the Supreme Being, even enough to fill one hundred billion
Buddha-fields, these offerings cannot equal the mind
of loving-kindness.

And again, in the Sūtra of the Questions of Vīradatta, we find:

Some make offerings to the Buddhas,
filling all the Buddha fields,
as innumerable as the grains of sand in the Ganges River,
with the seven precious gems.

Others fold their hands in prayer
and bow low with the mind of enlightenment.
Those who make such an offering are far greater:
Their offering is unexcelled.

In short, the mind of enlightenment endows you with immeasurable benefits and good qualities. There is a saying:

The person who meditates for merely an instant
on the mind of enlightenment
creates a magnitude of merit so great
that not even the Buddha can compute it.

One time, when Chen-ngawa was giving teachings on the importance of love and compassion, Lang Tangpa bowed before him and stated, "From this time forward, I will meditate only on love and compassion." The teacher removed his hat, and folding his hands in prayer, said three times, "This is most wonderful news!"

Another time, a disciple of Khampa Lungpa and the three spiritual brothers met with the teacher Geshe Tonpa. The teacher asked him, "What has Putowa been doing?"

"He has been teaching the Dharma to many hundreds of bhikṣus," he replied.

Geshe Tonpa responded, "This is wonderful!" And he asked again, "What has Geshe Puchungwa been doing?"

"He has been constructing the three foundations (stupas, images, and holy books), using his own wealth and donations from others."

Geshe Tonpa commented as before. Again he asked, "And what has Gonpaba been doing?"

"Gonpaba has been devoting himself solely to meditation."

Geshe Tonpa again replied as above. Then he asked, "And what has Khampa Lungpa been doing?"

"He is living in Drog-kha. Having covered his head, he does nothing but weep."

Geshe Tonpa removed his hat, folded his hands in prayer at his heart, and, weeping profusely, said in wonder, "He has truly been practicing the Dharma! There are many things I could say about the virtues of such practice, but if I were to express them now, he would not be pleased."

This is also the most important practice found in the teachings of Atīśa's oral lineage.

Orgyan Dusum Khyenpa has said:

Compassion, love, and the enlightened mind are inextricably
connected with the Three Collections: compassion with Vinaya;
love with Sūtra; and enlightened mind with Abhidharma.

They are also connected with the three trainings: compassion
free from attachment is associated with moral practice; love
free from hatred is associated with samādhi; and the mind
of enlightenment free from obscuration is associated with
the training in wisdom.

They are also connected with the three meditation experiences:
compassion free from attachment with bliss; love free from hatred
with mental clarity; and the mind of enlightenment free from
obscuration with meditation in which thought is absent.

Similarly, they wholly exclude any of the three poisons.
As they comprise the non-conceptual heart of the Buddhas,
they are called thugs, or 'spirit'.

These three—love, compassion, and Bodhicitta—are the essence
of the path of the Mahāyāna. There is no other.

## Love and Compassion in Action

When real love and compassion exist, the exchange of self for others
arises. Acting for the benefit of others, you do not ever even consider
your own life or body.

Long ago, our teacher the Buddha was born as a king named
Padma in the land of Ngari. The kingdom was struck by the plague,
and King Padma, being truly merciful, gave his life and body to alleviate the suffering of his subjects. Through the power of a wishing
prayer, he died and took rebirth as a rohita fish, for eating the flesh
of such a fish reverses the effects of the plague. As the fish he cured
everyone in his kingdom. Finally, he established all his subjects on
the path of final liberation from samsara.

Another time, the Buddha was born as a tortoise who rescued five
hundred shipwrecked merchants. Once on land, he sacrificed his body
to eighty thousand krema flies. Later, after becoming a Buddha, he

taught the Dharma to the flies, who had been reborn as eighty thousand gods, and established them in the vision of the truth.

Again, having become a king known as Tsugna Rinchen, he cut off his jeweled topknot and by doing so cut off the course of a famine and plague in the land of Drange. There are many similar birth stories.

Although Atīśa's teacher, Dharmarakṣita, did not officially receive teachings of the Great Vehicle during his lifetime, due to the great compassion he had established previously, in his heart he belonged to the lineage of the Mahāyāna.

At one time, Dharmarakṣita had a neighbor who became afflicted with a very serious illness. The doctors told the invalid that nothing could help him but the flesh of a living man. Hearing of this, Dharmarakṣita cut flesh from his own body and thus cured his neighbor. But as the realization of openness had not been born in Dharmarakṣita's heart, his wound caused him unbearable pain. Dharmarakṣita bore his pain patiently, knowing that even if he were to die, his own flesh had benefited another person. But because of the severity of the wound, he could not sleep.

Finally at the break of day he fell into an uneasy slumber. In his sleep, a fair-skinned man appeared to him, saying, "You will have to practice hardships such as this if you wish to obtain enlightenment! O wonderful, most wonderful!" The man in the dream then spit on the wound, after which he rubbed it, and the wound disappeared.

When Dharmarakṣita awoke, he found that the dream had been true. Later he explained, "The person in my dream was the Lord of Great Compassion, Avalokiteśvara."

Thus the realization of the ultimate, the true nature of being, was born in Dharmarakṣita's heart. He began to recite, like the sound of the wind, the teachings of the Middle Way written by Nāgārjuna. He soon realized with full force the ultimate nature of existence, and the genuine mind of compassion that holds others dearer than self arose in him.

Later, while Dharmarakṣita was teaching the Dharma using the tenets of Mādhyamika, a man began beating a dog with a stick. The Lama cried out, "No!" and fell from his seat. The others thought,

"No great harm has come to the dog! What pretense!" Knowing their thoughts, the Lama showed them his back. A welt had risen on his back in the same place that the dog had been beaten. Seeing this, all present expressed their great faith.

Another example is of the Master Ārya Asaṅga. For twelve years he lived in a cave and meditated on the Lord Maitreya without ever having a single vision of Maitreya, even in his sleep. Totally disconsolate, he finally left his cave. On the path he saw a female dog covered with festering sores and crawling with maggots. Great and unbearable compassion was born in Asaṅga's heart, and so he cut off a piece of flesh from his own body to feed the maggots. At once all his defilements fell away and he met the Lord Maitreya, the Protector, who took him to the Heaven of Tuṣita and taught him the works known as the Five Treatises of Maitreya.

Such are a few of the wondrous stories of those who have clearly realized the third stage of the Ārya Bodhisattva.

Also concentrate on the eight thoughts of a Great Being:

"May I someday be able to alleviate the suffering of all
sentient beings!"

"May I someday be able to provide great fortune for
sentient beings who suffer from poverty!"

"May I someday be able to benefit sentient beings by means of
my own flesh and blood!"

"May I someday be able to help all beings in hell,
abiding there for a very long time!"

"May I someday be able to fulfill the yearnings of sentient beings
by providing them with great wealth, both worldly and spiritual!"

"May I someday become a Buddha, able to destroy all traces
of the suffering of sentient beings!"

"In all lifetimes, may I delight in never doing anything that is
not of benefit to sentient beings. May I experience the ultimate.
May I never speak words that do not invigorate all beings. May I
never engage in a livelihood that does not help others. May I never
harm others by means of my body, friends, wealth, or power!"

"May the fruit of the wrongs of others ripen upon me, and may the fruit of my own virtue ripen upon others."

While these are actually just thoughts, because of their wondrous nature, they are also the meditations of great beings. Shouldn't we, although beginners, always meditate in the same way? If we do not cultivate the preliminary practices and love and compassion in this way, our practice in exchanging self for other is merely pretense.

Once you have earnestly generated love and compassion, it is important for you to establish them both in your very being. The Bodhisattva Śāntideva refers to this in several places:

In meditation, strive first
for the sameness of self and other.
—*Entering the Bodhisattva Path, 8.90*

Attuning your mind in this way,
taking delight in relieving the sufferings of others,
even if you enter the Avīci Hell,
you will be like a swan in a pond of lotuses.

When sentient beings are liberated,
what an ocean of delight it is!
How could this not make you content,
how could you not desire to liberate them?

Truly, even while acting for the welfare of others,
do not be proud or think yourself special.
Delight in the welfare of others alone, and
have no expectations for the fruits of your actions.

Truly, just as you protect yourself from unpleasant things,
however small, guard others likewise,
filling your mind with compassion. [8.107–10]

# Reflections

## Exchange of Self for Others

We all admire people who dedicate their lives to serving others, and occasionally we may reflect upon what it would be like to live such a life. We know the satisfaction we feel when we help someone else, even in small acts of kindness. How much joy might we experience in committing our whole being to benefiting others?

Considering realistically what such a life requires, few of us are willing to make the necessary sacrifices. The notion of exchanging self for others less fortunate challenges our most fundamental samsaric convictions of the central importance of self. Even the satisfaction we feel when helping others almost always has a selfish aspect to it; our motivation is seldom altruistic. We 'get something' out of helping or giving to others; we give to others because it feels good to do so, or perhaps in hopes of gaining gratitude or respect, or to make up for misdeeds in the past. Possibly we are motivated by the prospect of reward, such as an afterlife in heaven.

For the enlightened mind to flower, it is necessary to cultivate an unselfish and altruistic state of being. Of the meditation practices that promote this kind of development, the most effective involves Tong Len. The basic practice is simply presented in the root text:

*Alternately practice unconditional giving and taking on all suffering.*
*Mount them both upon the wind of the breath.*

Though the exchange of self for others in this practice takes place only in your thoughts, such thoughts have great and transforming power. The practice of Tong Len dissolves the individualism so basic to modern life, which often carries with it a sense of isolation and a feeling of having little in common with other people and their problems. Through the practice of Tong Len we can break down the barrier between self and other, and form a link for open-hearted communication with others.

Practicing on both relative and absolute levels, cultivating wisdom and compassion, we can use this teaching to awaken the seed of Bodhicitta within our hearts. Then the field of enlightenment lies open before us; vision becomes pristinely clear, allowing us to see the richness and beauty within the mind of compassion. Finally, when we awaken to the truth of liberation, rays of love and great joy permeate heart and mind, illuminating the darkness of samsara.

When the mind attains samādhi and taps its power to transcend all obstacles, we can bring forth the enlightened qualities of the Bodhisattva and use them to benefit all beings. Attuned to the Three Kāyas of the Buddha, we can serve beings with the beauty of true humility and inner balance. The chaotic conflicts of ego and selfish concerns fall away, and we live in a state of refined balance that words cannot fully describe.

# The Actual Practice: The Exchange of Self for Others

*T*o actually practice the exchange of self for others, the root text states:

> *Alternately practice unconditional giving*
> *and taking on all suffering.*

This is the actual basis of the path, and is vital for your practice. The Bodhisattva Śāntideva emphasizes this strongly:

Whoever desires to quickly rescue
both self and others
should perform this sacred, secret act:
the exchange of self and other.
  —*Entering the Bodhisattva Path, 8.120*

If you do not actually exchange
your own happiness for the suffering of others,
you will never attain Buddhahood,
or ever be truly happy in the world. [8.131]

In order to allay my own distress
and assuage the suffering of others,
I will give myself to others
and embrace others as I would myself. [8.136]

Having realized that I am full of faults
and others are an ocean of good qualities,
I must meditate on giving up self-grasping
and assuming responsibility for others. [8.113]

## *The Wish to Exchange Self for Others*

The master Nāgārjuna stated:

May everyone's sins ripen upon me
and may all my virtues ripen upon them.

In The Seventy Resolves, we find:

May I take on all the non-virtue done by beings overcome
by the mental darkness of the poisonous emotions,
and for their sake may I joyfully
descend into the hells.

May I satiate the world with the blissful nectar
of great peace, and may joy arise in every mind!
Whatever suffering sentient beings may undergo,
may I take it all upon myself! [6–7]

The master Vasubandhu states in his Various Counsels:

My life and my body
I must give to all sentient beings.

And again:

May the sins of all creatures
all ripen upon me.
Receiving these sins,
I take upon myself the wickedness of these poor beings.

As Atīśa's great Lama, Serlingpa, states in Stages of the Bodhisattva's Self-Mastery:

To protect the Way of the Sugata
as did King Mahāsattva,
I must consider only the welfare of others:
Most certainly I must exchange self for others.

The Master Dharmarakṣita states in his Self-Mastery: The Peacock's Antidote:

The Bodhisattva, as Prince Viśvantara,
gave up his son and daughter and his kingdom. In like manner,
may I give up everything, including garlands of precious gems
and all my attendants, so that poverty will be no more!

The Bodhisattva, as Prince Mahāsattva,
fed his own flesh to the tigress. In like manner,
may I joyfully give to the flesh-eaters
this illusory heap of flesh I hold so dear!

The Bodhisattva, as King Maitrībala, with his own flesh
sustained the yakṣas. In like manner,
may my heartfelt pity urge me to feed the Blood-Drinkers
with warm blood from my own heart, so difficult to let flow!

The Bodhisattva, as the Merchant Suparaga,
called upon the name of the Sugata at the watery abyss;
and did so again as the king of fish.
In like manner, may I give the gift of the sacred Dharma
to all beings destitute of the teachings!

The Bodhisattva, as Prince Gendun Chenpo,
reversed wrongdoing through his patient compassion.
In like manner, may I reverse samsara,
by showing the highest mercy and acting with great compassion
toward those whose nature is contentious.

When the Bodhisattva was a monkey,
he rescued the wicked ones from the well. In like manner,
may I never give up trying to help the wicked;
may I lead them with compassion, never desiring good in return.[8]

And also:

Let me follow the way of Upāli, who was finally the most noble,
and Aśvajit, whose care in practice transformed to beauty.
If I do not guide my parents to the path of enlightenment,
the stairway of selfish liberation will lead me downward
to great oppression.

Though you obtain the authority of piercing intellect
or become renowned like the foolish Nanda,
if you do not assume the responsibility of the teaching,
you will stumble, like a madman dancing.

Though you may look like a Lama,
if you do not take up the burden of the teachings,
but rather strive for your own desires,
superior beings will call you to task.

And again we find:

Bad omens occur in the world presaging what we do not desire,
as a darkened sky foretells the specter of battle.
Because the enemy's evil nature is to cause destruction,
you must don the armor of blessings.

Disturbing illusions occur in the world, such as
karma and kleśas, so very needless.
In order to be free from a life of self-grasping,
you must don the armor of exertion.

In the Wheel Weapon, we find:

Place all blame on one source
and concentrate on the great kindness of all beings.[9]
Take upon yourself what others do not desire,
and dedicate to others all your virtuous actions.

When the body, speech, and mind of others
are pervaded by the three poisons, take the poisons on yourself.
Just as the peacock is made splendid by poison,
let the emotional afflictions assist in enlightenment!

Give beings the roots of your virtue: Be like the crow,
cured by the medicinal nature of poisonous plants.
Having dedicated your life to liberate all beings,
may you quickly obtain the Awakening of the Sugatas. [96–98]

In Maitriyogin's Song of Adamantine Meditation, we find:

"Heed this! In order to deliver all beings
who have all been my parents,
may I put to good use the five poisons of the kleśas I still bear,
and may I draw forth all the poisons of sentient beings!

"Whatever virtues I may have, such as being without attachment,
may I dispense them equally to the beings of the six realms.
By means of the suffering I undergo as the result of various ills,
may I draw forth all the suffering of those realms.

"May I always distribute to all the beings of the six realms
whatever joy and benefit may come from being free from ills.
When I do this, how could an occasion ever arise
where I must struggle for even an instant
in this ocean of samsara?

"From now until I obtain enlightenment,
may whatever emotions I experience, whether as cause or effect,
become the means for bringing all beings to perfection.
May I devote myself to this end right now, on this very day.

"Whatever I accomplish this very day
through any suffering, however slight,
may I use it to immediately purify my mind!"
This is the yoga of Maitri!

Atīśa has stated:

There is a teaching for transforming the root of bad karma
through distancing yourself from it.
For others, however, such karma is the source of enlightenment:
This is the teaching taken up by the wise.

The All-Knowing Lama has stated:

Truly, all beings are my parents.
Just as I would benefit my friends and relatives,
so should I benefit others, generating the mind of enlightenment.
"May I practice virtuous action for the benefit of all beings!
May my virtuous actions make beings happy!
May all their suffering ripen upon me,

and may my own virtue ripen upon them.
May all embodied beings become Buddhas!"
Such thoughts arouse the Four Immeasurables
that develop and purify the enlightened mind.

Gyalsay Rinpoche has stated:

All suffering comes from desiring your own happiness;
perfect Buddhahood is born in the mind that benefits others.
Truly, this is the Bodhisattva's practice:
to exchange your own happiness and the suffering of others.
            —*The Thirty-Seven Bodhisattva Practices, 13*

   Immeasurable benefit comes from meditating well in this manner.
In Entering the Bodhisattva Path, we find:

Even the thought, "May I relieve
the headaches of sentient beings!"
is endowed with immeasurable merit,
being suffused with the motivation to be of help.

How much more so the merit arising from the desire
to relieve the immeasurable unhappiness
of each and every sentient being
and the wish for each to achieve immeasurable goodness.

Whose father or mother has ever had
the thought to benefit others in this way?
Has any god or rishi?
Does even Brahma have it?

Even in their dreams,
sentient beings have not previously
thought to truly benefit themselves,
so how can the thought to help others arise?

Previously this precious gem of mind—
this thought for the welfare of sentient beings—
has not come forth.
Its birth is a great wonder! [1.21–25]

And again:

It satisfies all desires
and dispels all the suffering
of those destitute of happiness,
caught up in so much misery.

It clears away even ignorance.
How could there be virtue to equal this?
How could there be a friend to equal this?
How could there be merit to equal this? [1.29–30]

Therefore, holding in your consciousness this precious state of mind that cherishes others, humbly wish for the opportunity to help them. In the same text we find:

I bow down to those Beings
who possess the sacred jewel of enlightened mind.
I take refuge in that source of happiness—in those
who offer happiness even to those who harm them.
                    *—Entering the Bodhisattva Path, 1.36*

## *The Method of Exchange*

In meditating and visualizing the exchange of self and others, you must take upon yourself the bad karma of others with all your heart, or no exchange occurs. If you do not give of yourself, you will not accumulate merit and wisdom. Both unconditional giving and taking on the suffering of others must take place. Thus, concentrate on taking upon yourself the suffering of others, as in the previous meditation. In Entering the Bodhisattva Path, we find:

Whatever the suffering of beings,
may it all ripen upon me. [10.56]

First clearly visualize your present-day mother, the one who bore you in her womb, who gave birth to you, who cared for you without rest. Concentrate on her great kindness, and pray that she will now meet with the doctrine of the Buddha and that the conditions will arise for her to practice the profound Dharma. Not only in this lifetime, but for beginningless lifetimes, she has gazed upon you with

loving eyes, embraced you with the mind of mercy, and protected you from harm.

Having meditated in detail on her very great kindness in securing your benefit and happiness as indicated above, consider what she has done in previous lives to help you. Reflect on how pitiful she is! Because of what she has done for you, she now wanders in circles in samsara, suffering in many different ways.

Concentrate on her kindness from the very depth of your heart, until tears stream down your face, and pray: "Let me now return the kindness and help she has showered upon me! I must remove all her difficulties!"

Concentrate thus: "I will take upon myself whatever harm comes to my mother—both the harm itself and any suffering due to that harm." Along with this thought, examine the various different ways she suffers: specific instances of heat and cold, hunger and thirst and the like, discomforts so routine in the realms of sentient beings.

Reflect as well on the universal forms of suffering your mother will have to undergo. Your mother, and all who depend on her, will inevitably meet with the omnipresent enemies we so fear and hate: birth, old age, sickness, and death. She will be separated from her beloved relatives; she will have the boundless suffering of not obtaining the things she desires.

Think also of the illnesses she is subject to: the hundreds of illnesses that come from the various combinations of wind, bile, and phlegm;[10] infectious diseases and unexpected accidents, diseases of the senses inconceivable in number: diseases of the mouth, the eyes, the ears, and so on. For, having received a body that is prone to destruction, no one ever escapes the three types of sufferings.

The sources of that suffering are both karma and the kleśas. The sources of karma include the ten non-virtuous actions (killing and the rest), the five indefensible sins, the five nearly boundless offenses, the four weighty sins, the eight errors, and whatever goes against the spiritual vows. Along with these are the inconceivable number of harmful acts performed almost without conscious awareness.

Then there are the sources for the kleśas. These include the root sources: desire, hatred, and ignorance that come from seizing on a self; the six root kleśas; the twenty proximate kleśas; and extending from those, eighty-four thousand other emotional fetters. Because she puts off meditation and dismisses spiritual vision, your mother is unable to deal with the innumerable and inconceivable obstacles to liberation and to omniscience that take form.

All this suffering, as well as the sources of suffering and the subtle residual patterns that support suffering, have come to exist in your mother's very nature. Now, cut this suffering from her, as if with a sharp razor. Take up this suffering and place it in the center of your heart. Once you have taken it upon yourself, hold it tightly. Do not do anything that might lessen it. Do not attempt to stifle your pain or hope that taking on the pain will somehow help you instead of her. Hold within your heart only the thought of pity for your mother. Clearly envisioning this, concentrate on removing all her sufferings and residual patterns of suffering, not leaving out anything.

When you do this, overpowering sensations of joy will arise. The motivating force behind this is the foundation of compassion, and from that basis, meditation on true self-sacrifice arises. Thus we find in Entering the Bodhisattva Path:

My body and enjoyments,
even all the virtues of the three times,
I will give for the sake of benefiting all sentient beings,
holding nothing back.

Giving up everything leads to nirvana:
Your own mind passes from sorrow.
The best way to give to sentient beings
is to give everything all at once. [3.10–11]

To benefit your mother in every way, to provide her with everything happy and good, you must give her all your own virtue and happiness without considering your own desires. Concentrate on your mother acquiring all the favorable circumstances for happiness and for practicing the Dharma. See her immediately gaining the ability to become a Buddha.

The actual process of self-sacrifice includes giving up your body and your enjoyments, as well as all your accumulation of merit. To give up your body means both your present body and all your future bodies. To give up your enjoyments means to give up everything you have, both now and in all future lives. To give up your merit means to give away all the virtue accumulated in the three times: past, present, and future. Giving your future body and enjoyment means that even if you have nothing to give now, in the future, having accustomed yourself to the thought of giving, you will be able to give up everything, including your body.

On this basis, you will eventually obtain the qualities of the Holy Ones. Obtaining these qualities is vital, as they make it possible for you to sacrifice yourself completely, even giving up your own head. And since you must have the precious wish-granting gem of a body in order to be able to give people what they desire, you will have the most beautiful body imaginable and be surrounded by the finest possessions existing within the worlds of the gods or mankind. You will always be accompanied by sweet sounds and have access to the finest food and drink. Everything in your life will be wonderful. The enjoyments you will have to give will be truly perfect, emanating throughout the extent of space.

Think with delight of all the virtuous actions done by others and that you yourself have done and ever will do. Then visualize giving away everything, holding nothing back. Visualize providing clothing for your kind mother as she did for you. Give her all the necessities to support a spiritual life: a suitable place to live and so forth. Clearly imagine that she has all the most spiritual qualities, as well as faith and wisdom, and the empowering conditions for awakening: a spiritual friend to teach her the path of the Great Vehicle, the teachings of the Great Vehicle, the path for practicing them, and the qualities for their fruition.

In short, visualize actually giving your mother all the immeasurable resources that exist in this world as well as in all other realms, including the transworldly ground of the perfect Buddhas. Generate intense yearning, full of delight in such giving. The motivation for such giving depends principally on love. Then meditate in the same way on your father and in turn, on all others.

Finally, meditate on the equality of all sentient beings. To do this, first clarify your focus by concentrating on a small group of people, including your father and mother and relatives, and then, by stages, extend this group to include your neighbors, those in your general region, the people inhabiting the same continent, and by stages all the peoples of the four continents. Then meditate on different world systems: one thousand worlds, then two thousand, three thousand, and so forth. After this, finally meditate on all sentient beings in all of space.

The Aspirations for Proceeding in Goodness states:

Vast as the sky
is the extent of all beings.
Only when all their karma and kleśas are brought to an end
will I cease my aspirations.

Since all sentient beings, from beginningless time, have existed as both your father and mother, concentrate as follows: "All beings have helped me immeasurably; their kindness is extraordinary! Yet now they are all being badly harmed by the various sufferings of samsara. How fitting it would be if I freed all these beings from suffering!"

Having meditated upon this strongly, focus on giving everything unconditionally and taking upon yourself all suffering:

"I take upon myself the suffering of those in the lower hells: the suffering that comes from being burned by fire, from weapons, from illness, and from other sentient beings. I take upon myself all the causes of going to the cold hells, from the hell of Arbuda, the Blister Hell, through to Mahāpadma, the Great Lotus Hell. I accept the consequences of the kleśas, including hatred and the most non-virtuous of actions—killing and the like.

"I take upon myself the suffering of the hungry ghosts: their hunger and thirst, their kleśas of desire and the rest. I take upon myself all their non-virtuous actions of middling force, such as stealing.

"I take upon myself the sufferings of the animals. I accept even the consequence of their eating each other, along with their kleśas such as ignorance and all their lesser non-virtuous actions.

"I take upon myself the karma that falls indiscriminately upon all of these beings: birth, old age, sickness, and death, so fundamental to the lives of those born as human beings in the higher realms; the quarreling of the demigods; the omens of death for the gods of the Desire Realm; the sufferings of transmigration and the fall of those in the two higher realms; and the kleśas of pride and jealousy and so forth. All of this I will practice using any means, seeing through trial and error what works and what does not work, steadily purifying my focus.

"I take upon myself all the adverse karma that creates obstacles for my enemies, whose actions cause them to be born into difficult lives; that creates obstacles for my spiritual friends, holy ones of the heart-lineage who teach the Dharma; that creates obstacles for the Śrāvakas, Pratyekabuddhas, Arhats, and followers of the Mahāyāna and prevents them from gaining the stages of the path.

"I take upon myself all the obscurations of the kleśas and the obscurations of the knowable, together with the residual patterns underlying these obscurations. I take upon myself all those misfortunes that suddenly appear to obstruct the lives of beings and frustrate their good actions. Gaining self-mastery in all aspects of taking responsibility, both general and particular, I will treat all equally."

Then consider the specific aspects of unconditional giving:

"I give my own body: flesh for those who desire flesh, blood for those who desire blood, feet for those who desire feet, eyes for those who desire eyes. I will be a slave for those who want a slave: I will do whatever they desire. I will give whatever I have that others wish for, giving food for those who want food, clothes for those who want clothes, vehicles for those who want vehicles—whatever is desired. I will give whatever virtuous actions I have done and am doing for others, rejoicing in others' virtue, giving as well all virtuous actions of the three paths in samsara and nirvana.

"I visualize each and every sentient being obtaining perfection with these gifts. Focusing intently, I visualize giving all beings every enjoyment of my own body, with as many manifestations of myself as there are atoms in a Buddha-field. I manifest and offer the wish-granting gem, the wish-granting tree, the nectar of the gods, the spontaneously growing crops of the fields, the wish-fulfilling cow,

the seven precious gems of the kingdom, the eight auspicious symbols, the precious adjuncts of royalty, and the offerings to be made to the gods, all of which fill the sky.

"I offer all this to the wondrous holy Lama of refuge, the Three Jewels, as well as to all the Bodhisattvas, that I might satisfy completely all the innumerable sentient beings without exception. In such a way, I ceaselessly give all virtuous actions."

This is the way to apply yourself to giving whatever may be desired. The Bodhisattva Śāntideva stated:

May I heal the sick
until they all become well.
May I nurse the sick
as both doctor and medicine.

May I rain down food and drink
to clear away the pain of hunger and thirst,
and during the kalpa of famine,
may I myself be the food and drink.

May I be an inexhaustible treasure
for those who are poor and destitute;
may I stay close by them
as whatever they should need.
    —*Entering the Bodhisattva Path*, 3.7–9

By giving whatever I can of this body,
I will bring happiness to sentient beings.
May I always devote myself to whatever gives them joy—
though it be to upbraid me, beat me, or kill me.

Let them play with my body,
making it a source of scorn and laughter.
Having given them my body,
what censure could I offer? [3.12–13]

May I be a protector for those without a protector;
a guide for those who enter the path.
May I be a boat, a bridge, a great ship
for those who desire to cross over.

May I be an island for those intent on an island,
a butter lamp for those desiring a lamp.
May I be a bed for those desiring a place of rest,
and a slave for all who wish to own a slave.

May I be a wish-granting gem and an ever-full vessel,
an all-healing medicine and a siddha-mantra;
may I be the wish-granting tree
and wish-fulfilling cow for all beings.

Just as the sky
and the great elements such as earth
sustain the life of all the many types of beings,
may I sustain all the boundless forms of life.

For all the realms of sentient beings
touching the ends of space,
may I be a source of life
until all pass beyond sorrow. [3.17–21]

Further methods for self-mastery are described in other works, and include practices that entail visualizing things such as the elements, the earth and so on. Meditation practices such as these also bring great joy. By such meditations, you can finally free all sentient beings from the causes of their suffering, freeing even those in the hells, tormented by intense heat and cold.

Having performed such immeasurable groundwork, you will establish pure realms for living beings and change entire ways of life, so that even the beasts of the field learn the path of the Mahāyāna, accomplish the two accumulations, purify the two obscurations, and finally manifest the qualities of the five paths and obtain the inestimable loftiness of the omniscient Buddhas.

Visualize freeing all beings, emptying the ocean of the three realms of samsara in this way. Then practice the meditation presented in the chapter Dedication in Entering the Bodhisattva Path, intensely developing joy in this practice.

As a simple practice for developing the mind of exchanging self for others the root text states:

*Mount them both upon the wind of the breath.*

When your breath flows out from you, see yourself calling out on the wind, "May all my virtue and happiness go to others, and may others be full of happiness." When the breath flows into you, concentrate on gathering to yourself all the sufferings and sins of others. Dissolve these sufferings into yourself, and concentrate on the thought that all sentient beings should be freed from the causes and effects of suffering. Along with being easy for the mind to grasp, this practice creates a mental state good for purifying the mind and for subduing disruptive thinking.

The Buddha taught that when you do this meditation, minor hindrances such as melancholy may at first arise. But if you persevere in controlling your breath as it goes in and out, you can gain complete control over your state of mind.

# Reflections

## Transforming the Emotions

*M*editating on the exchange of self for others opens us to a deeper sense of compassion. The process of exchanging self for others as developed in meditation must then be carried into each aspect of life. Every activity and every action must be imbued with compassion for all beings. Thus the root text counsels:

> *Tell yourself always remember only others;*
> *practice this principle in all you say or do.*

Carrying this practice through into everything we think and do, however, may be more difficult than it seems. As long as we are enmeshed in worldly concerns, we will continually be caught up in emotional turmoil. Although we may attempt to always act honestly and kindly and with a virtuous mind, our actions still unfold within a self-centered way of understanding.

Even if we take to heart the counsel to always remember others, we still must deal with our own problems. On a personal level, our lives present one difficulty after another, affecting work or family, friends or enemies. Those we love turn away from us or grow old; at any moment they may become ill and die. Certain difficult days seem unending; untold hours are lost to confusion, frustration, and emotional upheavals. Our thoughts and actions are part of samsara

and reflect its patterns. Where then do we begin to penetrate such pervasive obstacles?

Clearly, our problems begin with ourselves. But few people, especially those who perceive the pervasiveness of the world's difficulties, would accept that all these problems are due to their own actions. When we look more closely, we begin to recognize the interconnections between ourselves and others. Observing similarities and relationships that we did not see before, we begin to understand how our actions affect all those around us, extending outwards like ripples from a stone tossed into the water of a pond. Without being omniscient, we can look at the pattern of human nature in operation and know where certain actions will lead. We can take responsibility for deciding what patterns we wish to enact or promote.

The next step, taking upon ourselves the suffering of others, seems an almost superhuman activity, the self-sacrifice it would entail unthinkable for an ordinary person. And yet mothers make such sacrifices all the time for their children. Perhaps the magnitude of this self-sactifice is not so difficult and unimaginable as we think. Perhaps, in taking this step, we will find unexpected sources of support for sustaining and extending our capacities.

It is said that the Bodhisattva Avalokiteśvara, when first beginning to practice compassion, gazed over the land of Tibet and had a vision of countless beings being burned alive in an ocean of fire. He then went among the Tibetan people and made intense efforts to dispel their misery and bring them to happiness. But when he looked again over the land, he saw that he had not helped even a handful of beings. He was seized by sorrow, and for an instant the thought arose: "What is the use! I can do nothing for them. It is better for me to be happy and peaceful myself."

At that moment his head cracked into ten pieces and his body split into a thousand parts. In his agony he called out to the Buddha Amitābha, who blessed the Great Bodhisattva and transformed the ten pieces of his head into ten faces, one for each of the pāramitās. He transfigured Avalokiteśvara's body so that it produced one thousand arms; in each hand opened an eye, enabling Avalokiteśvara to engage the misery of samsara with the wisdom of the thousand Buddhas of the Golden Age.

## *Study and Practice*

You can begin the practice of compassion by looking clearly at the suffering that pervades your own life. Suffering comes naturally into the life of each being, and we can clearly document its range: from the aches and pains of the body to the minor annoyances of daily life, to great loss and confusion and the final sorrows of old age, sickness, and death.

Suppose you have a headache; not a big problem, but enough to make you uncomfortable and focused on your own feelings of discomfort. In turning your thoughts to others, you can see that everywhere around you, in every corner, every land, every realm there are beings suffering in the same way. In turning your thoughts away from your own suffering, the wish arises that no one should ever have to experience such pain or discomfort. It may not seem like much, but that is how the practice of compassion can begin.

Next, imagine what it is like to give what you cherish to others. One way to do this is to practice having the right hand make gifts to the left, and vice-versa, accompanying this action with sincere wishes for happiness and well-being. There is certainly some play-acting involved in this, but at this point the aim is simply to become familiar with the feelings that such a practice evokes.

It is deeply important to be patient with yourself in doing these practices, for they are the foundation for the Bodhisattva Path. They release karma and develop compassion; they lead to freedom from samsaric subjugation. If you can make this effort now, all other Mahā-yāna and Vajrayāna practices will come easily.

# After Meditation:
# Transforming the Emotions

*N*ow, transform the three poisons—desire, hatred, and ignorance—into virtuous activity. As the root text proposes:

> *From three objects, the three poisons,*
> *make three roots of virtue.*

When you are involved in what brings you pleasure, such as being with your friends and relatives, you experience feelings of attachment. When you are involved in what distresses you, such as having to deal with your enemies, you generate feelings of hatred. When you are involved with what is indeterminate, you generate feelings of bewilderment about what to accept and what to reject. These three kinds of events bring about the accumulation of karma, and the results propel you forward into samsara.

Therefore, concentrate on the thought: "Innumerable beings have generated the three poisons of the kleśas just as I have done. May I gather to myself all the three poisons they have generated, and may they attain the three virtues of being without desire, hatred, or ignorance." Rinpoche Sonam Dragpa said the following concerning this:

If the frame of mind is good in its essence, you can transform the kleśas and any non-virtuous actions into virtue, to say nothing of what is indeterminate. If the frame of mind is bad, then even

if someone wishes to cultivate devotion to virtue,
it is difficult for them to do so.

This is very true. Although you may be instrumental in advancing the spiritual progress of others at your own expense, if you feel self-satisfaction for this, you will make no spiritual progress. In thinking to advance yourself by helping others, you are actually accepting that it is enough for you alone to make spiritual progress even if others do not. If that is the case, even though in some sense you are developing yourself, are you really devoting yourself to virtue? Therefore it is said in the root text:

> *Tell yourself always: Remember only others.*
> *Practice this principle in all you say or do.*

At all times say to yourself:

"May all wrongdoing ripen upon me,
and may all my virtue ripen upon others."

The Most Noble Nāgārjuna taught this as well:

Offer every gain and victory to sentient beings,
as they are sovereign. Take upon yourself
all their troubles and difficulties.

In the teachings of the Kadampa, this is basic. Gyalsay Togmed Rinpoche thus taught:

May all the sufferings and sins of all sentient beings ripen on me,
and may all of my own happiness and virtue ripen on all others.

Express this very strongly and earnestly. The Lord of Dharma, Śākyaśrī, stated:

The suffering of others,
though it be as overwhelming as a mountain,
I take upon myself.
All my own happiness,
though it be as insignificant as a sesame seed,
I dedicate to others.

At first the strength of this intent emerges only haltingly as you express it. But as you become attuned to this state of mind, it will be as Lang Tangpa said at the point of death:

I wish to be born in hell! This is my wishing prayer of aspiration, made with all my strength. What I have achieved now I am unlikely to achieve again. Now, I have at least the appearance of purity, but later I may not even have this.

Even if your aspirations are weak and such a feeling for others does not arise, do not think it senseless to try. The Review of the Great Vehicle states:

Even should your actions to help others lack strength,
you must always think of others:
If that thought exists,
then the purpose ripens.

In order to develop the ability to take upon yourself the suffering of others, the root text states:

> *Start the process of taking on suffering*
> *with yourself.*

When your mind has not yet been purified through hearing and studying the teachings, so that you still think basically of yourself and are afraid to take on the suffering of others, you must first learn to accept your own suffering.

Concentrate on the thought: "In all my future births, may I never again have to experience the maturation of karma or the kleśas, or the suffering that is their result. May they ripen upon my mind and body in this birth. May I never again experience negativities that will mature later in this lifetime: May they ripen this year. May I bring to fruition in this month what would otherwise ripen this year; may I ripen today what would otherwise ripen this month. May I take on in this instant what would otherwise ripen sometime today."

By expressing this idea and meditating upon it, you gradually become accustomed to this process, until finally you can actually take on the suffering of others. In Entering the Bodhisattva Path, we find:

There is nothing that does not
become easy once you are accustomed to it.
Therefore, through learning to accept a little abuse,
you will gain patience even for great persecution. [6.14]

## Compassionate Openness

When you have thoroughly accustomed yourself to the process of taking on suffering, you will come to understand the complete unity of openness and compassion. Atīśa, in his Self-Mastery: The Crown-Jewel, states:

From beginningless time, openness being the way
the Dharma abides, patience toward beings merges with
the welcoming space of compassion. Even as compassion arises,
it arises from the Dharmadhātu; my child, even as it vanishes,
it vanishes in the Dharmadhātu.

All of samsara and nirvana are the mind itself:
All causes and conditions trace to mind. Who does not see this?
When you examine and consider mind, it is like a rainbow in the sky.
My child, realize openness and compassion accordingly,
like the rainbow colors of the sky.

From the profound depths of the ocean, turbulent waves arise.
My child, the waves emerge from the ocean
and then vanish into it.
Yet the moving waves differ from the ocean depth:
Who does not see this?

Likewise, from the spontaneity of openness,
the movement of beings and illusory compassion arise.
My child, the arising of compassion also aries from the nature
of openness; vanishing, it vanishes again into openness.

And further:

From within the radiant mandala of the sun
arises the light that illumines the world.
The sun and the light are very different: Who does not see this?
Openness arises in the form of great compassion,

yet compassion remains only openness.
O clever child, the Protector does not maintain
the existence of compassion apart from openness.

And again:

Is it a mistake to see openness as compassion,
or does compassion abide as openness?
O clever child, does openness arise as compassion?
Those who carefully examine this:
Do they distinguish compassion from openness
or from the syllable 'A'?

And again:

Alas! O clever child, whether beings go or stay,
they abide as isolated beings:
This is the abiding of mind itself within the middle nāḍī;[11]
this is the way openness abides, O clever child.

To cultivate compassion as that very nature:
O clever child, that is the yoga without distinctions.
If you cultivate compassion that understands in such a way,
you see this loving kindness as also only openness.

Meditation of openness not pervaded by compassion does not exist;
meditation of compassion is only openness.
Even the emptiness of the practice of abiding tranquility
belongs to this meditation.

The openness of this Great Vehicle is compassion;
the mark of this compassion is openness.
Therefore, understand the essential meaning as compassion:
So the Buddha has taught, and so should it be understood.

The Protector and his heirs have gone to the furthest reaches
to help both self and others.
They present the supreme unexcelled path to be traversed:
openness and compassion, method and wisdom conjoined.
Without this, who could traverse the way of knowledge?

The actuality of compassion, being open, has no self-nature;
it arises as compassion without cutting off its own capacity

of openness: indivisible in its aspects, like a rainbow or the image
of a moon in water. Those who know this well go beyond both
samsara and the peace of nirvana.

When analyzing appearance, all dharmas appear
like a dream at twilight; due to residual patterns,
they falsely appear as individual entities.
Each and every thing is non-objectifiable, open by nature.
Not holding on to the truth in this, you are endowed with wisdom.

The grasping, apprehending mind itself
is like the luminosity of space:
Though it appears to exist, if you examine it,
there is nothing to identify. Birthless, ceaseless, non-abiding,
passing from the extremes of coming and going—
to grasp at its signs is an error of the childish.

To see anything as existing anywhere is the extreme of eternalism;
the appeal to non-existence is the extreme of nihilism.
Even holding things to be dual and non-dual is inaccurate;
so rest in the nature of the balance of non-duality.

After meditation, all dharmas are like an illusion:
Though they are non-objectifiable,
happiness and suffering do appear on illusion's face.
Thus, within the impure realm of illusory thoughts,
take great care concerning cause and effect
and acceptance and rejection.

Alas, how pitiful! Beings whose understanding is obscured
do not realize that grasping at illusory appearances
as truly existing binds them to samsara.
The twelve links of dependent origination
are like the spokes of a chariot:
Again born, again turning! Alas, what a pity!

From beginningless time, we have wandered in samsara:
How could we not be linked with each and every sentient being?
The milk we have drunk at their breasts,
the essence of their bodies,
is greater in extent than all the water of all the oceans.

So it was that Norjinpa traveled far,
crossing vast distances, even the world of Brahma.
Having become an antidote for samsara's ills, he gave aid
so vast in extent that the sands of the river Ganges
cannot compare in vastness.

As all beings are our relatives,
to treat them with partiality, alas, is mistaken.
These are your dear mothers! They have stumbled into
the whirlpool of samsara:
How could you think of your own happiness alone?

They have closed their eyes to wisdom
and severed the feet of method; lost in the wilderness of samsara,
they are far from friends who could show them the path.
Lacking the provisions of virtue, they suffer,
stricken by illness. Alas! Our dear mothers are to be pitied!

The desire for your own happiness
hinges completely on wrongdoing;
it is from the mind of helping others that the Buddhas are born.
Your own happiness lies in not forgetting the suffering of others:
Now is the time to reach the stage of omniscience!

Before you have obtained the fruit of liberation for yourself,
how can you hope to free your wretched mothers?
With the mind that desires to be a Buddha for the sake
of freeing beings, always concentrate on Bodhicitta:

"From beginningless time, my dear mothers
have been bound up in this existence.
Through seizing on a self and through the causal power
of the kleśas, the whole mass of suffering of karma
and its effects have been produced.
From today on, I take responsibility for the welfare of all.

"May I give to all beings my own body and enjoyments,
together with all virtuous acts of past, present, and future,
so that my dear mothers need not make the slightest effort.
May I perfect the accumulations, purify the defilements,
and obtain omniscience.

"The roots of virtue arising in this way, I offer as well;
may they form an encompassing refuge to help all sentient beings.
With great compassion, may I follow my dear mothers back into
samsara, and may I quickly guide them forth!

"For as long as there exists a sky,
may I benefit beings, never disheartened.
Like the great elements of earth, air, fire, and water,
may I sustain all those who have form.

"May all those connected to me, whether by anger or faith,
exhaust all wrongdoing and quickly pass from samsara.
Having planted enlightenment, the healing, wish-granting tree
of virtue, may they harvest the flowers and fruit of Being
and pristine awareness.

"May those who merely bring to mind my name
assuage all their fears, their sufferings and traumas.
The thought of wrongdoing never active in my mind,
may I always be attuned to the two forms of Bodhicitta.

"Until I obtain the essence of enlightenment,
may all my karma ripen in this very life.
May the fruit of the teaching ripen this very day,
and may I henceforth never be cut off from the path of liberation.

"Wherever I am born, may I never forget the enlightened mind;
may I meet with the spiritual teacher, the Teacher himself.
Making effort so great that I take no account of my own body
or life, may I always achieve the welfare of others.

"O! Dear friends who depend on me!
The good path of this Great Vehicle is so difficult to find,
and so difficult to practice the right way as well.
May I inspire an army of efforts to strive untiringly day and night!"

This is the key to cherishing the path of the Great Vehicle:
With this you will travel the genuine path whatever you do.
Without this, you travel a lower path, however much you strive.
May all who have discrimination take up this noble aim.

ཁ་འབྲོམ་སྟོན་རྒྱལ་བའི་འབྱུང་གནས་ལ་ན་མོ།

*Dromton*

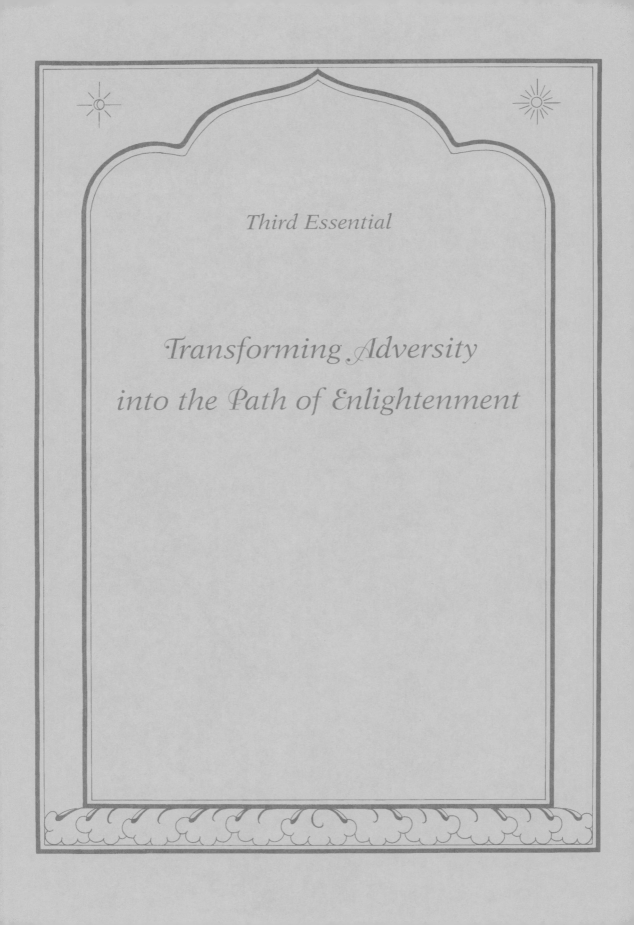

*Third Essential*

# Transforming Adversity into the Path of Enlightenment

## Practice of the Third Essential

*When all the world, both animate and*
*inanimate, is filled with evil, transform*
*all adversity into the path of enlightenment.*

*Place all blame on one source.*

*With firmly motivated concentration,*
*divert all benefit from yourself to others.*

*Openness being the greatest protection,*
*let openness reveal illusory appearance*
*as the Four Kāyas.*

*As the supreme method, apply the four practices.*

*Apply whatever happens to you to your meditation.*

# Reflections

## Meditative Action

*M*editative action in the world, the process of transforming all adverse conditions into the path of enlightenment, means to bring to bear in daily life both aspects of the enlightened mind as developed in meditation. Through focusing on compassion for all living beings, we bring compassion into our dealings with everyone around us; in focusing on śūnyatā, or openness, we gain the protection of its transformational character.

Today in these dark times of the Kaliyuga, practice of the Dharma is more difficult than ever before. Although our standard of living may be the highest known in human history, and we may lead very comfortable lives, little supports us in keeping a spiritual focus. Most of those we count on for encouragement, though they purport to follow a spiritual path, do not fully appreciate the value of a spiritual way of life. The environment itself is full of temptations that distract us and pull us off balance. As the insistence that ego be served gains strength, the power of desire is increasing, and our world is growing more fragmented, tense, and prone to dispute. Individuals seem more disappointed, more isolated and lonely, more hungry for peace and meaning than ever before.

In the face of these concerns, science offers little hope for solutions; while it traces out the operation of cause and effect at the

physical level with remarkable precision, it has nothing to say about the cause and effect of our underlying suffering. Religion is more likely to ask the right questions, but many dismiss religion as superstition or else incorporate it into the very structures that produce their misery. For those who take religious teachings seriously, there is the constant danger of turning fruitful forms of inquiry into exclusive sets of belief that are placed at the service of self-identity. As for political action, we have learned that as long as politics is dominated by self-interest, its solutions will be short-term and its accomplishments superficial.

Perhaps we will not gain enlightenment in this lifetime, but still the effort—or the fight—is worthwhile. The more evil forces seem to be pervading the world, the more appropriate the time to focus on the practice of transforming adversity into your path of action. Adversity, like all forms of experience, can be transformed through the process of meditative action. Motivated concentration on the two aspects of enlightened mind fills the mind with love and compassion and radiates their light and warmth to others. Love and compassion transform reality itself both externally and inwardly, for we create our reality, and we become what we create.

The aim is to turn the mind around, to put an end to self-delusion and unending confusion, to transcend all limited views and all limitations on the heart's natural capacity for love and joy. Even to set such goals is a rare privilege: the gift of the Buddha and the enlightened Mahāyāna lineage. Practicing the exchange of self and other makes this motivation a reality.

Striving to help all sentient beings, with no regard for dogma, regime, sect, or school, the Bodhisattva fights for all beings as a parent would fight for a beloved child. This way of life has tremendous joy and balance; ultimately, there is no more important work we can do. Fighting pain and suffering without discrimination, transforming ignorance to wisdom: This is the heart-activity of the Enlightened Ones, the heroes of the spiritual path, the true victors.

# Meditative Action

*I* bow down to the King of Physicians of skillful means:
By means of the exceptional medicine
of the wondrous enlightenment mind,
may self-grasping, the basis of all the chronic kleśas,
and all adverse circumstances be transformed
into the path of enlightenment.

*When all the world, both animate and inanimate,
is filled with evil, transform all adversity
into the path of enlightenment.*

The master Mātṛceṭa has stated:

When renunciates fall from their moral practice,
their desire to distance themselves from the treasure
of the teachings leads them to make few offerings.
They turn their backs on those unmarred by sin,
turn away from those endowed with moral practice,
and cultivate those who are full of malice.
Such renunciates then let householders guide their activities,
and thus they start to honor laymen. Acting in this way,
they might as well be householders themselves.
Thus commences the Kaliyuga, the age of darkness.

And again:

Those full of error, not esteeming knowledge and virtue,
offer those things that are not to be offered.
In making such offerings, these fools, guided by evil forces,
lead the world into certain suffering.
Those who have lost their own morals gain power
to threaten and destroy those with moral practice.
Delighting in sin, filled with the force of destruction,
these deceivers set about destroying the sacred Dharma.
Those who uphold their vows and who apply themselves
to the survival of the teachings are few,
and the doctrine of the rishis marches inexorably
toward extinction. Since fearsome disputes and battles
engulf the earth, the inclination to cultivate the land disappears.
Unbearably fierce winds arise, and thus no pure offerings
are produced to offer to holy beings.

Fierce robbers and enemies of the land abound,
and those with wealth and ease cannot enjoy it.
Truly beings suffer: All aspects of their lives become frightful.
The rains fall out of season, and hailstorms endanger travelers.
Cows do not give milk, the seasons are disrupted,
and grain does not grow upon the earth.
Medicines become ineffective: The more essential
they are, the weaker they become.
Controversies proliferate; arguments lacking logic
or truth take over, and evil prevails.

And again:

The times being frenzied, the balance of nature is destroyed,
leading the sun and moon to reverse their roles. Wives have
no wish to unite with their husbands, and so common women
take their place. Rulers abandon righteousness, and sons,
intent on wealth, despise their fathers. Alas! So vast
is the suffering of this age of great contention
that places of peace turn into perilous wildernesses.

Similar teachings were presented extensively by the All-Knowing
Longchenpa in the Dus-la-mngon-par-skyo-ba'i-rabs.

The dominant effect of the forces of the Kaliyuga is such
that people come to lack spirituality and proceed to corrupt
the natural environment. The inhabitants of this earth become
increasingly subject to the five poisons of the emotions
and thus take up all sorts of immoral activities.
This breeds great unhappiness, and people become
like savages in the deep jungles. One after another,
a stream of disasters and hardships strikes.

In the degradation of the present times, if you do not know how to
take adversity as your path, you lose the motivation to do what must
be done to act according to the Dharma. This method of taking adversity as your path is found in the central precepts of both the old and
new systems of meditation.

Orgyan Dusum Khyenpa presents the following in his Guide to the
Nyang gTer called Advice to the King:

When the time comes that you need to apply
a comprehensive antidote, you will certainly experience
great distress. Whatever frightful forms you encounter,
focus on the Three Jewels as the place of refuge.
When applying the antidote, keep in mind your teacher.
Always remember that if you lack the patience
of the enlightened mind, the root of the Dharma
of the Great Vehicle will decay.

Again, from the same source:

If it seems to you that a ceremony of fortunetelling or magic
is needed to counter adverse circumstances, keep in mind
that such practices run counter to the Great Perfection.
Whatever difficulties arise, remember that they are retribution
for former actions, and be happy at this. When any sort
of happiness arises, remember that it is due
to the blessings of the Three Jewels.

When you encounter those who hate you, keep in mind that they
are actually dear friends sent by the Buddhas and Bodhisattvas to
help you develop patience. When plagued by worries about your
family and loved ones, remember that they are chains that tie you
to samsara—obstacles sent by demons.

Remember that the sentient beings of the three realms—
every living creature—have all been your parents.
As your parents are wandering in samsara, remember
the Four Immeasurables. When major obstacles arise,
keep in mind the teacher who exhorts you to virtue.
Remember the great kindness of your masters,
and remember that you must depend on them
with great devotion, so as never to be separated from them.

When your body is ailing, keep in mind the object of refuge,
the one who guides you to the path of enlightenment.
Remember at all times that ordinary refuges possess
no real means to protect you. Keep in mind that when you
cling to belief in a self in the conglomerate of your body of flesh
and blood, you are letting demons enter your heart. Remember
that should they enter your heart, you must remain unagitated,
thus expelling them from your system.

Keep in mind that all that appears has no self-nature:
It is merely a dream, an illusion. As nothing has any self-nature,
this absence cannot be known, so keep in mind
the delusive nature of everything, both of self and other.
Bear in mind the need to turn that delusion
into the Dharma itself right now, this very moment.

Keep in mind that if you do not turn to the reality of the Dharma
right now, you will later have to wander endlessly in samsara,
experiencing unbearable hardships and suffering. Therefore,
give up all other actions, keeping in mind the urgent need
to practice only the Dharma. Remember that if you act
in such a way, you will completely root out samsara,
and remember that by rooting out samsara,
great bliss will arise ceaselessly.

And further:

If you practice the Dharma correctly,
the Dharma itself emerges through the force
of great blessings as your reality.
Thus, if you adhere to the consciousness of love,
delighting all beings will be your reality.

If you adhere to the consciousness of compassion,
loving all beings as if they were your own children
will be your reality. If you adhere to the consciousness
of equanimity, never being prejudiced towards friends or enemies
will be your reality. If you adhere to the consciousness of joy,
harmony in all modes of action will be your reality.

If you reject all intention to harm others, knowing little distress
will be your reality. If you do not accept the negative way
things seem to appear, lack of negativity will be your reality.
If you give up the grasping of attachment and desire,
effortlessly arising happiness of mind and body will be your reality.
If you stay in a remote retreat, spiritual experiences
arising in the mind will be your reality.

If you give up worrying about yourself, never being afflicted
by demonic obstacles will be your reality. If you look at the mind
with the mind, reality itself arising within you will be your reality.
If you always strive to practice, the qualities of impartiality
will be your reality. If you become acquainted with your own mind,
liberating practice will be your reality. If you realize samsara
and nirvana as the Dharmakāya, effortless meditation
will be your reality. If you do not give in to laziness
in your practice, having no regrets at the time of death
will be your reality.

And further:

If you do not subdue your enemies—the kleśas—
they will subdue you. You can be certain
that your mind will suffer when distracted
by many senseless things. If you do not protect
your devotion to virtue in Dharma activities,
even if you protect your relatives and loved ones
throughout your life, you can be certain
that you will be friendless at the time of death.
If you do not embrace the doctrine of the Victorious One,
and instead grasp at worldly profit
and renown, you can be certain
that you will again be cast into samsara.

The text continues:

The cycle of existence arises from not abandoning
the concept of 'I and mine', 'subject and object'.
Although all sentient beings are one in the mind of enlightenment,
we heartlessly tear self and other asunder.
Although all sentient beings have been our father and mother
in previous lifetimes, we heartlessly hold some to be friends
and others to be enemies. When we distinguish between samsara
and nirvana, we heartlessly take the side
of protecting the eight worldly concerns.

The text goes on:

With faith as dependable as a flowing river,
depend on the Lama and the Three Jewels.
With love and compassion like that of a mother for her children,
train all beings with loving-kindness. With unflinching effort,
as if your hair were on fire, protect virtuous actions of body
and speech. Analyzing carefully the operation of cause and effect,
conscientiously abandon non-virtue.

Should you feel rivalry with those above you,
seek out your spiritual friends, the gods and Lamas
who watch over vows, and guard yourself with modesty
and restraint. By developing even a little forbearance,
you will never harm others. Following such a path of action,
all that you do will be of benefit, and your body and speech
will be transformed into the Dharma. Never enumerate the faults
of others: Instead, expel all faults by taking them upon yourself!

Teachings like these explain all the aspects of both the ordinary and
extraordinary paths of taking upon yourself the suffering of others.

# Reflections

## Relative Enlightened Mind

*A*lthough these days it is common for people to explore some form of meditation at one time or another, few persist. Even when the desire to practice is strong, obstacles seem to continually arise, and the promptings of worldly desires tend to take precedence over the wish to deepen spiritual understanding.

We may be aware that the mind leads us away from spiritual practice into repeating patterns of frustration and disappointment that waste our precious time. Still we repeat the same patterns, hoping that this time the outcome will be different. When we experience the same types of difficulties yet again, we blame the economy, bad luck, our enemies, even our friends and family. Blaming personal problems on circumstances outside of ourselves, we lose control over our lives and fall into the habit of complaining rather than acting. We may manage to break free from a few destructive patterns, but the mind is tricky: We continually invent new ways to fool ourselves, slipping back almost imperceptibly into old patterns. Driven by desire, hatred, and ignorance, these patterns and the ever-present self-centeredness of mind begin to seem unshakable.

Under these conditions, we need to regularly remind ourselves that we are responsible for our lives and for what happens to us. Our time is limited and the opportunity to practice may soon be gone: We

cannot afford to waste any more time. While we have the power to act, we must do what we can to take responsibility. To start, we must do as the root text states, and:

*Place all blame on one source.*

The source of all our troubles is our egoistic mind. Although this is the last source we tend to consider, at some level we already know that this is true. Experience offers us ample data for observation; at this very moment, we could understand the true nature of our minds. But we hesitate to take these lessons seriously. We do not want to hear what events are telling us; we do not want to see the extent of the suffering we are creating for ourselves. Ultimately we do not want to have answers to our questions, because the answers challenge the structures of self and ego in which we have invested so heavily.

The self is samsara's strongest ally, for it refuses to acknowledge insights that threaten its authority. The self's claims of importance are the motor driving samsara and the real enemy of awakening to a healthier way of being. Unless we are somehow able to focus the light of inquiry on our views of self and ego, we will continue to grope in the darkness. We will never be able to halt the momentum of samsara or challenge the patterns linking our minds to suffering.

Here is where the real effort begins: insisting on continued investigations into the workings of the mind. While it is not easy to maintain this focused intensity or to resist the distractions of the self's insistence on prominence, we have the necessary inner resources that will support us in doing this.

At this fundamental level, the Dharma calls upon us to change our attitude. This very moment—right now—the opportunity is open to us. The very unfolding of our lives gives us wonderful material for study; the results of our actions give us direct feedback on whether our way of life is beneficial for ourselves and others. Turning our minds to the Dharma, we see that self-interest is our jailer and our unrelenting tormentor.

When we finally place all blame upon ourselves, we begin the process of learning how to escape the net of samsaric views and patterns. We realize that the key to freedom is already in our hands. Whenever we experience harm or suffering, we can trace it to its

source in our thoughts and actions, and learn to be independent of the patterns that have bound us.

By continually looking at the process of karma and the kleśas and continually activating the antidotes, we prepare the ground for our spiritual growth. In this way, we can overcome the strong drive toward self-protection that insists on the self's existence, identity, security, and control. We can uproot the very basis of samsara and rid ourselves of innumerable forms of suffering.

# Motivated Concentration
# on Relative Enlightened Mind

$C$learly wrongdoing results in the deterioration of all aspects of life—causing distress for the environment as well as for individual beings. Yet even when difficulties arise in great number, you can transform them into the path of enlightenment. Here meditative action, made up of firmly motivated concentration and application, comes into play. First of all, with motivated concentration, you can transform adverse circumstances into the path of enlightenment by means of both relative and ultimate Bodhicitta.

With respect to relative Bodhicitta: All suffering comes from failing to understand that self-grasping is the enemy, and that all sentient beings are our great and kind friends. The repercussions of such ignorance are great: Even now we are immersed in suffering. Since this suffering can be traced to the fault of holding to a self, the root text states:

*Place all blame on one source.*

Whatever sufferings descend on you are due to having conceived a self-centered identity; therefore, do not consider others responsible for your difficulties. In Entering the Bodhisattva Path, we find:

Whatever evils arise in the world
and whatever fear and suffering they bring forth

all arise from grasping at a self.
What good does this great demon do me? [8.134]

From beginningless time, we have taken as the self that which is selfless, and have cherished that self. Thus we have accumulated karma which also harms others. All the suffering of the adverse states of being in samsara arises in this way. The same text states:

O mind, you desire to benefit yourself,
and have passed innumerable kalpas in such pursuit—
but for all your great labor
you gave gained only suffering. [8.155]

Truly, as suffering is produced by the conception of a self, holding to a self is clearly the enemy. From beginningless time until now, this mind that conceives the selfless as self has produced all suffering. It continually causes envy toward those more eminent, scorn for those inferior, and rivalry toward those of equal status. Such a mind makes it certain that you will not find freedom from samsara and that you will undergo immense suffering and harm at the hands of beings both human and non-human. The same text goes on:

Mind! You have harmed me
in all my myriad samsaric births.
Now, having remembered your hostile actions,
I shall overcome your selfish aims. [8.172]

In looking at the process through which seizing on a self arises, it is like mistaking a multi-colored rope for a snake. Relying falsely on the assembly of the five defiled skandhas, the mind grows confused and sees a self where there is none. When you analyze the five skandhas, you can see that a self does not exist—either in the skandhas, outside of them, or anywhere else. Therefore, anything that could be called self-grasping should be abandoned the moment it is produced. From now on, do your very best not to produce the grasping that holds the self dear. The same text states:

In previous lifetimes
you destroyed me,
but now I see where you are headed
and I will completely conquer your conceit. [8.169]

Truly, whatever harm befalls you traces back to this demon of grasping the self. Thus you need to strive to subdue this demon at whatever cost. Should you wish to look at this more deeply, consider:

From beginningless time, we have mistaken friends for enemies and vice versa. Unable to distinguish who or what we should accept or give up, we have done nothing at all to activate an antidote for self-grasping; instead, we assist in it. Although in the past we have come in contact with those possessing liberation and omniscience, now we fail even to approach them. Surely the time has come to know who are our true friends and who our enemies.

Moreover, there is clearly no difference between seeing self-grasping as an enemy and abandoning it, and seeing all beings as our friends and cherishing them. Cherishing the self is our enemy, for by this destructive mind of grasping, we become attached to our own selfish ways. Growing hostile toward others and their ways, we hurt them and thus bind ourselves to this prison of samsara. We experience only the suffering of the three lower realms, so manifold that they cannot be enumerated.

What slaves we are to our desires! If we made a pile of the heads and limbs we cut off in the past to satisfy our desires, it would be bigger than Mt. Meru. As long as we are under the influence of desire, we will never be free from samsara and will have to undergo much suffering. Even now, we suffer. Our body is subject to the suffering of pain and illness; mentally we suffer by being defamed, despised, challenged, and disdained.

In short, everything we do not desire for ourselves or for our way of life comes forth, based on our dependence on the self's relationship to the external environment and to internal influences. We are cut off from the teachings of the lofty Dharma protectors. Base and inferior people say terrible things about us; disgusting creatures such as lice, fleas, and other vermin feed upon us. And the root of all of this is grasping at a self.

The harmful actions we have previously done to sentient beings now come back to haunt us. Nāgārjuna states in The Exposition of Bodhicitta:

From harming sentient beings,
you will take form as a hell being, animal, or preta,
and experience the state
of those who undergo many forms of misery.

The unbearable miseries of hunger and thirst,
of taking life and being killed in turn:
These are the fruits of harming sentient beings,
and they are difficult to reverse. [79–80]

Further, we find in Nāgārjuna's Wish-Granting Gem of Dreams:

Whatever you experience of suffering,
whether it is being killed or bound,
beaten or caught up in disputes:
This is the fruit of harming sentient beings—
thus the Sugatas have taught.

Those who are now physically strong and thriving
will be reborn in a lowly family, in poverty, and in harm's way.
Their lives will be short, their spouses will die,
they will lose their sight. All this
is the fruit of harming sentient beings.

Should you experience the miseries of the places
of evil states of being, such as the Avīci hell,
this too is due to your own faults:
It comes from harming sentient beings.

## Activating the Antidotes

We find in The Wheel-Weapon of Self-Mastery:

When those around us turn against us,
take consolation: This is caused by our own transgressions.
When our lives are full of sickness and physical woes,
it comes from having inflicted physical harm on others.
As the wheel-weapon of bad karma turns round,
now let all their ailments come to me.

When the mind is full of mental distress,
surely it is from having troubled others' minds.

The wheel-weapon of bad karma turns round:
Now let all their suffering arise in me.

When we are tormented by fierce hunger and thirst,
it is due to actions of greed, to robbing and swindling others.
The wheel-weapon of bad karma turns round:
Now let all their hunger and thirst arise in me.

When, powerless, we are tortured and enslaved by others,
it is due to having despised the lowly and used them as slaves.
The wheel-weapon of bad karma turns round:
Now let my body and life serve the purposes of others.

When people bombard my ears with harsh words,
it is due to the faults of having defamed and betrayed.
The wheel-weapon of bad karma turns round:
Now, let all harmful talk come to an end.

When I am born in a land where nothing is pure,
it is due to having thought about impure things.
The wheel-weapon of bad karma turns round:
Now I will only meditate on all appearance as pure.

When I am separated from close friends and helpers
it is due to having lured away the friends and associates of others.
The wheel-weapon of bad karma turns round:
Now I will not separate others from their friends.

When all the Holy Ones are displeased with me,
it is due to having turned from the holy and relied on bad friends.
The wheel-weapon of bad karma turns round:
Now I will give up my harmful friends.

When others unjustly belittle me and accuse me of sin,
it is due to having disparaged the holy.
The wheel-weapon of bad karma turns round:
Now the benefit of the doubt is theirs: I will cease disparaging others.

When all the provisions I need have been exhausted,
it is due to having felt contempt for the needs of others.
The wheel-weapon of bad karma turns round:
Now I will fulfill all others' needs.

When my mind is unclear and my heart is heavy,
it is due to having caused others to sin.
The wheel-weapon of bad karma turns round:
Now I will give up the conduct that causes wrongdoing.

When my mind is so disturbed I cannot function,
it is due to having made obstacles for the holy actions of others.
The wheel-weapon of bad karma turns round:
Now I will give up causing obstacles.

When I cannot please the Lama, whatever I do,
it is due to the bad karma of paying lip-service to the Dharma.
The wheel-weapon of bad karma turns round:
Now I must lessen my pretense in practicing the Dharma.

When people contradict me, whatever I do,
it is due to having dismissed the importance
of shame and remorse.
The wheel-weapon of bad karma turns round:
Now I will shun that which offers no support.

When my companions disagree with me as soon as they gather,
it is due to having shunned those whose habits annoyed me.
The wheel-weapon of bad karma turns round:
Now I will improve whatever bad habits I may have.

When all those close to me arise as enemies,
it is due to having harbored grudges.
The wheel-weapon of bad karma turns round:
Now I must increase the stream of regret and contrition.

When I am ill with chronic diseases and tumors,
it is due to my unlawful use or misuse of resources.
The wheel-weapon of bad karma turns round:
Now I must leave off misusing what belongs to all.

When I am racked by sudden headaches,
it is due to having broken the samaya vows.
The wheel-weapon of bad karma turns round:
Now I must abandon non-virtuous action.

When all that I study is confused in my mind,
it is due to procrastination in my Dharma studies.

The wheel-weapon of bad karma turns round:
Now I must become attuned to wisdom,
studying and reflecting on the teachings.

When sleep overwhelms me when practicing,
it is due to having accumulated defilements
regarding the sacred Dharma.
The wheel-weapon of bad karma turns round:
Now, for the sake of the Dharma, I must practice austerities.

When I delight in emotionality and my mind is unsteady,
it is due to not always thinking about the lures of samsara.
The wheel-weapon of bad karma turns round:
Now I must produce the great renunciation of samsara.

When whatever I have done rises up to lead me to ruin,
it is due to having disparaged the cause and effect of karma.
The wheel-weapon of bad karma turns round:
Now I must strive to accumulate merit.

When all the ceremonies I perform go wrong,
it is due to having hoped to benefit from hateful sources.
The wheel-weapon of bad karma turns round:
Now I must turn away from this perverse behavior.

When my prayers to the Three Jewels do not bear fruit,
it is due to having not trusted in the Buddha.
The wheel-weapon of bad karma turns round:
Now I must depend only on the Three Jewels.

When my thoughts are debased and inimical forces arise,
it is due to having transgressed against the gods
and the vows I have taken.
The wheel-weapon of bad karma turns round:
Now I must conquer all harmful thoughts.

When I wander vulnerable, like a stray,
it is due to having evicted Lamas and others from their places.
The wheel-weapon of bad karma turns round:
Now I must never turn anyone away.

When hail and other destructive forces rain down,
it is due to the bad karma of not keeping

my moral practice and commitments.
The wheel-weapon of bad karma turns round:
Now I must purify and keep all my promises.

When I am impoverished by my many needs,
it is due to not having been generous
and not honoring the Three Jewels.
The wheel-weapon of bad karma turns round:
Now I must strive to give offerings.

When I am born physically impaired and despised by the world,
it is due to having vented my anger by not erecting fine images.
The wheel-weapon of bad karma turns round:
Now I must erect images and be warmly accepting.

When I am in turmoil and full of attachment whatever I do,
it is due to having obstinately held onto a negative outlook.
The wheel-weapon of bad karma turns round:
Now I must expel this negativity.

When there is no way to achieve what I have aimed to do,
it is due to the karma of having taken up bad views.
The wheel-weapon of bad karma turns round:
Now I must direct whatever I do to the benefit of others.

When my mind remains unsubdued
though my conduct has been virtuous,
it is due to having been caught up in the ambitions of this life.
The wheel-weapon of bad karma turns round:
Now I must strive to fulfill my desire for liberation.

When, having examined my desires, I grow disheartened,
it is due to having dallied with shameless new friends.
The wheel-weapon of bad karma turns round:
Now I must be careful about my associates.

When I am ensnared by the foolish enticements of others,
it is due to having had strong desires and prideful thoughts.
The wheel-weapon of bad karma turns round:
Now I must lessen such disturbing manifestations.

When attachment or repulsion govern my response
in listening to or giving teachings,

it is due to having ignored the demonic faults in my heart.
The wheel-weapon of bad karma turns round:
Now, having examined what goes against the Dharma,
I must abandon it.

When all my good actions go astray,
it is due to my returning ingratitude for kindness.
The wheel-weapon of bad karma turns round:
Now I must bow down my head, grateful for kindness.

In short, the lightning and thunder of what I do not desire
crashes down upon me. I am like the smith killed
with the sword he forged himself.
The wheel-weapon of bad karma turns round:
Now I must beware of my own wrong actions.

Should I experience the suffering of the lower states of being,
I will be like an archer killed by his own arrow.
The wheel-weapon of bad karma turns round:
I must be careful of wrong action!

When the miseries of the householder crash down upon me,
I am like a cherished child that kills its parents.
The wheel-weapon of bad karma turns round:
Now I will stay always among the family of renunciates.

Like one who foils his opponent by seizing his hands,
I will seize this tricky thief:
Having done so, HAH! There can be no doubt:
This self-grasping is the delusive imposter! [9–49]

## Recognizing Fault

The same text goes on to identify the myriad ways we fool ourselves
and fall into error. Due to the delusive nature of self-grasping, we
must learn to apply the antidote immediately:

Carried away into the misery of the three lower realms,
we still chase after the cause, unconscious of its horror.
Roar like thunder down upon the head

of this perilous self-centered thinking!
Strike out the heart of this enemy, the Lord of Death.

We have immense desire for happiness
but will not work for what could cause it;
we have small endurance for suffering
but stubbornly think we deserve what we desire.
Roar like thunder down upon the head
of this perilous self-centered thinking!
Strike out the heart of this enemy, the Lord of Death.

When desired attainments draw near, our efforts grow weak;
we get involved in doing many things and never finish them.
Roar like thunder down upon the head
of this perilous self-centered thinking!
Strike out the heart of this enemy, the Lord of Death.

We gain many new friends, but our attention soon wanders;
we freeload off of others but are furious at those who pilfer.
Roar like thunder down upon the head
of this perilous self-centered thinking!
Strike out the heart of this enemy, the Lord of Death.

We turn our biting wit on others, but are mean-spirited ourselves;
we hoard what we do not need and grasp greedily at what we want.
Roar like thunder down upon the head
of this perilous self-centered thinking!
Strike out the heart of this enemy, the Lord of Death.

We do little for others, but boast about ourselves;
we cannot carry our own burdens but cause hardship for others.
Roar like thunder down upon the head
of this perilous self-centered thinking!
Strike out the heart of this enemy, the Lord of Death.

We want many great teachers, yet we shirk our commitments;
we want lots of students, but we take little time to help them.
Roar like thunder down upon the head
of this perilous self-centered thinking!
Strike out the heart of this enemy, the Lord of Death.

We make great promises, but have little background in helping;
we claim to be someone of status,
but shameless demons dominate our thinking.
Roar like thunder down upon the head
of this perilous self-centered thinking!
Strike out the heart of this enemy, the Lord of Death.

Though we have little knowledge, we pontificate on openness;
knowing little of scripture, we let our imagination fill in the gaps.
Roar like thunder down upon the head
of this perilous self-centered thinking!
Strike out the heart of this enemy, the Lord of Death.

Though we have many attendants, none will carry the burden;
though we have many managers, no one will help or support.
Roar like thunder down upon the head
of this perilous self-centered thinking!
Strike out the heart of this enemy, the Lord of Death.

Though we take a high seat, our qualifications
are less than those of demons;
though we consider ourselves most spiritual,
we are haunted by the demons of desire and hatred.
Roar like thunder down upon the head
of this perilous self-centered thinking!
Strike out the heart of this enemy, the Lord of Death.

Though our opinions are lofty, our actions are worse than a dog's;
as to our many 'virtues', they are long gone—lost in the wind.
Roar like thunder down upon the head
of this perilous self-centered thinking!
Strike out the heart of this enemy, the Lord of Death.

Those for whom we care we place within our inner circle;
those on the outside we laugh at for no reason.
Roar like thunder down upon the head
of this perilous self-centered thinking!
Strike out the heart of this enemy, the Lord of Death.

Though we don the monk's saffron robes,
we ask demons to guard and protect us;
though we take the sacred vows,

our actions accord with those of devils.
Roar like thunder down upon the head
of this perilous self-centered thinking!
Strike out the heart of this enemy, the Lord of Death.

Though our well-being is a godly gift,
we make offerings to the demons causing misery;
though our guide has been the Dharma,
we attempt to deceive the Three Jewels.
Roar like thunder down upon the head
of this perilous self-centered thinking!
Strike out the heart of this enemy, the Lord of Death.

Though dwelling in solitude, we are carried away by distractions;
having requested the most sacred Dharma teachings,
we turn to the use of omens and spells.
Roar like thunder down upon the head
of this perilous self-centered thinking!
Strike out the heart of this enemy, the Lord of Death.

Having cast aside the path of morality and liberation,
we embrace the householder's life;
having cast away the water of joy and happiness,
we solicit suffering.
Roar like thunder down upon the head
of this perilous self-centered thinking!
Strike out the heart of this enemy, the Lord of Death.

Having forsaken the good path of liberation,
we meander idly until the very end;
having obtained a precious human body,
we fulfill the conditions that lead to hell.
Roar like thunder down upon the head
of this perilous self-centered thinking!
Strike out the heart of this enemy, the Lord of Death.

Having put aside the special teachings,
we look for profit in business;
having left the school of religion, we idle in the cities.
Roar like thunder down upon the head

of this perilous self-centered thinking!
Strike out the heart of this enemy, the Lord of Death.

Though we have a good livelihood, we cadge from others;
having squandered our inheritance, we take from other people.
Roar like thunder down upon the head
of this perilous self-centered thinking!
Strike out the heart of this enemy, the Lord of Death.

Amazing! We have little persistence in meditation,
but are keen to have special powers;
though we have not gone far on the path of Dharma,
we look for the senseless power of seven-league strides.
Roar like thunder down upon the head
of this perilous self-centered thinking!
Strike out the heart of this enemy, the Lord of Death.

When someone gives us helpful advice, we see it as spite;
confused and backwards, we show gratitude to heartless deceivers.
Roar like thunder down upon the head
of this perilous self-centered thinking!
Strike out the heart of this enemy, the Lord of Death.

When others trust us totally,
we tell their confidences to their enemies;
if they have close companions, we shamelessly steal their hearts.
Roar like thunder down upon the head
of this perilous self-centered thinking!
Strike out the heart of this enemy, the Lord of Death.

We are jealous of the holy, rough and vindictive in our thoughts;
with those hard to get along with, we are basically short-tempered.
Roar like thunder down upon the head
of this perilous self-centered thinking!
Strike out the heart of this enemy, the Lord of Death.

Not trusting, not listening, we inflict only harm;
when others concede to us, we show no grace,
but keep our distance and argue even more.
Roar like thunder down upon the head
of this perilous self-centered thinking!
Strike out the heart of this enemy, the Lord of Death.

Those who give us good advice we find it difficult to be with;
those who bring us harm we readily embrace.
Roar like thunder down upon the head
of this perilous self-centered thinking!
Strike out the heart of this enemy, the Lord of Death.

Those who are great and holy we see as adversaries;
but due to our passions, we are eager to please the youthful.
Roar like thunder down upon the head
of this perilous self-centered thinking!
Strike out the heart of this enemy, the Lord of Death.

Embarrassed by our long-time friends, we keep them at a distance;
but grand new friends we proudly show off to all.
Roar like thunder down upon the head
of this perilous self-centered thinking!
Strike out the heart of this enemy, the Lord of Death.

Though we have no special powers, we feign them;
we lack compassion and take advantage of others' trust.
Roar like thunder down upon the head
of this perilous self-centered thinking!
Strike out the heart of this enemy, the Lord of Death.

The little we have learned we meagerly parcel out;
we scarcely know the sacred teachings,
but we broadcast wrong views widely.
Roar like thunder down upon the head
of this perilous self-centered thinking!
Strike out the heart of this enemy, the Lord of Death.

Attuned to attachment and hatred, we disparage others;
attuned to jealousy, we put down everyone else.
Roar like thunder down upon the head
of this perilous self-centered thinking!
Strike out the heart of this enemy, the Lord of Death.

We do not ask for teachings and have great contempt for scholarship;
we do not trust the Lama, and we disrespect the sacred texts.
Roar like thunder down upon the head
of this perilous self-centered thinking!
Strike out the heart of this enemy, the Lord of Death.

Not conversant with the Three Collections,
we make up false connections;
not purifying our perception, we preach what is inflammatory.
Roar like thunder down upon the head
of this perilous self-centered thinking!
Strike out the heart of this enemy, the Lord of Death.

We fail to condemn what goes against the teachings
but compose detailed refutations for what is well-explained.
Roar like thunder down upon the head
of this perilous self-centered thinking!
Strike out the heart of this enemy, the Lord of Death.

We are never chagrined in shameful situations,
but that which is exemplary, we hold to be shameful.
Roar like thunder down upon the head
of this perilous self-centered thinking!
Strike out the heart of this enemy, the Lord of Death.

We do not do a single thing we should be doing;
instead we do all we can do that is wrong.
Roar like thunder down upon the head
of this perilous self-centered thinking!
Strike out the heart of this enemy, the Lord of Death. [56–91]

## Self-Destruction

Again, in the Stages of the Bodhisattva's Self-Mastery, we find:

Conceptualization is the King of Demons:
Its nature is that of the Lord of Bad Karma.
It is the poisonous stem of self-desire;
it is the mind full of faults and laziness.

It is the skilled betrayer of the skillful means of this lifetime:
It perplexes the many guardians and protectors.
It is the trickster of the many gods and demons.
Do not let thoughts arise as the enemy!

The karma I have done is endless,
yet I pay no heed to the circle of protectors.

The wealth I have accumulated is senseless—
O to destroy it! O to bring this to an end!

The Lord of Death abides in my heart—
O life, I am destroying my self!
I myself am drinking the poison!
I must certainly confront this demon face to face!

And again:

By creating causes of contention in the present
we give sway to demonic impulses.
The suffering of disease takes over,
bringing great sickness and the misery of pain.

Some fall into the hells where they suffer great heat or cold,
others undergo the great suffering of destitution.
Some suffer fearsome hunger and thirst like that of hungry ghosts.
We bring about as much pain as poisonous snakes and rabid dogs.

When we have something of value, we defend our possession;
if we are without it, we roam about to find it.
Whatever we have done has only fed suffering;
in whatever we do, we have lost all meaningful direction.

We pay for the root of our problems, self-grasping;
we pay for our meager patience when suffering.
We pay for rending asunder the field of love;
we pay for cutting off the root of compassion.
We pay for disregarding the virtue of generating Bodhicitta;
we pay for depending on unsuitable friends.

　　Having identified such destructive behavior and the evils inherent in the kind of thinking that grasps at a self, you must at once rely on the antidote. If you do not, the previous destructive tendency will take over again and gain in strength. The same text goes on:

Alas! From beginningless time until now,
unable to subdue your own nature,
you let the messengers of karma and the kleśas gather
in the house of the demons of rotten disposition.

When you do not reflect upon your parents' suffering,
let alone the suffering of all sentient beings,
when you are superficial and careless—
Ah! You have not donned the armor of the antidotes.
That is a great mistake: Reverse it now!

Let understanding arise as follows:
When you have not subdued the demon of self-grasping,
Ah! Reflect upon the lives of your father and mother.
Ah! Conquer your hedonist ways!
Ah! Weep under the heavy weight of samsara!

If you do not muzzle the mouth of your own bad nature,
it will lash out as everyone's undoing.
Watch out! When the poisonous fangs sink into the flesh,
great pools of tears will flow!

If you put on the sacred armor of the antidotes
but do not cast out the thieving dog of your desires,
your belly will rot from within.
Watch out! The medicinal elixir will flow forth as poison.

When you have not cut the life-vein of the five poisons,
but give in to the mind of procrastination,
the whirlwind of your short life will carry you off.
Watch out! From the heart, you must repent!
This is a message good to learn.

And further:

We must secure in this short life
the seeds of our final birth.
But lacking the heart to make use of our time,
we are despoiled by inner demons.

Ruined once more by our great desire for pleasure,
we succumb again in just the same way.
If we still do not root out our bad nature,
this consciousness will bring us to ruin.

Not thinking of the welfare of others
but considering only what we need for ourselves,

we bring disruption on both ourselves and all others—
surely we will certainly fall into the hottest hell.

The same text tells how to depend on the antidotes:

When emotion-ridden thoughts arise,
be like a falcon chasing a flock of birds:
Pursue and scatter them,
and so bring them to ruin.

When perverse thoughts create yearning in your heart,
be like the spy who recognizes the enemy:
Investigate and identify them by shape and color,
and henceforth get rid of such thoughts.

When daydreams arise as your enemy,
be like an executioner taking hold of the condemned.
Having grasped them, cut short their life:
Crush them at once, and cast such thoughts away.

When laziness arises through desire for pleasure,
be like a teacher's assistant who fights off sleep.
Apply the strong restraints! There is no time to wait!
Move on to the action of liberation!

When you direct yourself to the prospects of this lifetime
be like one who sees cannibals feasting.
Rise up, drive them off,
and run far from the eight states of adversity!

When friends and distractions are sweeping you away,
be like one who sees corpses on a battlefield.
Run far from everyone, including your companions:
Resort to a forest retreat!

When the demons of desire and hatred distract you,
be like one running from a mad dog or a venomous snake.
Flee from the place of demons to the sphere of nirvana:
Turn your back on the joys and concerns of the world!

When eternalistic views lock you in their prison,
be like the king who agonized in the ravine.[12]

When death comes close, and your thoughts are bleak,
depend strongly on remorse.

When the desire to reflect on the teachings slips away,
be like the actor who must give a performance
with no time to rehearse. Thinking well on this,
develop great diligence.

Though you strive in the Dharma day and night,
if you do not get rid of evil influences,
your consciousness will be carried away by demons.
Reverse this now! Depend on the antidotes!

Though your intentions have been in accord with the Dharma,
should you revert to a life of wrongdoing,
your thoughts will be taken over by demons.
Call out now for the protection of the Three Jewels!

Should you dwell under a Lama's direction
in a center for the Dharma
beware of getting caught up in attachment or aversion
toward either teachers or students.
Retreat from these devilish thoughts!
Depend on a remote retreat!

Though you have practiced with full concentration,
if you still have not gained liberation, turn your thinking around!
How can you not find freedom through the teachings?
This is the profound view.

And again it is said:

The wise, if they desire to conquer their enemies,
from the beginning, despise the self.
Even if they are belittled by others,
they do not deny or defend themselves.

Even when harmed by others—
though they have done nothing to bring about that harm—
even when their body is torn free from the enjoyment of life,
they say, "This is the price of my own misguided actions."

Should others plan for your misfortune,
cursing and inciting demons to attack,
do not worry! They are no threat.
Satisfy them and make them happy.

If you find yourself too self-satisfied,
surround yourself with those who are like demons,
those who would plunder your own dear flesh:
Do not defend yourself, but satisfy their heart's desire.

When you make a gift and your kindness meets with its opposite,
do not be agitated for even an instant.
Be mindful of kindness; urge yourself to be patient:
Now you have the means of abandoning sin.

Do not spread hatred:
In banishing hatred, you truly practice love.
Is not this the contentment you asked for?
Is not patience obtained in just this way?

Associate closely with difficult people,
taking their aims as your focus.
Think of the wretchedness of samsara,
and meditate on great compassion.

When your resting place
is a rocky cave, or a hut that the raindrops enter,
a shrine, an animal pen in the empty wilderness,
or a narrow defile, you are unhappy.

Dissatisfied with your progress
when living in the teeming valley, you go to the mountains.
Once there, you have no wish to stay,
but quickly draw back from isolation.

Again and again you change your dwelling place,
displeased with your inner development.
If you always move around like this,
if this is the way of your practice, look closely:

Your resting place, wherever it may be, is the best,
the site of joy. Due to suffering endured for others,

you are not born in hell. Truly good fortune!
You will never be boiled there, or burned alive. How lucky!

You will not be born for a kalpa
in the hungry ghost's city of hunger and thirst. How lucky!
You will not be born for a kalpa
in a city teeming with worms and filth
in the midst of a great swamp. What fortune!

Thinking on these fearsome things,
are you not contrite?
Endure lack of food: Practice hardship!
Endure lack of clothing: Make yourself humble.

When you cultivate the antidotes
and despise pleasure and happiness,
when you focus on never doing useless things,
whatever you do advances enlightenment.

And further:

Do not place your hope in others
or fear anything, whether inner or outer.
When you think on senseless things,
later you cannot cut off the bad results that follow.

Swear to yourself not to grasp at a self:
Take an oath to give up bad things.
Promise yourself not to get involved with others:
Take an oath to prevail against desire.

"Lord, from now on, may I think upon all beings as my mother;
may I take all their sufferings upon myself!
May I take this suffering upon myself;
May I allot all blame to myself!"

Think! Think! Think of the horror!
Reverse it! Reverse the bad karma done before!
In such a way destroy the kleśas.
At all times and all places,
never take on the misery of self-grasping!

If you have done bad things, publicly proclaim them!
What you have hidden, bring it forth!
Take your internal turmoil and display it!
To cease all bad action, strive to get what you deserve!

When foul thoughts arise, pray
that your flesh be consumed by leprosy.
When demonic thoughts occur,
ask that adversaries overwhelm you.
When you engage in revolting actions,
ask for pus and blood to eat.
Broadcast this far and wide,
and subdue all self-grasping.

Do not beg for blessings through making offerings to demons;
do not rely on exorcists; do not fall for fortunetellers;
do not set the mind on destructive mantras;
do not abuse your sexual energies.

## Renouncing Physical Pleasures

The harmful influence of self-grasping has caused us to involve our
bodies in self-centered activity from beginningless time. Such physical involvement ensures a consequence: immersing us in blood and
mucus and all unclean things. This body is the source of all frightful
things, of all suffering. It is like a bubble of water, so frail it has little stability. Though we hold the body so dear, as much as we attempt
to guard it, suffering and harm inevitably overtake it. In Entering the
Bodhisattva Path, we find:

However great our efforts to protect this body
just so much do we fall into a state of torment. [8.174]

And we find:

This abscess having a human shape
brings unbearable pain to the touch:
When, in blind passion, I let it be grasped,
with whom should I be angry when I come to harm?

The childish do not want to suffer,
but they crave what causes suffering.
When harm comes to me through my own fault,
why should I bear ill-will towards others? [6.44–45]

Having understood this, seeing how your body is the enemy, it is clear that you must conquer the conception of a self. In the same text we find:

Because of my attachment to the body,
even the slightest danger produces fear.
Who would not hate as the enemy
this body that produces terror?

Because of the desire to put an end to
the body's hunger and thirst and illness,
we lie in wait on the forest path
to kill birds, fish, wild beasts, and other game.

For the sake of its profit and comfort
people even kill father and mother.
They steal the property of the Three Jewels
and so burn in the hell of Avīci.

What person who is wise
would worship, guard, and desire this heap of flesh?
Who would not see it as an enemy,
and who would not despise it? [8.121–24]

Though we have struggled from beginningless time solely for the welfare of our body, nothing useful has ever come of this. If you think carefully, you will see that the nature of the body is empty. How can you either help or harm it? How can there be joy or suffering?

The mind, being without reality and empty, is like the sky. Just as with the sky, there is no way to rely on it for happiness or suffering. Conventional appearance—and all its causes and conditions—is merely the appearance of dependent origination. Conventional appearance lacks meaning and substance: It is born and ceases in an instant, like a dream, like an illusion.

Until you understand existence to be like this, you should inventory every one of your faults—whatever dulling and senseless actions

you have previously done. What has gone before is the key to how well you will be able to focus on the antidote, determining how well you are able to focus on unconditional giving and taking on suffering.

This very day you must immediately do whatever you can to subdue this demon of grasping at and cherishing the self. Śāntideva has stated:

When you are beset by a host of emotions,
endure them patiently in a thousand ways.
Like a lion amidst foxes,
remain unaffected by the host of afflictions.

In times of great peril
a person guards the eyes.
Just so, when danger arises,
I must not let the emotions sway me.
   —*Entering the Bodhisattva Path*, 7.60–61

And yet again the same text states:

To die by fire
or even to have my head cut off
would be preferable to bowing
to the enemy, the passions. [7.62]

Shabopa has also stated:

In this lifetime that is now so short,
we must seek to subdue all demonic influences.

Anyone whose underlying motivation is to attain personal benefit is just an ordinary person; only when you act with the intention of achieving the welfare of others are you given the name Dharma practitioner. Thus, you should learn to accept and reject as did Geshe Ben in his practice. Geshe Ben stated:

With the lance of the antidotes, I stand vigilant at the gates
of the castle of my mind. When the emotions grow fierce,
I am fierce. When they relax their hold, I relax mine.

Having seen that grasping the self is your enemy, you must give it up. Regarding this, Shabopa has said:

The Buddha taught: "The Dharma wards off demonic influences."
Thus, when you see that grasping the self is your enemy
and that other sentient beings are in the clutch
of this same self-grasping, you will have understood
the great kindness of beings, and you will pity and cherish them.

## All Sentient Beings as the Teacher

So it is that all sentient beings, from beginningless time, have been
your father and mother an immeasurable number of times and have
repeatedly shown you only great kindness. In the Exposition of
Bodhicitta, we find:

These sentient beings were formerly
my father, mother, friends, and relatives.
Always they have been so helpful to me:
For what they have done, I must be grateful. [74]

The great kindness of all others is the foundation for having a long
life, for being healthy, for meeting with the Dharma and so forth.
These are but a few of the good things that come from having honored all sentient beings for their previous kindness. In the Wish-
Granting Gem of Dreams, we find:

In such a way, karma brings forth harm and benefit:
It is the cause of both immeasurable happiness and suffering.
As this is so, sentient beings are our Lama.

And again:

The perfections of health and lineage,
a beautiful body, long life and power,
wealth and a beautiful spouse—
all are the result of have benefited sentient beings.

And again, it states in the Exposition of Bodhicitta:

Being born in a happy world or a miserable world,
or being born in the desire or non-desire realms,
such fruit has its seed in having brought
harm or benefit to sentient beings. [76]

Even in all future times, beings will show you great kindness: All the perfections and happiness of the highest states come from depending on sentient beings. Nāgārjuna has stated:

By bringing joy to sentient beings
you will certainly obtain a kingdom
greater than the vast domains of the greatest chakravartin kings,
or the abode of Indra.

Those who benefit sentient beings
will in the end obtain the perfections of a Buddha.
How can their wonderful nature be compared to those
who obtain the state of the heartless lower gods?

And again:

Through supporting sentient beings
you obtain the unparalleled state of the perfect Buddha.
How much more wonderful this is than to obtain the state
of Brahma, Indra, or a mighty world protector.

What is more, when you delight sentient beings, you also please the Bhagavans: the Buddhas who are the supreme refuge. Such is their great kindness. The Buddha states in a Sūtra:

When you benefit sentient beings, you honor me;
any other kind of honor is not the way. The true way
of showing honor is never to cease acting towards beings
with compassion. Actions done without compassion
turn you into the lowest sort of person. True compassion
never extends from those who would do harm. Those who
cultivate compassion for sentient beings are the ones
who honor me, the ones who embrace and cherish the teachings.

And again:

When you benefit sentient beings greatly, you show me
the greatest honor; when you do great harm to sentient beings,
you also do me the greatest harm. With respect to happiness
and suffering, I desire what sentient beings desire:
Thus, when people harm sentient beings,
it is as if they did the same to me.

The Buddha emphasized this in many teachings. Nāgārjuna has also stated:

I seek to delight the Victorious Ones.
How shall I do this? For a very long time,
the Victorious Ones have felt distress
at the suffering of beings:
Therefore, I must make sentient beings joyful.

Śāntideva states:

Being our unswerving friends, the Buddhas
act for our immeasurable benefit.
Apart from honoring sentient beings,
no other means exists to please them.
   —*Entering the Bodhisattva Path, 6.119*

The happiness of beings delights the Munis;
when others are harmed, they are displeased.
So, by pleasing others I delight all the Munis,
but by harming them, I harm the Munis as well.

When the body has been set on fire,
the sense objects do not bring delight;
just so, if you harm sentient beings,
there is no way the Compassionate Ones will be pleased. [6.122–23]

Apart from honoring sentient beings,
no other means exists to please the Buddhas. [6.119]

Nothing is more effective for generating merit and wisdom and for purifying our defilements than helping sentient beings. Thus, Entering the Bodhisattva Path points out the great kindness of all beings:

If simply to think of benefiting others
is greater than worshipping the Buddhas,
what need to mention actually striving
to benefit every single sentient being? [1.27]

And again:

The Victorious One has taught:
"The field of sentient beings is the Buddha-field."

Those who do all they can to honor beings,
in this way reach perfection. [6.112]

The merit born of faith in the Buddha
is due to the greatness of the Buddha.
Just so, to honor beings with loving-kindness
is to honor the greatness of sentient beings.

Since both have attained the qualities of the Buddhadharma,
Buddhas and sentient beings are said to be equal. [6.115–16]

   The great kindness of sentient beings comes from their serving as
our sole support for the attainment of perfect enlightenment. Thus
Ārya Nāgārjuna states:

If sentient beings did not exist,
what would be the purpose of giving gifts?
If embodied beings did not exist,
how would we train ourselves?
How could we develop moral practice?

The same is true for evil-doers:
All who cultivate heroic patience for their sake
will obtain whatever they desire.
For whom else could we make such efforts?

If embodied beings did not exist,
how could there be love, compassion,
joy or equanimity? Yet these are the genuine basis
for the bliss that comes through entering samādhi.

The joy of liberation is described
as an underlying propensity and potential,
whether known directly or indirectly.
If there were no beings, how could you gain
this knowledge that purifies the kleśas?

As those things in harmony
with the perspective of enlightenment
are thus caused by sentient beings in this way,
as I desire perfect enlightenment,
I must view sentient beings as my teacher.

To summarize, in Entering the Bodhisattva Path, we find:

Sentient beings and the Victorious Ones are alike
in achieving the qualities of Buddhadharma.
I revere the Jinas: Why do I not
have the same reverence for sentient beings? [6.113]

The opportunity to attain Awakening is due in the same degree to the kindness of the Buddha and the kindness of sentient beings. Thus, after intensely cultivating feelings of love and compassion for sentient beings who have shown you such great kindness, take their suffering and sins upon yourself and give them all your virtue and happiness.

# Reflections

## Dealing with Demonic Forces

*I*n the practice of Tong Len, thoughts of compassion are directed to all beings. The root text advises:

> *With firmly motivated concentration,*
> *divert all benefit from yourself to others.*

Although we might at first assume that compassion directed toward innocent sufferers would create the greatest benefit, focusing on demonic forces may prove even more effective. By directing compassionate thoughts and actions to the forces of evil, we undermine the power of the egoistic mind and can even conquer evil itself. Many Bodhisattvas, considering evil beings to be those most in need of compassion, choose to reside in hell rather than the heaven realm, demonstrating the power of love and compassion for as long as it takes to help the hell-beings liberate themselves from suffering.

To assist the reader in developing such potent compassion, Zhechen Gyaltsab introduces a practice similar to the practice of Chod or "cutting through" brought to Tibet in the eleventh century by the Indian master Padampa Sangyay. Chod takes the practice of giving to its furthest limits: Practitioners literally offer their body to demons in order to cut off all attachment to ego and self-interest. This practice has a special power, for the physical body is the most

difficult of all possessions to give up. If we can make such an offering on the basis of having developed right view, right meditative practice, and right action, we are practicing compassion in a way that also promotes the growth of Prajñāpāramitā, perfect transcendent wisdom. In all schools of Tibetan Buddhism, such practice has been accorded exceptional honor.

In Western traditions, an opposite approach to overcoming evil is usually followed: Rather than attempting to transform evil with compassion, evil is considered something to be feared and destroyed. In the annals of many religions, we read of diabolic forces that possess their victims' bodies and souls, and cause even good people to become evil. Offering oneself to a malevolent being such as a demon seems counterproductive and even dangerous. How could giving to the forces of evil strengthen the forces of good rather than evil?

## The Practice of Chod

When fear and hatred motivate us in our attempts to destroy evil, the negative nature of such motivation, rather than destroying the forces of evil, lends them strength. Such action actually opens a gate for demons to enter.

The practice of Chod draws on the positive forces of love and compassion. Because these positive energies are much stronger than the negative emotions that fuel the forces of evil, Chod practice undermines evil and strengthens goodness. Instead of letting demons play with us like toys, we invite them as our honored guests and transform them with loving-kindness and compassion. In making offerings to such beings, we transcend the residues of selfishness and purify the defilements.

Chod practice addresses demons, whether inside or outside our minds, as dreamlike creations. A demon takes form through ignorance and emotionality, through lust, greed, passion, anger, and aggression. These emotions are familiar to each of us, for the ego is born of such patterns as well. It would be shortsighted to think that we are different from the demons or somehow more deserving of good fortune.

Cutting through the ego with the sword of openness, Chod practice puts self and ego on the same footing as the demons. If our giving is wholehearted, it is the demons who have a problem, for with the destruction of self-interest, the demons will disappear along with the illusion of self. The karmic chain is cut, and enlightenment manifests as the natural state of being.

# Dealing with
# Demonic Forces

*I*f at present you are being harmed by any living creature, either human or non-human, remember that those who cause you such harm have been your parents and relatives from beginningless time and have benefited you in countless ways. Now it is your turn to benefit them, ignoring the grievous tales you could tell of their great wrongdoing. These beings are now wandering in samsara and experiencing immense suffering: Through the force of mistaken appearances, they do not realize that they were once your blood relatives.

Urged on by your own bad karma, these beings are now committing a great wrong in harming you. The result will be that in the future they will again experience great suffering; and as they are so self-centered, their suffering will last for a very long time. Considering your experience, meditate fiercely with love and compassion, patiently focusing on all these beings, who are so to be pitied.

By meditating in such a way, a fine understanding of the karma of demonic activity arises. Once you accept demonic beings as having been your mother, then you are their child. With that conception of mother and child in operation, how can you come to any harm?

If you were to treat all beings as if they were your mother, all would treat you as if you were their child. Since reality is shaped in just this way, this practice alone will let you free beings from suffering. In The Verse Summary of the Prajñāpāramitā, we find:

Many ills and demonic forces arise in the human world;
but these are calmed by waves of truth,
through compassion and the wish to help. [20.24]

Thus, reflect as follows: "In the past, I clearly must have only harmed these beings who are harming me. Now I must defuse this harm and gain their welfare." Meditate strongly on giving unconditionally and on taking upon yourself all suffering, and consider: "Whether they are man or beast, I will strive to do whatever I can to benefit these beings."

If you are not able to actually benefit beings by your actions, sincerely reflect upon this and express the following: "May all these beings who are causing harm be freed from suffering! May they be happy! May they quickly become awakened!" From now on, whatever virtuous activities you perform, concentrate on acting for the welfare of all these beings. This practice is of great importance. It is also the principle of the four liberating techniques of Panchen Śākyaśrī:

1. Not looking out for your own welfare beyond a single day's sustenance

2. Performing each of the ten positive Dharma activities every hour of the day

3. No matter what the circumstances, not acting to protect yourself except through meditating on openness

4. Benefiting others in return for any harm they do to you.

Finally, there are the twelve meditations of the Lord of Dharma, Godtsangpa, which include the vow to benefit others in exchange for any harm they might do to you.

Holy beings, in performing beneficial actions, always concentrate on giving great benefit in return for harm. When such motivation exists, the benefits of this practice also arise effortlessly. Thus we find:

> *With firmly motivated concentration,*
> *divert all benefit from yourself to others.*

Strongly concentrate on benefiting those who harm you. The samaya vows undertaken in the practice of self-mastery, such as those set forth here, and the commitment to benefit those who do you harm, must be further broadened by prayers of aspiration. Gyalsay Rinpoche stated:

Some people under the spell of great desire
would steal another's wealth or compel others to steal it.
We must dedicate to such as these our body, our possessions,
our virtue of past, present, and future:
This is the Bodhisattva's practice.

Others would even chop off the heads of innocent victims.
Taking upon ourselves such sins as these
through the power of compassion:
This is the Bodhisattva's practice.

Some people would show contempt in various ways
even for those who have taught for three thousand years.
To proclaim their good qualities again and again
with a loving mind: This is the Bodhisattva's practice.

Some people, even in the midst of a large assembly,
would find fault with others, singling them out to abuse them.
Being conscious of being their spiritual friend
and bowing down humbly before them:
This is the Bodhisattva's practice.

Some people would see as their enemy even those
who have treated them as dearly as a son.
Treating them with the loving-kindness of a mother
toward a sick child: This is the Bodhisattva's practice.

Some people would treat with the scorn of arrogance
those of equal or of lower rank. To approach such people
with the respect and reverence one would show to a Lama:
This is the Bodhisattva's practice.

—*The Thirty-Seven Bodhisattva Practices, 14–19*

When you are led by ambition to do anything harmful, or when you fail to generate the mind of compassion and benefit, you are not engaged in the practice of self-mastery. Lang Tangpa has stated:

Before I had purified my mind, I went to a teacher of the Prajñāpāramitā in Kham, knowing that he was a Dharma brother, as close to me as my inner being. Great joy had arisen in me and I was expecting perfect mutual regard. But it did not happen like that—instead, he beat me with a stick. But whatever he did to attack me, I did not respond with anger: The loving-kindness I had felt before did not change. That is purification of practice.

Even if you are actually despised and vilified, you must be like Lang Tangpa, who never grew angry.

There was once a rich householder who had a sickly child. He consulted a fortuneteller, who told him that if the child became the son of the master named Geshe Zangpo, he would become well. The householder's wife at once took their son into the presence of the Geshe, saying: "This is your son! He is ill!" She then fled, leaving her son behind.

Geshe Zangpo did not say anything, but entrusted the child to another woman to care for. The child soon became well, and rumors spread as to the child's parentage. After some years had passed, the parents returned, and after showing great respect to the Geshe, and after making offerings to him, they said they would take the child back.

There is a similar story in Geshe Nayzurwa's biography, concerning a situation that arose through jealousy.

Though you have done nothing wrong, if you accept accusations of wrongdoing, you are dealing correctly with your own past wrongdoing. Once, at Radreng Monastery, a good monk by the name of Zangpo who had gone to the kitchen to grind some tea into powder was accused of stealing some missing plates. He went to the abbot and said, "I am innocent! They are giving me a bad name!"

The abbot advised him, "Accept the blame. Then offer tea to all of the monks. Later you will be proven innocent." The monk did as he was advised, and that night he experienced signs of having purified many sins. Some time later, a number of plates were found, and the

monk was proven innocent. His respect for the abbot greatly increased, and he was most grateful for having followed the abbot's advice.

Even if the being harming you is a demon, concentrate firmly on the thought: "From beginningless time I have eaten your flesh, drunk your blood, crunched your bones, and worn your skin countless times. If I were to heap together the remains, even the three thousand worlds would be too small a container.

"Countless times I have killed and beaten and robbed you. This adversity I am now experiencing is therefore in repayment and is a great kindness to me. Now, I will return this kindness with my own flesh and blood. I will give to you unstintingly all that you desire."

Visualize in front of you those who are doing you harm. Open your body with your mind, and with your entire being think: "Eat what you desire of my flesh and blood and bones!"

Then express this verbally, with the force of your whole mind behind it:

"If you would enjoy this flesh of mine, eat my flesh. If you would enjoy my blood, drink my blood. If you would enjoy my bones, gnaw on my bones. If you would enjoy my skin, wear my skin. If all has congealed, eat me raw. If not, eat me cooked. If your throat is large, swallow me whole. Carry away what you wish. Take whatever you desire. Do what you will."

Having expressed all this from the depth of your heart, continue to concentrate in the same way.

The Stages of the Bodhisattva's Self-Mastery states:

When you are struck by the demonic force of illness,
you can turn aside the ferocity of Vajrapāṇi and the rest;
you can distance yourself from the fury
of Mahākāla and the others. Reflect as follows:

"Today I meet my retribution!
I summon protection and refuge at the time of death!
Today I must distinguish samsara and nirvana.
Gather, gather, and eat my flesh!
Gather all who would take my breath!

Come to help in flaying me alive!
Come and wear my skin as hide!

"You my parents, dear as my life,
come revel in the flesh and blood of your child!
You, my fathers and mothers, so very kind,
come! Let me repay you for your goodness now!

"In the past, holding my body and mind so dear,
I was forced to wander yet again in the world.
In the past, pleasure in certain actions swept me away,
causing me to be struck yet again by disease.

"In the past, I harmed others who harmed me,
so that now a mountain of burdens weighs me down.
In the past, I did actions to regret—
now, with death approaching, my mind is still disturbed.

"In the past, I closely guarded my own self,
and remembered only a few words on refuge.
Now, not even the power of the three objects of refuge
can help me turn aside this ego-self.
Not even they can master it or force it to be gone!

"For their compassion to protect me,
I must demolish inner grasping!
I must demolish outer grasping at things!
I must demolish my positions of attachment and hatred!
Hereafter, I must have no hostility.

"Now I will hold the banquet of repayment,
inviting guests from throughout samsaric realms:
from all the fearful deities to those in the eighteen realms of hell.
All will enjoy what I have of body and diversions,
breath and vigor and vitality.
I will gather all that they might need.

"Come, O eighty-thousand demons!
Forever may you frolic in delight
in this flesh and blood I have held so dear!
In return for this food, do not pursue me hereafter!
You eighty-thousand revelers, draw near!

You fifteen despoilers of children, come close!
Come forth, all you flesh-eating yakṣas!

"May the male demons, messengers of Māra, come forth!
May the female demons, fiends of action, come forth!
May the demon king of evil spirits
and the lord of the earth come forth!
May you all draw near to revel in my flesh and blood!

"From the aperture of Brahma at the crown of my head
down through my fingers, to the soles of my feet,
I will not hold on, I will not be attached:
I will cheerfully satisfy all, so eat!

"Eat my flesh, drink my blood, crunch my bones!
Ingest the marrow of my head and limbs;
ingest my joints and innards and juices.
Eat my brain, my flesh, and all the rest.
Partake of my body, both inside and out!

"Not holding back, revel until you have your fill;
take all you can to eat or drink:
Through this appeasement may you disappear,
obliterated! The root cut out!

"I call out fiercely, call distinctly!
Attend to me! Chom-chom myog-myog bdag-la-ya!
rBad-rbad thum-thum bdag-la-ya!
HŪṂ DZA! May you now be gone!
May the wheel of samsara stop in its tracks!
May the mountain of bad karma crumble!

"I have cherished this body in the past:
Now this very self must be shattered!
You who possess the force of foul destruction!
You, the toxic dealer in flesh and blood!
You, fierce demon who takes away the breath!
Samaya! Blessings!

"In conquering the self we become greater
than the Buddhas of the three times.

But if we do not conquer the self,
we are ruined by our own actions.

"Now, knowing this, I desire to be free
from the chains created by all self-destructive actions.
If I do not free myself from them, may all the demons gather here,
sending heaps of illnesses, gathering wind and bile and phlegm
and fierce, unbearable suffering!

"When I pass from the cycle of samsara, this world of appearances,
send to me all that is not desired.
May I cut short the karma and kleśas of beings,
as well as all their suffering!

"Right now, with certainty, in the center of my heart,
may I bring to fruition the suffering undergone
by all sentient beings. May I thus eradicate
the cause and effect of bad karma of all beings.
May I perfect renunciation and realization!

"May all the virtues that exist in me
be dedicated completely to all beings,
and may that be the cause for all beings
to obtain perfect realization.

"May I thus bring about the perfect renunciation
and realization of all beings.
Attaining the essence of the Dharmakāya,
the glory of love and compassion,
may both merit and wisdom come forth.

"As I will remain in the world
until I obtain enlightenment for all,
may all experience, all the kleśas, their causes and effects,
mature in my consciousness in this lifetime.

"May the kleśas, together with their causes and effects,
mature in this lifetime—this very year.
May they mature this very month;
this very day; this very instant!

"Today, when I experience fierce pain
from an illness of short duration,

may this illness be all the illnesses of all beings,
that I take on as my burden alone.

"Now, a lightning flash advances:
the essence of giving and taking.
Ah! The joy as I call out! Certain joy for sentient beings!
I take upon myself their suffering!

"Now I cut off all hope for myself!
It is not right for anyone
to suffer even a little pain—
and so I gather all maladies to me.

"Understanding illness, I will cut through it.
Understanding pain, I will heal it.
Understanding the pangs of hunger and thirst, I will assuage them.
Though my body be unwell, the joy within my mind will grow."

When you give in this way, those who would harm you will have their hunger and thirst assuaged—eating your flesh, drinking your blood, and gnawing on your bones, from your feet to your skull. As a result, your joy of body and mind will be inexhaustible, and the strong motivation of the two aspects of the enlightened mind will immediately be generated in your consciousness.

Again, having manifested your body as before, give of your body again, feeding all the various forms of demonic creatures who eat flesh and blood. Having satisfied them all, concentrate on their becoming happy and virtuous.

Because all wrongdoing arises from cherishing the self, see the self as your enemy. Accept whatever harm comes to you. As all benefit and happiness come from sentient beings, view them all as your blood relations, and benefit them in whatever you do. Regarding this, Lang Tangpa stated:

Of all the teachings I have heard, this is the most profound:
"All faults are mine; all good qualities belong to sentient beings."
The key is this: Offer every gain and victory to others;
take upon yourself all their troubles and difficulties.
This is the only way to bring about understanding.

This is stated clearly in Entering the Bodhisattva Path:

And so you must certainly act
for the welfare of others:
For as the word of the Buddha is infallible,
you shall see the benefit of such conduct later.

If, in the past, you had practiced
the exchange of karma,
you would not now
find yourself lacking the bliss of the Buddha.

Just as you have come to grasp as 'I'
the ovum and the drop of semen that came from others,
now, in just such a way
be attuned to others.

Having come to a deep understanding of 'other',
take whatever it is
that appears to be your body
and use it to benefit others.

When your mind tells you, "I am happy,
another unhappy; I am high, another low;
I will benefit myself, but not the other!"
why not feel jealous of yourself?

Separate yourself from happiness;
take upon yourself the suffering of others.
Ask yourself, "Why do I act the way I do?"
Examine your own faults:

"May I transform even the wrongs done by others
into my own faults.
As for my own faults, however slight,
I will confess them to everyone.

"Extolling the glory of others
and denigrating my own worth,
may I be like the lowliest servant
employed for the benefit of all.

"I must not praise my nature, so full of error,
for any transient advantage:

May even my few good qualities
never become known to others."

In short, whatever harm you have done to others
for your own benefit,
let this harm now fall on yourself,
for the welfare of sentient beings.

Do not present yourself forcefully
in the way of those with arrogance;
rather, present yourself like a new bride,
bashful, timid, and restrained.

Mind, you must act and stay like this!
You must not act as you have done before!
In this manner, I shall control you.
You shall be overcome and brought to a halt. [8.156–67]

# Reflections

# Motivated Concentration on Ultimate Enlightened Mind

*T*he key to developing the ultimate mind of enlightenment is the realization of śūnyatā: the recognition that appearance is similar to a dream or an illusion. The Bodhisattva gains strength from this clear insight into the nature of samsara. Thus we find in the root text of the seven essentials:

> *Openness being the greatest protection,*
> *let openness reveal illusory appearance as the Four Kāyas.*

This is not an easy insight to maintain, for it challenges the very basis of our reality. To see existence as being without substance is like turning the world inside out: Our reality is no longer real; it seems almost crazy. Such a view of reality can be so unendurable that even devoted disciples of the Dharma may turn away. But for those who have the motivation of the Bodhisattva to free all beings, it is not possible to reject this knowledge.

Ever intent on the goal of liberation for all, the Bodhisattva embraces śūnyatā as the best of friends. With penetrating insight, courage, and patience, this heroic being enacts a path of action inseparable from great compassion. We can sense the wealth of such a practice: Seeing its beauty we become transfixed by its jewel-like radiance. Its nectar flows through our being, healing past pain and

bringing new joy. Turning body, speech, and mind toward this vision, shaping our resolve through prayers to the enlightened lineage, we see the truth of realization opening before us and become at last beings who are truly capable of helping others.

This is the gift of Prajñāpāramitā, Mother of the Buddhas. In an era when the world urgently needs relief from suffering, these deeper dimensions of knowledge, born of wisdom traditions that may soon be lost, are precious jewels whose value we cannot afford to ignore.

When you take on the practice of openness and compassion, the great Bodhisattvas stand at your side, ever ready to help you: giving you strength, enriching your compassion, encouraging you in your efforts. In the same way, the blessings of many great panditas and Bodhisattvas magnify your compassion so that you can share it with all beings. With their support and your own deepening motivation, you need have no concern: You can easily overcome the destructive emotions and shape your conduct and thoughts in accord with the practice of the Bodhisattvas.

Once you have started to develop the great compassion of Bodhicitta, a seed is planted in your heart and blooms into a flower of manifold blossoms, like the opening of a rose or lotus. Once the lotus of enlightenment comes forth, Bodhicitta transmutes the destructive nature of samsara: Nothing remains to oppose the growth of beauty.

So trust your wisdom, trust the Buddha, trust the Bodhisattvas and the path of Dharma. You have been given the seed of understanding; now do not toss it away. You have been given a glimpse of another way; now take care never to return to the samsaric path. Samsara has many workers on its side. Now it is time to move to the side of Dharma.

Encourage yourself continually. Recognize that this is the time to work on behalf of all sentient beings. Giving to the Dharma is the same as giving to all sentient beings; either way, strive to make work on behalf of all beings a part of your practice. The influence of this dark Kaliyuga is spreading, but there are many ways to protect yourself if you take the Path of Heroes.

# Motivated Concentration on Ultimate Enlightened Mind

*A*s you proceed to purify the ultimate mind of enlightenment, also continue to transform adverse conditions into the path of enlightenment. The root text states:

*Openness being the greatest protection,*
*let openness reveal illusory appearance as the Four Kāyas.*

The kleśas (the destructive emotions) are the cause of our existence. Their operation is reinforced by contributing conditions—the damaging aspects of the world of form and the formless inner essence of beings. All mental distress and suffering are based on the harmful nature of these causes and conditions. Yet emotionality and suffering are nothing but the illusory appearances of mind; they do not truly exist in any way at all. In being relative, appearances are like the terror you feel when dreaming of being trapped in a fire or carried away by a flood. Such are the reverberations of holding as true that which is not true.

Since nothing, ultimately, has any existence whatsoever, if you look at the actual nature of the kleśas or suffering, you will see that they are non-arising even from the first. This 'birthlessness' is the Dharmakāya: the Body of Dharma. Since they do not arise, no cause could possibly exist for their final cessation. This 'being without

cessation' is the Sambhogakāya: the Body of Ecstatic Awareness. In being without birth or cessation, there is also no middle ground. This 'non-abiding' is the Nirmāṇakāya: the Body of Manifestation. The inseparable actuality of these three is the Svābhāvakāya: the Body of Intrinsic Nature.

This is the instruction on how to identify the Four Kāyas in viewing illusory appearance as the Four Kāyas. It is similar to the meditation that focuses on openness, whatever the circumstances, as found in the four liberating techniques of Paṇchen Śākyaśrī.

It is vital to meditate on śūnyatā—openness—as the best protection, whatever circumstances may arise. Thus we find:

The best protection is ultimate truth:
No other methods of protection are needed.

Again, Āryadeva has stated:

If you have cultivated openness,
you will never be harmed by the Lord of Death,
so how could you be harmed
by any of the other demons?

And we find in The Verse Summary of the Prajñāpāramitā:

Imagine that all sentient beings in fields
innumerable as the sands of the Ganges were demons,
and that from each strand of their hair demons emanated:
Even all of them together could not hinder the wise.

Bodhisattvas, endowed with strength and wisdom,
cannot be assailed by the four Māras.
They cannot be agitated for four reasons:
They abide in openness; they never abandon sentient beings;
they act in accord with their words;
and they have the blessings of the Sugatas. [27.2–3]

And again:

Those who manifest in action the perfection of wisdom,
embracing humility and acting with sagacity,
will never be harmed by poison, weapons, fire, or flood.

Māra and his host of demons
will find no opportunity to harm them. [3.1]

Concentrate on this view that cuts off both hope and fear concerning your spiritual progress. When you meditate on the two aspects of enlightened mind, do not be concerned with the outcome. Consider, instead, the great kindness of those who harm you, for their actions are inducements to purify the two aspects of Bodhicitta. We find in Entering the Bodhisattva Path:

As if a treasure had appeared in my house
without my making any effort to obtain it,
I must rejoice in my enemies,
who help me to perform enlightened actions.

Due to them I have had the chance to practice;
therefore it is right that they should be the first
to obtain the fruit of my patience.
Truly they are the cause of my patience. [6.107–8]

And again:

How could I achieve patience if all were like
the physician who always seeks to help me?
No, it is by depending on those
whose minds are full of fierce hatred
that I generate patience. They are the ones
as worthy to be honored as the sacred Dharma. [6.110]

The objects of desire are distracting. Once you free yourself from them through the antidotes, you will no longer be inclined to fall prey to the emotions. Yet because the emotions call you to action, you need to consider them as being manifestations of the Buddha. In the same text we find:

Praise and the like distract me;
they also lay waste my sense of sorrow.
Leading to jealousy of those with good qualities,
they destroy the perfections.

Therefore, those intent on deflecting the praise
that would come to me protect me against
falling into lower states of being.

Intent on liberation,
I do not need the bondage of fame and respect.
How could I be angry at those
who free me from such bondage?

Their desire for me to suffer
is identical to the blessings of the Buddha.
As they bar the door to my fall,
how could I be angry at them? [6.98–101]

Truly, wrongdoing is the cause of bad karma, and suffering is its fruit. As suffering arises in this way, if you do not wish to suffer, you must give up wrongdoing, which is the cause of suffering. Any inducement to give up such action is a great kindness.

Those who harm you due to your actions in previous lives will certainly only suffer in the future by going to lower states of being. Thus, if you are now able to lead them from the abyss of bad states of being, it is again due to their kindness. As they show you only kindness, concentrate on the fact that whatever they do to you is certainly the wondrous action of the precious Lama. As stated in the Song of Tselay Natsog Rangdrol:

The whole of the visible world is the mandala of the Lama:
The purity of appearance demonstrates complete compassion.
All that happens in the world is a manifestation of the Lama:
All actions benefit beings with what they need.

All beings born in the world are the manifestation of the Lama:
The Dharmakāya, as the heart of the Sugata, pervades everything.
All joy and happiness are a manifestation of the Lama:
a gift of siddhi, granting whatever the mind could wish for.
All the distressing conditions of illness
are also manifestations of the Lama,
for the experience of suffering purifies wrongdoing.

And again:

When you do not realize all goodness and evil as the Lama,
the impartiality of pure appearance has no means to arise.
Without the experience of pure appearance,
the visible world manifests as the enemy.

Therefore, those who have trained their minds thoroughly
understand everything as an emanation.
If you do not understand adverse conditions
of inimical forces as the Lama,
avoiding one obstacle will only lead you into the arms of another.

When the mind does not renounce grasping at a self,
it will return in the same form.
The key is to thoroughly understand
that whatever arises is the compassion of the Lama.

In summary, Śāntideva has stated:

For the sake of delighting the Tathāgatas,
henceforth I will diligently serve the world.
Though many beings should strike me,
may I put my own life at risk to delight the Lord of the World.

The masters of compassion consider all beings
to be identical to themselves: Of this there is no doubt.
Seeing compassion as the nature of sentient beings
is to see the Buddhas as well.

Why do I not honor beings as does the Protector?
It is this that pleases the Tathāgatas;
and thus also is my own welfare achieved.
It is this that clears away the suffering of the world.
Truly I must always practice in this way.

     *—Entering the Bodhisattva Path, 6.125–27*

 As the Buddha has taught, take delight in fulfilling the desires of
those who would do you harm, and see the harm they cause you as
actually being the beauty in their hearts. Even if you should come
down with the fiercest form of leprosy or the like, consider that without this suffering, you would not be mindful of the Dharma when
planning your life. Reflect that such suffering compels you to be
mindful of the Dharma and is thus the supreme action of the precious Lama. Atīśa stated:

Adverse conditions are our spiritual friends;
demons are manifestations of the Jina.

Illness sweeps away all sins and defilements;
suffering is the call of the Dharma.

Moreover, illness and suffering help you to generate the mind of renunciation. Thus we find in Entering the Bodhisattva Path:

Without suffering there is no renunciation;
therefore, mind, stand firm! [6.12]

The remorse and feelings of renunciation you experience are in direct proportion to your mental suffering. At that time, pride and the other destructive emotions are cleared away.

With sentient beings as the root of the path of the Great Vehicle, compassion becomes the guide. Knowing what to accept and reject with respect to the cause and effect of karma, you become endowed with many virtues. The same text states:

Moreover, suffering has good qualities:
Through repentance we do away with pride
and generate compassion for samsaric beings,
abhorring evil and delighting in virtue. [6.21]

In short, this way of relying on the Lama is similar to generating both aspects of the enlightened mind. Thus, when you concentrate decisively and sincerely on supporting those who cause you harm or suffering, you generate both aspects of Bodhicitta.

# Reflections

## Accumulation and Purification

*T*o break samsaric patterns, we need to focus on making virtuous activity the ongoing standard of our lives. Accomplishing this is not easy, for to ensure success, we need to identify what constitutes virtuous action and learn how to incorporate virtue into all aspects of thought, word, and action. Since we cannot hope to do all of this at once, we begin at the conceptual level by reading about the lives of virtuous people and reflecting on how to strengthen our own virtuous qualities.

As a practice, we can imagine ourselves performing virtuous acts, particularly those that develop the pāramitās. For example, when focusing on the pāramitā of giving, we can imagine giving everything good to others. Making imaginary offerings turns the mind away from self-interest toward the needs of others. This practice develops humility and releases the tightness that comes from holding firmly to the concerns of the self.

Keeping in mind our past selfishness and wrongdoing—all self-centered or self-serving action—we can see that we have been active participants in a system of suffering. We can see how the self-centered mind has created beings who are little better than demons, although they too are only slaves of samsara. We can symbolically accept and purify our part in this suffering by making offerings to

the demonic creatures of the world as well as to the enlightened ones who strive to help us. Symbolic giving then naturally progresses to giving of a more substantial nature.

The more we accumulate merit through giving, the more we gain familiarity with giving as a gesture of our whole being. With such full engagement, the senses open and qualities such as patience and endurance develop more easily. Like the performer who trains in daily rehearsals, we can train ourselves in an enlightened way of being, eventually learning to communicate the power of compassion. Like the accumulation of beauty as an artist applies successive brush strokes to a painting or a composer adds new harmonies to a symphonic theme, merit builds on itself, each action inspiring the next.

Through the accumulation of merit and wisdom, virtue reaches new heights of goodness, until eventually the environment itself is completely transformed. Its wholesome and beautiful clarity sustains practice, and prevents interference from old destructive patterns. Balance comes naturally, and benefits flow to ourselves and to all beings. Emotionality ceases to be a problem, and a sense of all-pervasive responsiveness makes all burdens lighter. Tension is released, and companions on our journey to enlightenment appear spontaneously, without having to be invited. When we begin to think of all we do in terms of performing a virtuous activity or purifying nonvirtue, all activity becomes a meditation, and we move closer to generating Bodhisattva compassion and insight into śūnyatā, the twin aspects of the mind of enlightenment.

# Application:
# Accumulation and Purification

*D*ifficult circumstances are transformed into the path by the two essential features of application: accumulation and purification. Thus the root text states:

> *As the supreme method, apply the four applications.*

The four applications are the best methods for fashioning difficult circumstances into the path:

1. The accumulation of merit and wisdom
2. The purification of wrongdoing
3. The gift of torma to evil forces
4. The offering of torma to ḍākinīs and Dharma protectors.

## *Accumulation of Merit and Wisdom*

When reflecting upon ways to accumulate merit and wisdom, consider: When you suffer, you think that if your suffering would only disappear, you would be happy. But whenever you desire your own happiness, only suffering comes of it. This pattern persists because until now you have not taken it upon yourself to accumulate the true causes of happiness.

If you want happiness instead of suffering you must accumulate the merit that is the cause of happiness. Reflect upon this earnestly. The master Śūra has stated:

What is great virtue?
It is that which causes happiness.
With it you gain the superior qualities
of beauty, great generosity, and nobility.

Virtue is a good friend,
a kindred spirit that goes with you everywhere.
Certainly, virtue will repay you
with perfect qualities.

When you have firmly obtained a state of glory,
the masters of the world sing your praises,
and your guidance gives widespread benefit to others.
Thus, increase your practice of virtue,
and through your virtue, abandon pleasure in wrongdoing!

This teaching is from the Precious Teaching Like a Jeweled Casket, a text that sheds extensive light on this practice. Learn these teachings well, and make a point of meditating with humble faith in the precious Lama. Concentrate on this practice earnestly, as much as you can.

Honor the precious Lama, respect the Sangha, give torma to all creatures and gifts to the destitute. Offer butter lamps and tsa-tsas, perform prostrations, circumambulations, and so forth. In short, however you can, gather merit and wisdom, through body, speech, and mind. Put energy into going for refuge, into making the Bodhisattva vow, and especially into the seven-limbed practice and offering the mandala. Pray very strongly to put an end to hope and fear:

"If I will practice better by being sick,
I pray to be blessed by illness.
If I will practice better by being healthy,
I pray for the blessing of health.
If it is better for me to die,
I pray for the blessing of death."

Orgyan Dusum Khyenpa has also taught:

Practice the ten virtues and be attentive to the effects
of your actions. Great force comes from karma:
By the great force of truth, wrongdoing is abandoned
and the antidotes for the kleśas are brought to bear.
Make fierce effort to perform virtuous actions,
for without the accumulation of merit, a good mind
does not materialize: A good mind becomes active
as you accumulate merit. Until your mind is full
of goodness, strive for virtue and shun wrongdoing.

And again:

However sick you might be, whatever difficulties or miseries
you may be undergoing, always present the mandala
and the five types of offerings to the Three Jewels,
and afterwards take refuge. The recitation of prayers
for the accumulation of merit and wisdom, the offerings
of torma and the like, create the background for taking refuge.
If these actions do not immediately benefit you,
do not assume that this means that the teachings
of the Dharma are not true, or that blessings do not come
from the Three Jewels. Concentrate on the thought
that you will be healed when your bad karma
has been extinguished. Do not look for omens
or answers in fortunetelling or other such things;
go only for refuge as the Buddha taught.

## Purification of Wrongdoing

The second application for transforming adverse circumstances into
the path is the purification of wrongdoing. When you are suffering,
you tend to think that if your suffering would only disappear, you
would be happy. But think again! If you do not want to suffer, you
must abandon the actions that are the cause of suffering. For this
apply the Four Forces:

1.  The force of renunciation and remorse over past wrongdoing

2.  The force of turning from wrongdoing by committing yourself
to never again doing such actions, even at the cost of your life

3. The force of reliance: of going for refuge to the Three Jewels and generating the enlightened mind

4. The force of the all-encompassing antidotes, known as the Six Gates, which produce wholesome actions by serving as antidotes to the forces of defilement: meditating on openness; reciting specific mantras; concentrating on the names of the Buddhas and Bodhisattvas; constructing images of the Three Jewels or repairing old images; doing prostrations and circumambulations; and reading and reciting the profound Sūtras and Tantras.

The practice of the Four Forces stimulates the impulse to admit wrongdoing and thereby to purify wrongdoing. The Teaching of the Four Dharmas states:

The Buddha said: "Maitreya, endowed with the four dharmas,
you can purify all the wrongdoing you have committed
and become completely pure. What are these four?
The force of renunciation, the force of reliance,
the force of the all-inclusive antidotes,
and the force of total commitment."

Entering the Bodhisattva Path also states clearly that by following such a course we are certain to purify wrongdoing. Again, in the Sūtra of Golden Light, we find:

Whoever for thousands of kalpas
has been unable to resist wrongdoing,
in one session of heartfelt confession
can purify it all.

In the Instructions from a Spiritual Friend, we find:

Whoever has been previously negligent
and later learns to take heed,
is as beautiful as the moon clear of clouds:
like Nanda, Aṅgulimāla, Ajātaśatru, and Udayana. [14]

During the time of the Buddha, these men were purified of their sins when confessing on the basis of the Four Forces: Nanda, who was very attached to his wife; Aṅgulimāla, who killed nine hundred and ninety-nine people while following an evil teacher; Ajātaśatru, who killed his own father; and Udayana, who killed his own mother.

As stated in the Sūtras, the first two obtained Arhatship in their lifetime. Ajātaśatru became a Bodhisattva, and Udayana was reborn as a god and obtained the fruit of entering the stream.

## Offerings of Torma

The third way to transform adverse circumstances into the path is to make offerings to evil forces.

Having understood that those who harm you are your mothers and fathers, you must draw them to you and offer torma to them. With great conviction, call to them:

"When in the past you caused me adversity,
you showed me great kindness, assisting me to train
in the two aspects of Bodhicitta. Now, help me
to ripen upon myself the suffering of all sentient beings!
Help me to free all sentient beings from suffering!"

When you pray very strongly, body and mind emit tranquility and joy, and the desire to be happy and helpful is fully realized. But if you are unable to do this, then after offering torma, concentrate on cultivating love and compassion toward those who are harmful, and tell them:

"If you create obstacles for those who are acting for the welfare
of sentient beings, you will later be born in hell. Therefore,
since I am attempting to benefit you by means of the Dharma
and in whatever ways I can, please do not create obstacles
to my Dharma practice."

## Offerings to the Protectors

The fourth way to transform adverse circumstances into the path is to make offerings to the Dharma Protectors.

Keeping in mind the dynamic nature of the charismatic activity of all the Dharma Protectors, Lamas, and yidams, make torma offerings to them. Pray for them to help you quell circumstances contrary to the Dharma so that you can practice in harmony with the Dharma.

Pray for their help in using whatever happens in your life to advance on the path. Never pray for happiness or joy or to be cured of sickness or to silence demonic influences. The Buddha taught that without the existence of illness and demonic forces, without misery along with happiness, we would have no way to know which circumstances go counter to the Dharma and which accord with the Dharma.

Many different practices and ways of offering torma are found in the Sarma and Nyingma teachings. Extensive teachings on ways to transform adverse circumstances into the path are found in the Bla-ma'i-dmar-khrid of Orgyan Dusum Khyenpa.

## Transforming Adversity

During your practice, or in between sessions, obstacles may suddenly arise to cause you distress. In order to bring such adverse circumstances into the path, the root text states:

> *Apply whatever happens to you to your meditation.*

If you should suddenly fall ill or if inimical forces should arise against you to cause you intense suffering, consider the innumerable similar situations occurring in the many worlds. Concentrate on compassion for those who are subject to such difficulties, and gather to yourself all their suffering. The Crown of Sūtras states:

The heirs of the Jina, when taking action, employ
the various senses to whatever may be.
They manifest action in order to benefit sentient beings,
and offer advice appropriate to each type of being. [6.9]

The Sūtra on the Purification of Activity contains similar teachings on using each aspect of life to help sentient beings:

I will employ all my senses and the various objects of the senses
for sentient beings. I dedicate all that I do with body, speech,
and mind—with words and actions in harmony—
to ways of benefiting all sentient beings.

Think as follows: When entering a house at night: "May all sentient beings enter the city of liberation." When sleeping: "May I obtain the Dharmakāya of the Buddha." When dreaming: "May I realize

that all things are like a dream." When awakening from sleep:
"May I wake up from ignorance." When rising: "May I obtain
the Dharmakāya of the Buddha." When dressing: "May I put on
the attire of modesty and constraint." When fastening a belt
around my waist: "May I be fastened to the root of virtue."

When sitting down: "May I obtain the Vajra seat." When leaning
back: "May I have the support of the tree of enlightenment."
When lighting a fire: "May I burn away the fuel of the emotions."
When the fire is burning: "May I burn with the fire of wisdom."
When preparing food: "May I brew the elixir of awareness."
When eating: "May I obtain the sustenance of good qualities."

When going outside: "May I pass from the city of samsara."
When descending stairs: "May I enter the world to serve
the welfare of sentient beings." When opening a door:
"May I open the door to the city of liberation." When closing
a door: "May I close the door to bad states of being."

When setting out on an excursion: "May I enter the path
of the Āryas." When going uphill: "May I establish
all sentient beings in the happiness of the high states of being."
When going downhill: "May I dry up the stream
of the three lower realms." When meeting others:
"May I meet with the Buddhas." When putting down each foot:
"May I proceed to benefit all sentient beings."
When raising each foot: "May I draw beings from samsara."

When seeing someone wearing jewelry: "May I obtain
the ornaments of the signs and marks." When seeing someone
not wearing jewelry: "May I become endowed with the qualities
of purity." When seeing a full vessel: "May I become full of good
qualities." When seeing an empty vessel: "May I empty myself
of faults." When seeing beings who are enjoying themselves:
"May I take joy in the Dharma." When seeing beings who are
dissatisfied: "May I become dissatisfied with all composite things."
When seeing a happy person: "May I obtain the happiness
of Buddhahood." When seeing a person suffering: "May I relieve
the suffering of all sentient beings." When seeing illness: "May I be
freed from the illness of the kleśas." When witnessing gratitude:
"May I repay with gratitude all the Buddhas and Bodhisattvas."

When witnessing ingratitude: "May I never show gratitude
for wrong views." When witnessing a threat: "May I be able
to cut off all outside threats." When witnessing praise:
"May I praise all the Buddhas and Bodhisattvas."

When observing someone reciting Dharma: "May I obtain
the eloquence of the Buddha." When gazing upon a holy statue:
"May I be without defilement in seeing all the Buddhas." When
looking upon a stupa: "May I become a reliquary for all beings."
When seeing a merchant: "May I obtain the seven precious jewels."
When seeing someone doing prostrations: "May I obtain the
invisible crown of the worlds peopled by both gods and humans."

Concentrate again on the fact that all who harm you are actually
being very kind, for their actions assist you in practicing the two
aspects of enlightened mind. Further, when you see others suffer,
immediately take this suffering upon yourself. Strongly and sincerely contemplate: "Whenever anyone is overcome with negative
emotionality, may I gather to myself all such destructive emotions."

To summarize, the Great One of Oḍḍiyāna, Padmasambhava, has
stated:

It is vital to precede all things with the generation of the mind
of enlightenment. Those who generate the mind of enlightenment
meditate on all sentient beings as being identical to their mother;
they strive in their practice in order to serve all sentient beings.

No beings exist who have not been your father and mother,
and so you must involve yourself in benefiting them all.
Cultivate love and compassion for all beings
and always concentrate on developing Bodhicitta.
Whatever there is to be done, and whatever you do,
learn to do it for the welfare of sentient beings.
You must learn to cherish others more than life itself.

Generating the enlightened mind is itself the root of the Dharma.
Through the desire to reach the all-knowing Awakening
of the Buddha, you come to learn that there is no self-nature,
either in the apprehension of a self or the apprehension
of phenomena. Whatever virtuous actions you do,
understand that all things are like an illusion, like a dream.

Follow my advice, and meditate on everything as being openness,
never yearning for the practice of the six pāramitās
or for great compassion. By the strength of having meditated
on openness, you will come to understand that even the generation
of the six pāramitās and the generation of great compassion
are like an illusion. The meditation of openness
will also serve to assist all pure dharmas as an antidote
for the emotions. Whatever virtuous action you do,
propel it by the mind of enlightenment. Thus you will never
separate yourself from the six pāramitās. In this way, concentrate
on increasing virtue and decreasing the stream of non-virtue.

Whatever you do physically, direct your actions toward virtue.
Whatever you say, direct your words toward virtue.
Whatever you think, direct your thoughts toward virtue.
Whenever any action of body, speech, or mind
moves toward non-virtue, reign it in.

Again, remember: If you do not protect yourself
with the armor of alertness and mindfulness,
the sword of the destructive emotions will cut you off
from the higher states of being and keep you
from gaining liberation from samsara.
Accordingly, in the four kinds of activity,
be sure to protect yourself with alertness and mindfulness.

In the same source we find:

The distinction between the greater or lesser vehicle
is not a matter of view—it is compassion that makes the difference.
Therefore, meditate on great compassion. For the sake of self
and others, never turn away from actions to eradicate the misery
of samsara. Meditate on extricating yourself from samsaric
activity, and meditate on compassion for the well-being of others.

First of all, train yourself to feel that all sentient beings are just like
you, and practice making the suffering of others your own suffering.
Then train yourself to feel that all sentient beings are more dear
to you than your own being, and practice the great compassion
that cuts through your sense of powerlessness to help others.

The term "follower of the Mahāyāna" means embracing sentient
beings as being more dear to you than life itself. Thus, if you seek
your own happiness without being mindful of the suffering
of other beings, if you cherish yourself rather than others,
the Great Vehicle will not appear for you. It is when you
have trained in the enlightened mind of love and compassion
that you are never again born in the lower realms, and you become
a non-returner.[13] This is the essence of my teaching.

Wherever you go, make certain that you never disengage
your mind from Bodhicitta. In whatever you do or will do,
learn to cherish others and to act for the welfare of sentient beings.
Even if you have many spiritual qualities gained through having
guarded your samaya vows or through having purified yourself,
even if you gain great powers from the efficacy of mantra,
if you do not cultivate Bodhicitta, you will not become a Buddha.
Again, if you generate the enlightened mind in the stream
of your consciousness, all the siddhis, both ordinary
and extraordinary, will arise. This is my only teaching.

Whether you meditate on openness or on something else,
if your meditation does not serve as an antidote
to the emotions and to whatever is common,
it will become a cause of falling into samsara.

Whatever you learn, think, and explain that serves as an antidote
to the emotions and assists in producing the pure Dharma
in your consciousness is called a teaching of the Mahāyāna
and is without error. People may call you learned when they look
at your knowledge of the teachings and call you wise
when they look at your work for others and your meditation,
but if any of the eight worldly concerns are behind
any of your actions, they are not actions of virtue.

After meditating on all that appears as being like an illusion,
it is vital not to allow attachment to grow. If you are free from
attachment, you need nothing more: It can be said that you
are a great yogi. The source of the happiness and welfare
of all sentient beings is the doctrine of the Buddha—therefore
you must listen to and investigate closely the Sūtras and Tantras.

Take care to distinguish virtue from wrongdoing,
since actions and their fruit—happiness or suffering—
come forth from those seeds. Without the protection
of discipline, the root of the Dharma will decay.
So, guard your samaya vows as you would guard your eyes.
Again, if you do not practice the Dharma with conviction,
your work is wasted, and whatever you have done
becomes worthless. Thus, it is vital that you act
decisively and without reservation.

Some people, though they profess to be adepts and practitioners
of the Mantrayāna (practitioners of Tantra), act very coarsely.
This is not the conduct of a follower of the Mantrayāna.
To follow the Mantrayāna is to act in accord with the Great
Vehicle, cherishing all sentient beings with totally impartial
compassion. Having professed to be a follower of the Mantrayāna,
if you do not shun non-virtuous action, you are not qualified
to practice. A follower of the Mantrayāna must act
with the disposition of great compassion. If you do not produce
compassion in your innermost being, you may profess
to be an adept, but you are following the way of the worst heretics.

The deeds of the Mantrayāna are those of the Great Vehicle,
and the deeds of the Great Vehicle are actions done
for the welfare of others. To act for the welfare of others,
you must obtain the Three Kāyas which are the fruit,
and to obtain the Three Kāyas, you must gather
the two accumulations of merit and wisdom.
To gather the two accumulations, you must train
in Bodhicitta and meditate on the unification
of the development and completion stages.[14]

Any practice of Mantrayāna that lacks the practice
of Bodhicitta is worthless—it would not be fit to be part
of the Great Vehicle. While it is said that approaching
the Mahāyāna path through the view of philosophy
or through the practice of mantra are very different strategies,
there is but one system. Should you lack either correct view
or conduct, you will become a Śrāvaka. Descend from above

by means of the highest view, and ascend by means
of your conduct: These are my directions.

Transform whatever you do into the path of enlightenment
through concentrated application of Bodhicitta as has been taught
here. The master Śrī Gyalpo, Paltrul Rinpoche, has stated:

When happy, you should be displeased;
when miserable, delighted. For when you are happy,
the five poisons of the kleśas rage; when you suffer,
you are working out bad actions previously performed.
Suffering is the compassion of the Lama.

When praised, you should be displeased; when criticized, delighted.
For when you are praised, you become arrogant and proud;
when you are despised, it is your own faults falling upon you.
Being belittled is the blessing of the gods.

When prominent, you should be displeased; when lowly, delighted.
When you are prominent, jealousy and pride are generated;
when lowly, care and devotion to virtue are expanded.
The inferior position is the highest seat.

When you are wealthy, you should be displeased;
when poor, delighted. When you are wealthy,
gathering and guarding your things causes you to suffer;
when you are poor, your austere practice offers the teaching of gods.
The body of a beggar is the essential aim of the Dharma.

When given gifts, you should be displeased;
when robbed, delighted. When you are given gifts,
the burden of repayment increases;
when you are robbed, karmic debt is cleared away.
Contentment is the treasure of the Arhats.

When you have friends, you should be displeased;
when you have enemies, delighted.
Friends create obstacles to the path of liberation;
enemies create an object for the practice of patience.
Practice of the equalizing meditation of compassion is what counts.

The Bodhisattva Kunga received the five forms of siddhi from
Padampa of India through prayer:

"Bless me to be without country and with no means!
Bless me to be without food and without shelter!
Bless me to be without companions and without friends!
Bless me not to be seen by anyone!
Bless be not to have even one iota of good fortune!"

Having so pleaded, he is said to have obtained siddhi through meditation. This has been taught in the Drugpa Kargyud bZlog-sgom and similar teachings.

Using similar means, do whatever you can to travel the genuine path and subdue your consciousness. Padampa taught:

Until you know that merit is a demon, you will never free yourself
from suffering. Until you turn your back on the security
of your fatherland, you will never sever your connection
with what is not Dharma. Until you purge yourself
of the eight worldly concerns, you will not free yourself
of the causes of samsara.

Until you know that whatever is not Dharma is unnecessary,
you will never free your mind from attachment and desire.
Until you understand that material possessions are an obstacle,
you will never turn your mind from desire. Until you discontinue
your enslavement to food and clothing, you will never take up
the practice of devotion to virtue. Until you give up living like a
householder, you will not find the time to practice the Dharma.

As long as you do not commit yourself to the path,
you will be disappointed in this lifetime. As long as you
are attached to a spouse, your wish for the sacred Dharma
will be halfhearted. As long as you are unable to dwell alone,
you will be overwhelmed by the obstacles of difficult practices.
As long as you do not give up diversions,
the Dharma will not come forth—whoever you are!

Drubchen Orgyanpa has stated:

Seeing another's greed, move yourself to supreme generosity.
Seeing another's laziness, move yourself to great effort.
Seeing another's attachment, move yourself to be
your own greatest friend. Seeing another's great hatred,

move yourself to great patience. Seeing another's great ignorance, move yourself to great wisdom. Seeing another's wrong views, move yourself to great purity of vision. Seeing another's scattered mind, move yourself to be dependable. Seeing another's evasive mind, move yourself to great renunciation. Seeing another's suffering, move yourself to the great mind of enlightenment.

All these ways of taking adverse circumstances as the path cut off both hope and fear. Once they have transported you to the path free from hope and fear, you will have purified any bias toward friend or foe. As Lang Tangpa taught: "It is like straightening a crooked tree."

## *Prayer for Purifying Adverse Conditions*

Alas! These days the world and its inhabitants
are filled with evil; the glories of the vessel
are polluted by the rising tide of filth within.
There is no time to stop the rising flood,
for the clouds gather thickly,
boiling like murky and noxious potions.

Subject to the five poisons of the kleśas,
the inhabitants of the world
are led away from good toward all kinds of wickedness.
These are the conditions assisting
the root cause of desire and hatred—
like fire spreading in a forest,
they ravage the self and ravage others.

At times like this, having produced the strength of the antidotes,
if I do not bring adverse conditions to the path of enlightenment,
the poison of random thoughts and seizing on a self will rise within,
and its bile will destroy the living root of genuine freedom.

From beginningless time, this great demon 'self'
has abided in my heart, wreaking harm in countless ways.
If I do not subdue the conception of self, the root of this corruption,
how can anything I do offer hope for happiness?

Now, having brought to mind its persecution,
I will urge on the massed armies of openness and compassion:
May they march forth right now, rooting out the forces
of capricious thought and grasping at a self.
May they be victorious!

The harmful mind, obsessed since beginningless time
with the welfare of the self, has continually harmed others.
Thus I am bound in the prison of samsara:
Even now, that which I do not desire falls like rain.

Are we ever satisfied with what we have?
Though we undergo hundreds of miseries,
we do not know to be alarmed.
Unable to bear our burdens,
we look for others to bear them for us.
Look at the wicked mind,
full of thoughts that reap destruction!

In this lifetime, we are racked with illness, hunger and cold,
beatings and bad news, and all that we do not desire.
Such is the cost of holding the self to be the root of mind and body.
Must others, too, pay the price of our afflictions?

Due to the influence of this 'self'
I am sure to be torn to bits by weapons of unthinkable suffering.
Truly, all I do not desire comes to destroy me,
brought on by the demon of seizing on a self.

In the past, I did not distinguish friend and foe:
Alas! a mistake! From this day on, deluded and evil mind,
I will watch your every move. You are like a poisonous weed.
From this day on, I will root out your unbearable misery
with the blade of the antidotes.

All beings are in essence my cherishing parents:
surrounding me with unconditioned love from beginningless time.

Even now, they assist me in attaining enlightenment:
They are my actual spiritual friends,
helping me to purify the two defilements.

Bringing about their benefit delights the Jinas.
Bearing all harm away from them is the best austerity.
Being devoted to them, we transcend samsara and nirvana:
They are equal to the Jinas as fields of virtue.

Bound tightly by the chains of the eight worldly dharmas,
I have nearly fallen into bad states
of being by the power of bad karma.
By making me strive to close the gate of selfishness,
the enemies who harm me
are like manifestations of the Buddha.

Due to the present miserable conditions,
I will rid myself of heedless pride and other fetters.
Weary of samsara, ready to renounce it,
I will generate compassion for beings.
Turning away from wrongdoing and never despising virtue,
I will purify my defilements and become
as worthy to honor as the sacred Dharma.

Having contemplated the great kindness of all beings
and having generated the strength of love
and compassion to repay their favors,
I take upon myself their suffering,
their sin, and their emotionality,
and I dedicate to them the roots of all my virtue:
past, present, and future.

To make up for my former inclination
to retaliate with enmity and do harm to others,
I offer you this heap of flesh and blood—this illusory body;
from this day on, be sated in your revels!

In any case, all this is false, like a dream or an illusion:
identical to non-arising, non-cessation, and non-abiding.
All delusive appearances are like the armor of view
fitted out for us and extending as the Four Kāyas—nothing else.

This is the supreme practice of the arising
of openness and dependent origination,
encompassing the Four Applications,
counted as the gold of skillful means:
This is truly transforming all adverse conditions
into the path of genuine enlightenment.
May they be turned into a hundred pure vessels! Ah, yes!

In summary: May whatever adverse conditions
suddenly arise be truly and immediately purified
through the antidotes of alertness and mindfulness.
And through concentration and application,
by means of openness and compassion,
may they, O friends, be transformed
into the path of enlightenment!

Here is completed the section that explains
the method of transforming adverse circumstances
into the path of enlightenment.

།ག་རུ་འཆད་ཁ་བ་ཡེ་ཤེས་རྗེ་རྫལ་ན་མོ།

*Guru Chekhawa*

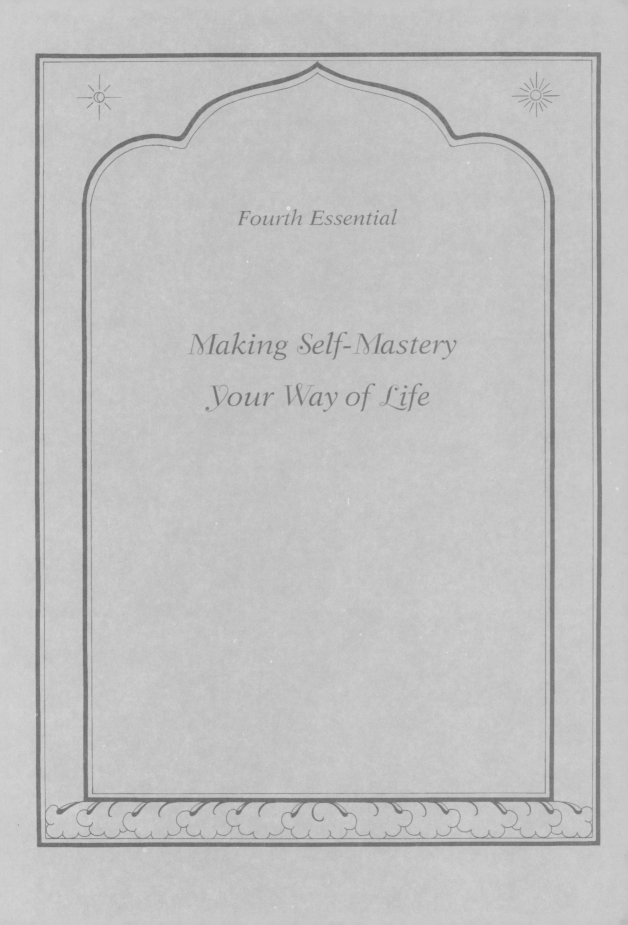

Fourth Essential

Making Self-Mastery
Your Way of Life

## Practice of the Fourth Essential

*To distill the essence of the instructions:*
*practice the five powers and refine them.*

*The Mahāyāna teachings for transferring*
*the life-force depend on these same five powers:*
*Commit yourself to practice them!*

# Reflections

## Practice as a Way of Life

We know from long experience that the patterns of mind that shape our lives are self-reproducing. Anyone who has tried to break a harmful habit or focus the mind in the face of emotional disturbance knows that mental patterns have a powerful longevity and can affect every aspect of our lives.

The acts of body, speech, or mind, once completed, are like seeds that take root and then inexorably sprout and grow. At first the growth takes place unseen, but eventually the young shoots emerge from beneath the surface. Blossoming, they produce new seeds that take root in turn. The question is this: What is the soil that nourishes the seeds of our actions? Western science answers: the body. But is this a satisfactory explanation?

Our understanding of the mind (as measured by our ability to control the mind) is quite limited. Perhaps the power of the mind operates in more subtle dimensions than we can normally perceive, unfolding patterns that never lose their hold and condition all that will arise in the future. Perhaps there are unseen forces at work that shape the circumstances of each emerging life. Perhaps the patterns that project forward with so much power from our every action are not only prompting the repetition of similar actions, but also recreating the circumstances on which those actions depend—including

the actor. Perhaps there is no firm wall separating the one who acts from the action taken; the one who imagines and what is imagined.

It seems that patterns—once programmed—will continue to replicate themselves. This is, however, not the last word: Clearly patterns can be broken. We can draw upon inner resources to change even our most ingrained habits. For instance, in these times when violence thrives all around us, we tend to think in terms of a violent response. But with strong resolve, we can counter this pattern of self-centered reactions to whatever arises. Rather than allowing ourselves to react violently, we can determine to respond to harmfulness with benevolent words and actions. In this way the cycle of violence and hatred can be broken.

When resolve to change our destructive patterns comes into play, we naturally become more mindful. Mindfulness is inherently a strong force for change. When we take care to be mindful in all that we do, we can make virtuous action our norm in every area of life. As positive patterns take the place of destructive ones, virtuous action itself becomes the pattern. Goodness has great power: By accustoming ourselves to virtuous action, even if only in our imagination, virtue begins to become our reality.

As the pattern of virtuous action strengthens, the thought of renunciation arises. With the thought of renunciation, the whole pattern of life changes from one of suffering and emotionality to one infused with the qualities of enlightened mind. When we can fully renounce a self-centered way of living and being, aspiration for the enlightenment of all beings arises naturally.

# Overview
# Practice as a Way of Life

*I* bow to the feet of the incomparable Lama
who expresses the condensed essence
of the Supreme Vehicle, extensive and profound:
the elixir of the teaching flowing from the heart of compassion,
the path entirely without error,
as entered by the heirs of the Victorious One.

Two processes set forth this practice as a way of life:

What is to be done in this lifetime
and what is to be done at the time of death

Regarding what you should do in everyday life, the root text states:

> *To distill the essence of the instructions:*
> *Practice the five powers and refine them.*

Practice of the five powers is essential, as together they incorporate all the profound instructions for practicing the sacred Dharma. These five are:

1. The power of projecting resolve
2. The power of familiarity

3. The power of the seeds of goodness

4. The power of renunciation

5. The power of aspiration.

First, the power of repeatedly projecting intense resolve:

"From now on—today, tomorrow, this month, this year—until the time of my death, I will embrace the two aspects of enlightened mind, never resting until I attain the Awakening of a Buddha."

This very day, should anyone slander you, insult you, beat you, or in any way harm you, concentrate strongly on the many reminders that death is immanent and reflect upon your commitments. For example, recall the times you have gone outside at the break of day to do some essential task and then awakened to find out that you had been dreaming.

Whenever you meet with adverse conditions, use the power of resolve to keep in mind the antidotes. If you concentrate with intense resolve on acting in accord with the pure Dharma at all times, then body, speech, and mind will align with the nature of the Dharma.

Long ago, in the city of Kyormo Lung (west of Lhasa), at a very inauspicious time, a certain Jonangpa found out that he had to start on a journey. He reflected, "Although unpleasant things may occur today, should anything unfortunate happen, I will not lose sight of the Dharma." After concentrating on the Dharma with great resolve, he set forth.

Along the way, a band of fierce and frightful men approached from a ravine. He was about to call for help when he remembered his inner vow. Instead of calling out, he said to them quietly, "You are so kind to have appeared! Please take everything I have!" He then joyfully divided his things among them, after which he went on his way.

Truly, resolve is very important. Thus we find in Entering the Bodhisattva Path:

The Muni himself taught
that resolve is the root of all facets of virtue. [7.40]

Second, the power of familiarity:

This entails accustoming yourself to virtuous action. With alertness and mindfulness, look carefully at everything you do and determine whether your actions have been virtuous, non-virtuous, or indeterminate. Be honest about your non-virtuous and indeterminate activities: Never try to make actions done for your own purpose appear to be done out of devotion to virtue. Purify your actions again and again, so that you are never separated from the two aspects of the enlightened mind. In short, train in the enlightened mind as the principal form of virtuous action. Śāntideva has stated:

Those who do not know this secret of the mind,
the foremost principle of the Dharma,
though they desire to obtain happiness and to conquer suffering,
wander continuously and aimlessly.

Hence I must guard my mind well
and take care of it.
Unless they help me to guard the mind,
what use to me are the many practices?

If I had a gaping wound,
I would take great care in the midst of a bustling crowd.
So, when mingling with wicked people,
I must always guard this open wound—my mind.

If I take such great care of a wound for fear
that I might suffer some slight hurt,
why do I not guard the open wound of my mind
for fear of being pulverized by the crushing mountains of hell?

If I persist in this practice,
then though I dwell among harmful people,
or even in the midst of women,
I will not slacken the zealous observance of my vows.

Let me be without gain, honor,
body, or livelihood—
let all other virtues decline,
but may I never be without the virtues of the mind.

With hands folded in prayer I beseech those
who desire to guard the mind:
Guard both mindfulness and awareness:
Make every effort you can!
　　—*Entering the Bodhisattva Path*, 5.17–23

Again, the same text states:

There is nothing that does not become easy
once you are accustomed to it. [6.14]

Third, the power of the seeds of goodness:

This entails generating the two aspects of Bodhicitta during times
of practice (either when you are generating Bodhicitta that has not
yet arisen or increasing Bodhicitta that has already been generated).
Included in the process of generating the enlightened mind is the
making of a mandala, placing offerings before images of the Three
Jewels, purifying defilements, and gathering the accumulations of
merit and wisdom as much as possible. Pray to the Lama and request
the spiritual help of the Dharma Protectors. Study, contemplate, and
meditate, and accumulate the ten virtuous Dharma actions. In short,
constantly concentrate your energies of body, speech, and mind on
virtue, and never be satisfied with virtue already attained. In the
Verse Summary of the Prajñāpāramitā, we find:

As long as you have not perfected the root of virtue,
you will never attain the blessed openness of śūnyatā. [20.10]

And again, Padampa has stated:

Though you accumulate merit, without the steadiness
of meditation you will take birth again.

The two aspects of the enlightened mind arise in dependence on
one another: When you realize the openness of śūnyatā, compassion
also arises from its strength. In the Exposition of Bodhicitta, we find:

When yogins become
attuned to openness,
they will without doubt
delight in the welfare of others. [73]

Padampa was asked, "If you have realized openness and then do something harmful, are you committing a sin or not?"

Padampa replied, "When you have realized openness, it is senseless to do anything wrong. Realization of openness and the generation of compassion are born at the same time."

The same can be said with regard to compassion, as in the case of the great Lama Dharmarakṣita.[15]

Fourth, the power of renunciation:

Because life after life has been marked by thoughts of self-cherishing and strong emotions, we have wandered in samsara from beginningless time. Remind yourself:

"O self, I have gone along with your unwholesome thoughts, and in return you have made me experience great misery. You have caused great suffering and wrongdoing and prevented me from generating in my consciousness the pure Dharma that I so desire. Everything you do goes against the three vows: This is what you give me in repayment for taking your side. Truly, I find no joy in associating with you. Now I must concentrate instead on stopping your destructive action."

By keeping self-grasping and selfish thoughts at a distance, you will ultimately cast them off. Śāntideva has stated:

Truly, I must never retreat
from conquering the kleśas.
This is what I yearn for:
to conquer the harmful emotions without exception.
Holding firmly to my outrage,
I will engage in battle with the kleśas.
                        —*Entering the Bodhisattva Path, 4.42*

And again:

If you do not completely give up the self
you cannot cast off suffering,
just as one who does not put out the fire
is unable to prevent a conflagration. [8.135]

Fifth, the power of aspiration:

This entails heartfelt prayer. At the end of any virtuous endeavor, pray strongly and sincerely:

"Acting by myself, may I lead all sentient beings to the stage of Buddhahood." More particularly: "From now until I become a Buddha, I will never forget the two aspects of the precious mind of enlightenment, even in my dreams. May they grow stronger and stronger! Whatever adverse circumstances arise, may I be able to turn them into aids for cultivating the mind of enlightenment!"

As you offer torma to the Lama, the Three Jewels, and the Dharma protectors, pray like this continually, and dedicate all your virtue for the welfare of others. The Heap of Jewels states:

As all dharmas accord with conditions,
you will abide where your highest aspirations take you.
By setting forth the highest wishes,
you acquire corresponding results.

We find in Entering the Bodhisattva Path:

Whether openly or indirectly,
never do anything that is not in accord with the welfare of others.
Dedicate everything towards enlightenment,
for the sake of all sentient beings. [5.101]

In the Crown of Sūtras, we find:

The wishing prayer of the resolute
accompanies their devotion to the mind of enlightenment. [19.74]

Thus you should pray with all your heart and mind. These five powers are said to be the teaching that gathers all the Dharma into a single syllable: HŪṀ.

# Reflections

## The Time of Death

*A*ccording to the basic laws of karma, our future lives will be shaped by our actions in this life, just as future circumstances are colored by present actions. Reincarnation has a powerful logic supporting it, for it is clear that nothing can appear without a cause. How else can we account for the way that different patterns of behavior, emotions, mind, and body are organized? How else can we explain their interplay?

People who reject the concept of reincarnation often use the argument that there are many more people in the world today than there were even a few hundred years ago. This argument, however, does not take into account the possibility of birth from other realms. Nor does it consider that, with the cause and effect of karma continually in operation, we may not necessarily be reborn in so fortunate a state again.

Because we are now human, we like to think that we will always be born as a human. But even if born human, does a human shape necessarily define human potential? Unfortunately, many of those born in the human world seem to be actually living in the lower realms, subject to perpetual brutality, burning torment, and despair. Moreover, if we act like animals in this life, looking only to satisfy our desires, what is to keep us from becoming an animal in the next?

Anecdotal evidence of reincarnation is available in great quantity, and those who are inclined to accept reincarnation find such evidence quite persuasive. If it does not meet the standards of proof of the physical sciences, the same could be said for many connections we make in our daily experience.

Modern science is based on the principle of cause and effect, but science limits its range, insisting on looking only at physical processes and only from a materialistic viewpoint: If consciousness is tied to the body, then it stops at death, and we might as well take what we can from life. Thus people tend to look at life as little more than a way to gain as much pleasure or happiness as they can, whether through accumulating wealth, fame, or pleasant sensations. Most people try not to think of unpleasant things such as sickness and death.

Death does not come close or touch many in this society until they are adults. Children may lose a few pets, or elderly relatives may pass away. But the death of relatives generally happens in as insulated an environment as possible, in hospitals where children are not allowed. With the growing violence in society and the images of mayhem presented daily in the media, we may be aware that death can touch our lives at any time, but few of us directly engage the stark finality of death. The full impact of dying may not strike us until we grow old or sick and approach the time of our own death. Unprepared at this critical time, the mind becomes clouded and experiences extraordinary pain and fear.

How much better to have prepared ourselves than to come to death frightened and confused. While there are rituals for dying and death as found in such texts as *The Tibetan Book of the Dead*, and transference rituals or Phowa, as found in the sixth section of Paltrul's Kun-bzang-bla-med-zhal-lung, it is far better to have purified the mind beforehand. With a purified mind there is no doubt of rebirth in a higher realm.

# Instructions for the Time of Death

What are the teachings for the time of death? The root text states:

*The Mahāyāna teachings for transferring the life-force*
*depend on these same five powers:*
*Commit yourself to practice them!*

When those who have undergone self-mastery are terminally ill and certain of approaching death, they first activate the power of the seeds of goodness by giving away all they have: either to their Lama and the Three Jewels or wherever it will be of most benefit. They give up everything, with no thought of hanging on, without a hair's breadth of attachment. This is very important, for if at the time of death you hold on to even the smallest thought of attachment, you will be thrust into lower states of being.

Long ago a monk who was very attached to his begging bowl was reborn immediately after death as a snake. This snake was born inside the monk's begging bowl and did not move from it. When the body of the monk was taken from his grass hut to be cremated in the cemetery, the monk's attendant picked up the begging bowl. Seeing a snake inside the bowl, he at once threw it down. Enraged, the snake spewed fire from its mouth, setting fire to the hut. The snake died in

the blaze, and was at once reborn in hell. There he burned with the fire of karma. Since at the same moment the body of the snake was burning in the grass hut and the body of the monk was burning in the cremation house, it is said that the monk was consumed by flame three times at once.

Another monk who was attached to his Dharma robes was also reborn as a snake. This happened also to a young man of Ngari Lomon, who was attached to his slingshot. There is also the tale of a Tibetan lady whose attachment to turquoise led to her being reborn as a tortoise. There are many such stories. Therefore, the Great One of Oḍḍiyāna has stated:

Listen! At the time of your death, when the bardo appears,
if you have cast off the grasping of the mind attached to everything,
you will enter steadily into the clear nature of the precepts.
You will be transported to the sphere of space,
self-knowing, birthless. When you are about to separate
from this compounded body of flesh and blood,
you will understand that it is impermanent: an illusion.

Before you die, if you are able, make offerings, following the seven-limbed practice. If you are unable to make actual offerings, make the following prayers with one-pointed mind.

With the power of aspiration pray: "By the force of whatever roots of virtue I have accumulated throughout time, may I never forget the precious mind of enlightenment in all my lives to come. May it grow stronger and stronger! May I meet with the true Lamas who reveal this Dharma! May the blessings of the Lama and the Three Jewels make it so."

With the power of renunciation, reflect: "Clinging to the self, I have suffered innumerable births. Now I am experiencing the suffering of death. But ultimately, as neither self nor mind truly exist, there is no death. I must destroy the harmful mind that seizes on the self, that thinks: 'I am sick! I am dying!'"

With the power of projecting resolve, reflect: "I will never disengage from the two aspects of the precious mind of enlightenment, whether at the time of death, in the bardo, or in all my births to come."

With the power of familiarization, clearly establish both aspects of the mind of enlightenment in accord with your previous meditations.

Although the principal practice is to focus singlemindedly on the five powers, several additional practices can assist you: Sit in the posture of Seven Gestures. If you are unable to do so, lie on your right side, with your cheek resting on your right hand. With the little finger of the right hand, press the right nostril shut, and while breathing through the left nostril, engage in the preliminary practices of love and compassion. As the breath goes in and out, practice unconditional giving and taking upon yourself all suffering. Then reflect that both samsara and nirvana, birth and death, are but the appearance of mind.

Rest in the understanding that the mind itself does not exist anywhere, so that the mind does not cling to anything. In this way, the two aspects of the enlightened mind will grow strong, and you will be able to control the breath in your meditation as you are dying.

Many effective precepts deal with the time of death, but it is said that there are none more wonderful than this. Whoever practices transference of consciousness (Phowa) using these practices will undergo a most auspicious passage, for these practices free the consciousness from the confused shifting it ordinarily undergoes at the time of death.

Nothing could be more wonderful at the time of death than to have the consciousness be guided by the thought of cherishing others rather than yourself. The Buddha once told of a mother and child who were both swept away by a river: The single thought of the mother was that her child be saved; the single thought of the child was for the mother. Through the arising of such thoughts, both were reborn in the heaven realms. The story of the one who pulled the chariot in hell, and the story of the Dzawo's 'daughter' told previously are similar in outlook. Moreover, if you generate the pure mind of cherishing others, in each future birth, and even in this life, wondrous omens will occur.

Long ago, at the ferry of Jasa, six nobles attempted to cross the river in a boat made of hides. An envoy joined them at the last minute, and after they had gone some way, the boat began to fill with

water. The boatman said: "The load is too heavy for the boat—one of you who knows how to swim must jump overboard. If you toss me off, one of you will have to take over steering!"

When it became clear that none of the passengers knew either how to swim or how to steer the boat, the envoy said with firm conviction, "Rather than all of us dying, I will die alone." And so saying, he jumped into the water. At once a rainbow appeared; flowers fell from the sky, and though he did not know how to swim, he did not drown. Rather, he crossed the river like an accomplished swimmer. It is said that he had not previously done any Dharma practice, but when such a pure mind arises at the time of death its effect is very powerful. What more needs to be said?

If cherishing others does not arise naturally, there are other profound teachings to help focus and connect with the enlightened mind at death. Some of these entail breathing practices and visualizations, while other instructions for transference of consciousness (Phowa) call for the use of various substances. An example is to rub on the crown of the head a mixture made with the burned ashes of whole cowry shell, ground lodestone, and honey from wild bees that have fed on psychotropic plants. Blessings can also be transmitted by using sacred substances such as the ring-bsrel relics of the Buddha and the gdung and ring-bsrel relics of the highest siddhas, or the ring-bsrel relics that do not mix with anything.[16] Practices on Phowa found in the Tantras are also very effective.

## The Noble Path of the Mahāyāna

The noble path of the Mahāyāna is a treasure,
the instructions of the Lama are a river of milk
churned by the Bodhisattvas into the pure butter
of practice that gives results in a single lifetime.
This is none other than the practice of the five powers.

The power of resolve does not decline until the end of existence:
the flowing force of the wind of space, never turning back
no matter what occurs. Its great waves move the sun and moon:
the two aspects of Bodhicitta that immediately dispatch
dark troubles far away.

Through the power of familiarity, the two aspects of Bodhicitta
flow like the Ganges River of the gods, rushing downstream
until they enter the ocean of purity, not far distant,
where the shining foam from wave upon wave of actions
benefiting self and others never loses its iridescent luster.

The power of the seeds of goodness in the fields
is nourished by the warmth of moisture
of the accumulations of merit and wisdom,
flowing in two great healing waves.
When the seeds sprout, at the tip of the stalks
are the wondrous Five Paths.
Certainly the golden ears of corn
of the Two Kāyas will quickly come forth.

Again and again we find ourselves shackled
in the prison of samsara, beset by myriad miseries.
The cause of our torment: this fearsome, decrepid heap,
this grasping at the self. Quickly, quickly,
through the power of the antidotes, may it be vanquished!

Through the power of pure aspiration, the wise charioteer,
driving the wondrous precious chariot of many virtues,
enters without difficulty the city of knowledge:
Surely all sentient beings will gain relief.

Spreading wide the wings of the five powers,
we fly free of existence within this illusory,
impermanent, magic wheel.
Traveling with the force of the wind,
sweeping through the sky of the Dharmadhātu
we cross with ease the abyss of the six realms of beings.

O! Blessed with this vase of treasures, the profound precepts!
O great wonder! With this awakening, virtue comes to life!
The petty concerns of samsara grow pale.
I must strive from the depth of my heart to practice:
There is no time to waste!

།འཇམ་མགོན་བླ་མ་མི་ཕམ་རྣམ་རྒྱལ་རྒྱ་མཚོ་ལ་ན་མོ།

*Lama Mipham*

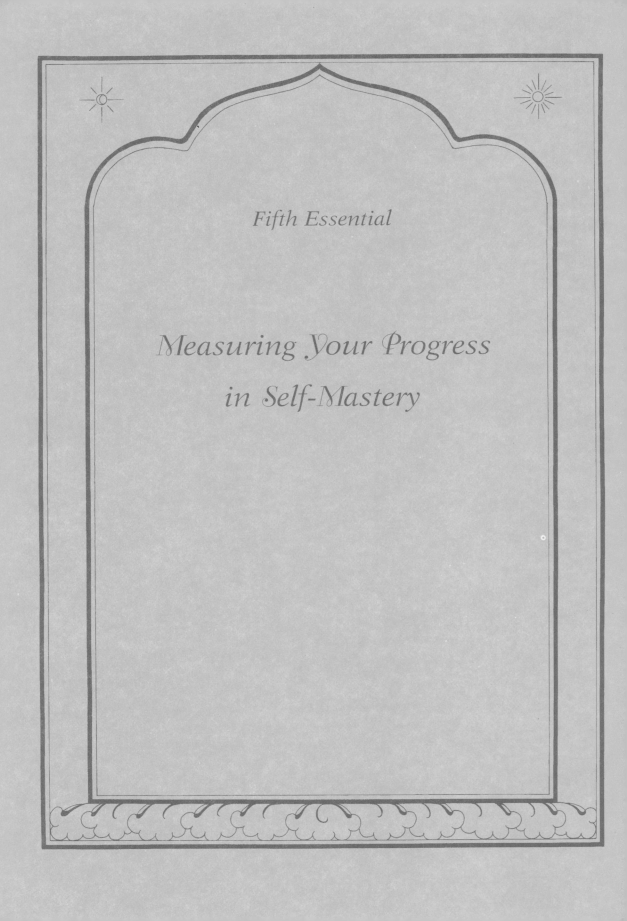

Fifth Essential

# Measuring Your Progress
# in Self-Mastery

## Practice of the Fifth Essential

*Unite all Dharma in a single aim.*

*Accept the better of two witnesses.*

*Let a joyful mind sustain you.*

*When you can practice even when disturbed,
this is called practicing well.*

# Reflections

## Evaluating Your Practice

*E*very day, every hour, conflicting thoughts bombard our minds, pulling us this way and that, often leaving us confused and unfocused. Even individuals who are truly successful in their fields are often only marginally more able to focus their energy and intelligence. First come the emotions and desires, then the worries and concerns, then the plans and regrets. This chaotic and disorganized way of using our intelligence would be deeply disturbing if we were not so accustomed to it.

While at some point we may sense the futility and dissatisfaction underlying our way of being, we find it difficult to identify what we might change or become discouraged when our changes have little effect. Why is it so hard to get to the root of the problem? Throughout history human beings have concerned themselves with finding happiness and a sense of meaning and fulfillment. Why have their efforts not been more successful? Why is the solution to our problems so difficult to discern?

The teachings of the Buddhadharma invite us to look more closely at these questions and to become aware of what is going on in our minds and experience. The teachings show us how to make use of the patterns we find in the mind, turning them into a field for inquiry, so that we can gradually clarify our disordered thoughts by strength-

ening awareness. When we practice teachings directed towards self-mastery, we invite our intelligence to shine through our thoughts and color the realm of the senses.

## The Power of Samsara

When we begin to practice, we soon realize that samsara is more powerful and more thoroughly entrenched than any conventional 'establishment'. Samsara establishes itself through all we desire—gain, happiness, praise, and fame—and their opposites which we try to avoid. Whatever our spiritual ideals, we are not readily able to put them into practice; whatever our ideas of spiritual progress, we find ourselves losing interest and lessening involvement as worldly concerns attract our attention.

It would seem ridiculous to wish for the opposite of what we usually look for—to hope for loss, unhappiness, disgrace, and blame. And yet learning to be content in any circumstance is a key to true happiness. When this becomes clear, we can appreciate what great masters of the Vajrayāna have always known, that difficult circumstances are the ground for spiritual growth. The process of self-mastery is the process of learning to subdue self-centered concerns and give to other beings no matter how great the sacrifice. The teachings point to this one aim; when we accomplish it, the destructive emotions lose their hold, and true happiness can arise.

To practice in this way is not easy. In fact the task is so overwhelming that only true heroes would even think of carrying it through to completion. Yet even when we experience one setback after another, we do not have to grow discouraged. Today we may be able to spend a few minutes focused on the Dharma, free from at least some of our samsaric patterns. Tomorrow it may be a few minutes more. Perhaps we can keep a focus on Dharma central to our intentions for an hour or two a day, perhaps longer. In this way we give ourselves a message of encouragement: If we look from moment to moment, nothing is fixed. True, we have been programmed by samsara, but we can also reprogram ourselves. The virus may have replicated, the infection may be global in its scope, but the antidote is here in our own awareness.

Once some degree of faith in the Dharma has been born in us, a feeling of gratitude may awaken in our hearts. We sense that we have found a true friend who has our own best interests at heart; that we may actually be able to find answers for the problems that have seemed so fixed and firmly rooted—not only in our own lives, but in the lives of all beings throughout time.

Our self-centered stance, the logic of the self, has been bound to the view that each of us is isolated and separate. But when we understand that our conditioning involves us intimately with samsara, our perspective shifts radically. We realize that each action we do for others helps bring the enlightened nature into being. There is no mystery in this, only the clear expression of a unity taught by masters of the enlightened lineage.

# Instructions on Evaluating Your Practice

*T*hose whose hearts come under the sway
   of wisdom and compassion
will undergo even the fires of the Avīci Hell
for the welfare of others.
I bow to the Jina who joyfully entered that hell
as if it were an ocean of lotuses,
and to the Lamas, his heirs.

Referring to the fifth essential for self-mastery, measuring your progress, the root text states:

*Unite all Dharma in a single aim.*

All the spiritual practices of both the Great and Lesser Vehicles can be condensed into a single aim: to subdue attachment to the self. When you purify your mind to conform to spiritual conduct, your self-grasping will decrease in correspondence to your meditations. But if your desires lead you to act in ways that do not counter your attachment to self, if you aim instead at accomplishing the eight worldly concerns, whatever you have done to guard your morality or to hear, think about, and meditate on the teachings will be essentially useless.

The measure of spiritual activity is whether it acts as an antidote for self-grasping. If it does, this is a sign that you have purified your consciousness through the practice of self-mastery. The Great One of Oḍḍiyāna, Padmasambhava, said:

When your attachment to self is limited, this is a sign
you have trampled your demons. When your emotionality
is limited, this is a sign you are deactivating the five poisons.
When your sense of 'I and mine' is limited,
this is a sign you have rooted out demonic forces.

And again:

In short, being unattached to your own body is a sign
that you are free from the depth of desire. If you are unfazed
by suffering, this is a sign you understand appearance
as an illusion. If you have greatly diminished
the eight worldly concerns, that is a sign
you recognize the mind itself.

Such inner signs also show themselves externally,
like leaves appearing on a tree. When the signs
are apparent to others, it is like ripe fruit
that shows signs of being ready to eat.
But many practitioners lack inner virtues,
and those endowed with realization
are very rare indeed. Thus it is vital
to generate great effort in meditation.

The Kadampas state that specific signs indicate whether you are proceeding in accord with the Dharma or not, and give strict ways to determine this. The root text states:

> *Accept the better of two witnesses.*

One kind of witness, observing you, might say, "This is a pious person who embodies the Dharma! This person is practicing the Dharma well!" But most people are not truly objective; others do not usually make reliable witnesses. Ordinary worldly people cannot see what is in your mind; they see only the outward show of virtuous action as it manifests in body and speech. Admiring these outward

signs, they may express their admiration, but this does not prove that your actions actually manifest admirable inner qualities.

Therefore, you yourself must examine your own inner nature, taking stock of your wholesome activity as best you can. Measure your degree of faith and renunciation, wisdom and compassion, effort and so on, as if you were about to die this very night. If you conclude that there is nothing more you could have done, if in examining the measure of your attainment and practice you have nothing to be ashamed of, that is your principal witness.

This witness examines the mind honestly, for it owes nothing to the unreliable outer witness. Accordingly, embrace your own mind as the principal witness, making the strongest effort never to overrate yourself.

Among the extensive teachings on these matters given by the Great One of Oḍḍiyāna, Padmasambhava, is the following:

For those who enter the door of the Dharma, many pathways
lead to error. While there are spiritual teachers who have liberated
their consciousness by hearing and thinking about the teachings,
there are also deluded teachers whose understanding is based
on intellect alone. While there are those who have gained
genuine experiences in their practice, there are also those
who go astray and let their spiritual practice lag.
While there are those with good discipline who follow through
on their spiritual intentions, there are also the hypocrites,
who rely on the deceptive appearance of doing good.
While there are those whose views are true to the precepts,
there are also those who pay lip service to the Dharma,
but whose teachings are in error. While there are those
who are faithfully devoted to practice, there are also the frauds
who speak falsely of their practice.

Again, there are those whose whole nature is imbued
with the Dharma as it should be. But there are others
who assert that the Dharma is something 'beyond'
our comprehension and use their eloquence
to put forth teachings that reflect only ordinary consciousness. This
is cleverness, not Dharma.

Dharma must pass into Dharma.
You must travel the path of the Dharma.
By means of the path, you must clear away illusion.
Only then does illusion arise as wisdom.

Understanding that all the Dharma can be gathered
into one vehicle, realize there is nothing to accept or reject:
This is the Dharma passing into the Dharma.

Whatever your situation, when you generate the mind
that goes for refuge, when you also unify method and wisdom
and unify the stages of development and completion,
this is traveling the path of the Dharma.

Bonding the path of view, meditation, and action with its result:
This is the path that clears away illusion. Striving to practice
from the innermost heart of view and meditation:
This is illusion arising as wisdom.

The hearts of holy beings are always honest. Therefore, should they be the ones to praise, honor, or applaud you, they can be considered the most reliable witness of all. On the other hand, those who do not have self-knowledge, who do not know what to accept and what to reject, and even those with some understanding who see themselves with less than perfect honesty, are not suitable to be even their own witness.

*Let a joyful mind sustain you.*

The measure of having purified the mind is when you are never fearful or depressed, even in difficult circumstances. Then, whatever happens, good or bad, everything assists you in self-mastery, and this in turn assists you in being continuously joyful. Thus we find in the root text:

The karmic energy of previous practice,
awakened, led me to be greatly inspired.
Disregarding suffering and insults,
I requested the precepts for subduing self-grasping.
Now, when I die, I will have no regrets.

Further, Nāgārjuna has stated:

For one who knows the ways of the world,
there is gain and loss, happiness and suffering,
fame and disgrace, praise and blame: the eight worldly concerns.
These are not objects of my mind; they do not concern me.
—*Instructions from a Spiritual Friend, 29*

Worldly people wish for four principal things—gain, happiness, praise, and fame—and try to avoid their opposite. By training the mind to wish for what people do not desire—loss, unhappiness, disgrace, and blame—your desires will come to pass, and nothing but delight will arise in your mind. Having meditated joyfully on the appearance of adverse circumstances, learn to take upon yourself joyfully all the misfortunes of others as well.

> *When you can practice even when disturbed,*
> *you are practicing well.*

A skilled rider will not fall from a horse even if disturbed, but for an unskilled rider, any sudden movement can lead to difficulties: to being jerked about, kicked, or worse. By remembering your aims, you will have no need to hold on tightly, and you will not become annoyed or distressed when adverse circumstances arise. Rather, these same circumstances will help you in gaining self-mastery. This is the measure of a purified mind. Strive to act in such a way.

To put it briefly, when the two aspects of Bodhicitta arise clearly and effortlessly in all circumstances—upon the advent of friends or enemies, happiness or suffering, or any sort of harm—this is self-mastery. The closing four lines of the root text, quoted above, describe signs of having gained these key elements in developing the enlightened mind.

Some may say this is a sign of no more need for practice, but this is not so. Until you obtain the highest Awakening of a Buddha, you must continue your practice in developing the mind of enlightenment.

## *Nourishing the Sprouts of Bodhicitta*

The thousand sharp plowshares of the profound instructions
have cut through all emotionality and self-grasping:
The sprouts of Bodhicitta grow well.
May the blessings of the benefits
for self and for others be far-reaching!

Having benefited greatly from bountiful merit and wisdom,
you need no false modesty; when the gods of long life live alone,
their conscience is clear. Having examined this well,
accept the witness of your own mind.
May the blessings of the path of the Dharma be far-reaching!

Whatever conditions and appearances arise are like fuel for fire:
They are meant to assist on the path of enlightenment.
Whatever happens, do not cut off the flow of mental delight.
May the blessings of self-mastery be far-reaching!

In short, whoever can deal with sudden disruptions
will be like Mount Meru, forever immutable.
When well-developed signs of meditative heat arise
in the stream of the twofold Bodhicitta,
may the blessings be far-reaching!

།འཇམ་དབྱངས་མཁྱེན་བརྩེའི་དབང་པོ་ལ་ན་མོ།

*Jamyang Khyentse Wangpo*

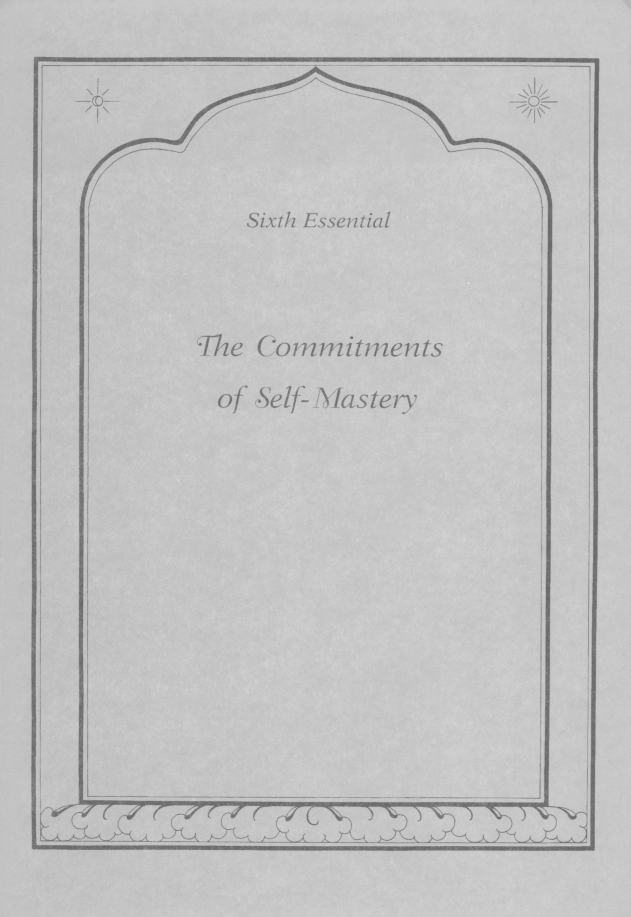

Sixth Essential

# The Commitments
# of Self-Mastery

# Practice of the Sixth Essential

*Always practice the three basic principles.*

*Change your attitude, and be unassuming.*

*Do not talk about others' infirmities.*

*Stop all negative thinking about others.*

*Purify the strongest emotional attachment first.*

*Give up all hope of getting anywhere.*

*Stop poisoning yourself.*

*Do not tie yourself to a rigid sense of
right and wrong.*

*Never get caught up in cycles of retaliation.*

*Do not lie in ambush.*

*Do not strike at the heart.*

*Do not place the load of a dzo on an ox.*

*Do not practice magic.*

*Do not aim to finish first.*

*Do not bring a god down to the level of a demon.*

*Do not seek pleasure at the expense
of another's pain.*

# Reflections

## Keeping Your Commitments

*A*n increasing number of Westerners, after learning something about the Tibetan Buddhist tradition, are then becoming involved in its practice. For many, practice includes taking vows: for receiving specific 'empowerments' from Buddhist teachers, for the recitation of special prayers, for participation in ceremonies, for becoming monks or nuns, or for directing the mind toward the service of others through reciting the vow of the Bodhisattva.

While such vows are an integral part of the Tibetan Buddhist tradition, it is not unusual for people who take vows to see themselves as being somehow special. For instance, after taking the Bodhisattva vow, some individuals consider themselves Bodhisattvas, and with that understanding, go on about their regular lives. They tell themselves that as long as they are trying to live a good life and do not harm others, that is enough. Having done a little meditation practice or studied a bit, they may think they are more advanced in the teachings than they really are. The true practice of the Bodhisattva, however, is not only to dedicate every aspect of existence to all other beings, but to actually act in a way that fully expresses this dedication.

The real practitioner is the person who serves others, never considering personal self-interest or comfort, or even his or her life itself. This does not mean that we can expect spiritual teachers to

serve us if they happen to be Bodhisattvas, or that it is not important to honor and serve those who follow the Bodhisattva path. Rather, it directs us to always keep in mind the main precept:

> *Give all victory and gain to others;*
> *take upon yourself all troubles and difficulties.*

These days, however, we can scarcely make sense of this way of practice, and it may no longer be possible to replicate the results that practitioners of these teachings once achieved. Are the Buddhist masters asking too much from ordinary human beings? Even simple acts of spiritual practice such as taking refuge, doing prostrations, or meditating may seem too much to fit into our busy lives or too awkward to carry through when living in a secular society. And yet people rarely feel awkward in putting their lives "in the hands of God." Perhaps we do not want to have to work for the blessings of paradise.

## Maintaining Focus and Resolve

The nature of existence is such that the vast majority of people need some sort of religious focus, a need that intensifies as various tragedies touch our lives. But if we view most religious teachings as outdated, little better than superstitions, we will tend to pick and choose among religious beliefs, disregarding what appear to us to be illogical taboos or ignorant practices, without seeing anything wrong with this approach.

We must be careful, however, not to judge too quickly. Unless a practice is clearly harmful on a vast scale, we may be judging wrongly, choosing to believe something that will strengthen our self-centered tendencies rather than helping us to progress spiritually. When choosing a teacher, it is essential to always look carefully at our own motivation, while also investigating statements and claims about a teacher's spiritual development and what he or she can offer us. These days there are many false teachers, particularly those who say they are teachers of the Mantrayāna. Having received a few teachings, they may then consider themselves beyond the constraints of ordinary morality, no longer bound to follow earlier spiritual vows or commitments.

It is important to remember that the Mantrayāna or Vajrayāna teachings rest on the foundation of the path of the Bodhisattva, the way of compassion and wisdom. The vows of the monk or nun, the Prātimokṣa vows, are binding for a lifetime, while the Bodhisattva vow, to gain enlightenment for the sake of all living beings, is binding for all lives to come, until the attainment of enlightenment.

Even today it is possible to find those who have traveled this path of heroes; we have models of kindness and compassion, and we have the history of the great lineage holders to inspire us. Drawing on these resources to nourish our sense of devotion, perhaps we can give the teachings an opportunity to work their wonder.

# Instructions on Keeping Your Commitments

*I* bow to the feet of the incomparable Lama, Khyentse:
Wisdom and Loving-Compassion,
ornament of sun and moon,
who presents the mountains and islands
of dhāraṇī and samādhi in fine array
on the pristine site of pure moral practice.

Referring to keeping your commitments, the sixth essential for self-mastery, the root text states:

*Always practice the three basic principles.*

These three principles are:

1. Never to break the commitments of self-mastery
2. Never to engage in disruptive acts
3. Never to apply double standards.

Even if some of the commitments you have made seem insignificant to you, do not neglect any of them in your practice. Do not tell yourself: "I have no time! I am too busy training my mind!"

The process of self-mastery is built on inclusion. From the first of the Prātimokṣa vows to the samaya vows of the Vajrayāna, you must guard your commitments and never relinquish any of them. Thus the Great One of Oḍḍiyāna has stated:

The foundation fashioned by commitments is like a fertile field;
whatever you do, you must never destroy it.

If the morality that sustains your commitments is not pure, you will never obtain the perfect foundation needed for attaining the path. Thus in the Entrance to the Middle Way, we find:

When someone breaks the foundation for moral practice,
that person will fall into adverse states of being,
even though endowed with prosperity through giving. [2.4]

Should this occur, you will lose the chance to meet again with the sacred Dharma of the teacher who exemplifies the actual path. The Sūtra Concerned with Moral Practice states:

Truly, without eyes you cannot see form;
likewise, without moral practice you cannot see the Dharma.

You also will not be able to pass from samsara and thus gain the fruit of having attained the path. The same text states:

Truly, without feet how can you enter a path?
Likewise, without moral practice, you will not find freedom.

On the other hand, if you embody moral practice, you complete all the causal conditions of attaining the path. The sDud-pa states:

By means of morality, the nature of the many lower states
of being and the eight adverse states are cast off;
thus one always finds freedom.

Moral practice is the support of all the good qualities of pure spirituality. In the Instructions from a Spiritual Friend, we find:

Just as the earth supports both animate and inanimate existence,
moral practice is said to be the foundation of all good qualities. [7]

By depending on all the accumulations of merit and wisdom, you will increase them. The Entrance to the Middle Way states:

These good qualities, the field of moral practice, increase,
and the fruit of your offerings is never depleted. [2.6]

The many gateways of meditation open accordingly, as is said in the Lantern of the Moon Sūtra:

When you are no longer fettered by the emotions,
you obtain samādhi quickly—
this is the benefit of pure moral practice.

Further, pure aspirations generate their results. In the Sūtra of the Meeting of Father and Son, we find:

By guarding your pure moral practice,
you will attain all your aspirations.

Finally, you will achieve perfect enlightenment without difficulty. The same Sūtra states:

Because pure moral practice generates many seeds,
it is not difficult to attain perfect enlightenment.

The Stages of the Bodhisattva states:

Bodhisattvas, having completely accomplished
the perfection of moral practice, will become complete
and perfect Buddhas, endowed with perfect, genuine,
and unexcelled enlightenment.

In this way you become endowed with the immeasurable qualities of the Bodhisattvas, as is mentioned in the Sūtra Concerned with Moral Practice and in many other places:

Those endowed with moral practice will meet the coming Buddhas;
those endowed with moral practice will be supreme
among all ornaments; those endowed with moral practice
will abide in complete joy; those endowed with moral practice
will be praised by all the world.

## The Commitments

While there are many systems of vows for those who maintain different tenets, in the Mahāyāna, the seeds of the mind of renunciation

and the seeds of the mind of virtue are inherent in the actual vows. Śāntideva has stated:

Committing yourself to the intention to forsake non-virtue.
is said to be the perfection of moral practice.
—*Entering the Bodhisattva Path, 5.11*

More specifically, there are the vows of the Prātimokṣa, of the Bodhisattva, and of the Mantrayāna. The nature of these is indicated in the Padma'i-lam-rim-chen-mo:

It is said: "Recoiling from harmful action,
engaging in helping others, through skillful means
you arrive at unification."
Through the moral practice of the Prātimokṣa,
you recoil from harming all sentient beings.
With the vows of the Bodhisattva,
above and beyond no longer harming beings,
you set in motion the activity of benefiting others.
With the commitments of the Mantrayāna,
you turn away from all harm. You engage in helping others.
And through exercising exceptional skillful method
and wisdom, you arrive at unification.

The distinctive method and wisdom of the Mantrayāna is great bliss, the unchanging and innate indication of the unification of E-Wam. Bodhisattvas who hold the vow of Mantrayāna praise this as if with one voice.

How does one person practice all three vows? The same scripture states:

Each system is exclusive and complete in itself.
Each deals with the totality of what must be brought
to an end and what is to be accomplished.
Each is endowed with specific qualities.
Yet they are not contradictory in their essential nature.

Thus, through the commitments of the Prātimokṣa, the kleśas are abandoned; through the commitments of the Bodhisattva, the mind is purified. Through the commitments of the Mantrayāna, whatever you do is the path. Though each system is independent,

they are united in dealing with the emotional afflictions
in the consciousness and in furthering what must be brought
to an end and what is to be accomplished.

When the kleśas cease to harm you, your good qualities
will increase and assist you. Though the commitments
and ways of guarding them are different for each system,
essentially the three sets of vows are not contradictory.
Instead, they mesh, for any one way of controlling the kleśas
is effective on all non-virtue.

When you have truly understood this, it is vital to guard this knowledge and not let slide anything you have learned, even the smallest thing. To disdain the basic commitments is a great wrong.

At one time when the Bhagavan was teaching, a youth dressed as a religious novice came to listen to the Dharma. The Buddha at once said to him: "Having harmed the teachings of Kāśyapa, would you now bring harm to my teachings as well? Listen to the Dharma in your own form!" The novice at once went away, but sometime later a creature appeared with the head of a snake on a body that looked like the trunk of a great e-le tree. All those close by ran away in great fear.

One monk, however, did not give in to fear, and instead of running away, said: "This must be the novice who appeared yesterday! Well then! what is the meaning of this?" The Buddha replied, "This poor creature was once a monk, a disciple of the Buddha Kāśyapa. At one time while traveling in a rough area, he caught his robes on a branch of an e-le tree that was overhanging the path. This made the monk so angry that he went against the teachings and cut down the tree. And so the events you see have come to pass."[17]

Therefore guard your commitments, even those that seem the most insignificant. Do not let anything you have learned be lost. In Entering the Bodhisattva Path, we find:

Following my vows and commitments,
I must practice humility. [4.12]

Gyalsay Rinpoche has stated:

Without moral practice, you cannot help yourself—
what a joke to wish to help others!
Therefore, guard your moral practice,

never yearning for samsara:
This is the Bodhisattva's practice.
—*The Thirty-Seven Bodhisattva Practices, 28*

## Avoiding Disruptive Action

The second objective, to avoid disruptive acts, calls for you to never think of yourself as better than others. Be sensitive to others' beliefs, even if you consider them to be superstitions. Never destroy places considered to be dedicated to any gods, and never cut down trees considered to house tree spirits or disturb watering places said to house water spirits. Also, never associate with dissolute beggars, those who have given up their vows. Make certain that nothing you do contradicts the Kadampa teachings of Geshe Tonpa of Radreng Monastery.

We find in the songs of Kunpang lHatsun Chenpo:

The teacher of the World, Śākyamuni,
gathered around him the inhabitants of the three realms:
This is the sign that he knows the minds of others.
Can you do that?

The Master of Oḍḍiyāna, Padmasambhava,
subjugated and liberated the foes who sought to harm him.
This is the sign that he conveyed consciousness into the pure fields.
Can you transform things like that?

The King of Siddhas, Shavaripa,
slaughtered the wild pig of ignorance.
This is the sign that he cut the root of samsara.
Can you cut through things like that?

The King of Secret Mantra, Indrabodhi,
made no distinction between night and day
and surrounded himself with attendant queens.
This is the sign that he fused attachment with bliss and openness.
Can you join things like that?

The Master of Yoga, Lwavapa,
slept all day and night.
This is the sign that he coursed in clear light.
Can you sleep like that?

The Yogi of Great Attainment, Virūpa,
drank all the beer of the realm.
This is the sign that he frolicked
in the nectar of immortality.
Can you play like that?

Marpa, the lotsāwa of lHodrag,
accumulated the amusements of a householder.
This is the sign that he incorporated
all worldly pleasures into the path.
Can you integrate things like that?

The Master of Sky-Dancers, Melongpa,
ran naked through many ravines.
This is the sign of removing the shame
of taking illusion as reality.
Can you remove things like that?

Thunder of Freedom, Kunlegpa,
took on many unpredictable forms.
This is the sign of destroying
the illusion of subject and object.
Can you get rid of things like that?

But watch out! Until you obtain firmness in practice,
do not despise cause and effect.

Again, the All-Knowing Lama has stated:

Those who run naked in the midst of crowds cause confusion;
though they think they are practitioners, their thoughtlessness
disrupts all around them. Rely on discretion,
for this is the essence of the secret teachings.

People who nurse the sick so that they can demonstrate their goodness are not really good at all. But those who nurse others without
thought for themselves, who nurse even those with contagious diseases, are wonderful indeed.

Also, keep from getting caught up in any non-spiritual activity. In
Entering the Bodhisattva Path, we find:

Should you become involved in many
entertaining diversions
and various kinds of foolish patter,
abandon your attachment to them.

Should you delight in doing useless things
such as poking at the earth with a piece of straw
or idly drawing lines in the ground,
remember the teachings of the Sugata!
Tremble, and give them up.

When you have a yen to move about
or have the urge to talk,
first examine your mind,
and then act wisely in a steady manner.

When your mind is caught up in attachment
or caught up in anger,
do not speak, do not act:
Stop! Stay as still as a tree.

When you are idle and reckless,
swollen with pride and self-satisfaction;
when you think about exposing the faults of others,
and your mind is cunning and deceitful—

When you are inclined to praise yourself
or inclined to despise others,
bringing about disputes and condemnation:
Stop! Stay as still as a tree.

Should you desire gain, respect, or fame,
servants, sycophants,
or personal homage:
Stop! Stay as still as a tree.

Should you be inclined to forget about helping others
and look out for your own self-interest instead;
should there arise the desire to talk:
Stop! Stay as still as a tree.

Should you be intolerant, lazy, and fearful,
obstinate and rude; or should there arise

the wish to have your own way alone:
Stop! Stay as still as a tree.

Truly, having examined the mind that strives
for senseless things and is caught up in emotionality,
the hero, the Bodhisattva, should stop short
and firmly take hold of the antidotes. [5.45–54]

Again the same text states:

Do not spend time alone with another's spouse;
or ride or sit or sleep alone with such a one.
After observation and reflection, give up
whatever is disruptive to the general good. [5.93]

And further on it states:

To guard against a worldly mind
conduct yourself in ways
that do not conflict with what is taught in Nāgārjuna's works.
Having seen the teachings, act rightly. [5.107]

When these lessons have not been truly assimilated, bad habits
will undermine even the Bodhisattva. In the Twenty Verses on the
Vow, we find:

When you depend on external things, no learning will ensue.

To summarize, strive to act according to the advice the Great
Abbot Bodhisattva gave in his parting counsel for the renunciates of
the future:

O, all you venerable monks, listen!
The Prātimokṣa vows presented by the Teacher
are a refuge and a protection for you all.
Those who embrace the discipline of the Teacher
are worthy of the offerings of beings.

Should any of you venerable monks be irresolute,
you will weaken the doctrine of the Teacher.
In acting to delude beings,
such degenerates go to awful states of being.

As demonstrated in the Sūtra of the Wheel,
the karma of demons arises in just this way.
Therefore, give up such weakness,
for it does not make the kingdom joyful.

For a monk to act like a king
is demonic: Such activity
will cause the destruction of the doctrine of the Jina.
Such pleasures are not fitting.

Those who pass judgment create disturbance.
Elevating their own desires,
they lay low the virtuous monks
and debase the law of the land.
This is demonic activity that harms the
doctrine of the Teacher, and must be given up.

It is not suitable for a monk to stay with women.
When a monk stays in a secular household,
all the householders despise him,
and that monk proceeds on a wicked course.
This demonic activity should be renounced.

The Sūtra of the Prātimokṣa Rules,
compiled after the enlightenment of the Teacher,
sets forth the teaching for the Sangha.
Show it great respect!
Superficial action has but superficial benefit,
so protect the sacred Dharma of the Teacher!

And again:

In the future, Śramaṇas, those called virtuous of endeavor
will not be endowed with the four dharmas of the virtuous.
They will incite the wrathful,
and anger will defeat the virtuous.

They will curse those cruel to them,
and cruelty will rip asunder the doctrine of the Jina.
They will beat those who have abused them,
and the Śramaṇas will be led into battle.

These are the monks of the devil:
They will quickly destroy the doctrine of the Teacher.
As you may not be informed regarding demonic action,
I proclaim this testament to virtue: Act on it with care!

Patient, holy, dependable:
The ascetic, with austere and righteous practice,
should always live in a monastery.
In the future, venerable monks
will meet with the obstacle of anger arising:
So subdue and pacify your conduct.

Here in the Land of Snow, I have clarified
the precious teaching of the Buddha
so that those who come after us
may also grasp this wondrous doctrine of the Teacher.

And again:

In accordance with my teachings,
not failing in moral discipline like non-followers,
but practicing Bodhicitta as do Dharma practitioners,
cultivate both stages of Secret Mantra.

## Avoiding Double Standards

The third basic principle is to never apply double standards. Give up any hope that you can continue to pursue your own happiness while also making some effort toward self-mastery. You must purify your mind in all ways.

Do not think it enough to be patient with your friends but not your enemies. Do not think it is enough to patiently bear harm coming from human beings but not harm from demonic forces—or the other way around. And even if you learn to accept all these, you must also learn to patiently accept the suffering of illness and the like. Even bearing all that is not enough. The Great One of Oḍḍiyāna, Padmasambhava, has stated:

You need ideal faith like a river, neither drying up
nor overflowing its banks. You need ideal compassion

like the sun, not distinguishing friend from foe.
You need ideal giving like pure water, impartially available
for all to drink. You need ideal commitment:
like a flawless crystal globe.

### *Change your attitude, and be unassuming.*

People tend to consider themselves more important than anyone else. This tendency needs to be reversed, so that you cherish the welfare of others only. You also need to be discreet about even the smallest manifestation of your spiritual growth. Thus, your outer conduct should be patterned after those who live in accordance with the Dharma. Be humble, and let your spiritual progress go unperceived by others. We find in Entering the Bodhisattva Path:

"I am ever linked with others!"
O mind, know this well.
Now you should think only of
acting for the welfare of all sentient beings. [8.138]

Again, the same text states: "As much as you are able, stabilize the mind." [5.34]

Again, Padampa has stated:

Practice the secret way, O people of Dingri!
There are many obstacles to achieving the true signs of practice.

And again, the Great One of Oḍḍiyāna, Padmasambhava, has stated:

Whatever spiritual experience or realization arises,
conceal it from others, and do not try to explain it.
In this very lifetime, you have the possibility
of obtaining the siddhi of Mahāmudrā.

### *Do not talk about others' infirmities.*

Do not speak ungraciously of others, whether concerning worldly infirmities such as blindness or mental problems or even spiritual faults such as lax moral practice. Rather, always speak cheerfully and with a peaceful, smiling face, expressing whatever is optimistic and helpful. Regarding this, we find in Entering the Bodhisattva Path:

When speaking, your words should be soft and gentle,
pleasing and engaging, clear in meaning,
free from attachment and hatred;
your language should be appropriate and cheerful. [5.79]

Atīśa has stated:

Words that do not sweetly touch the hearts of others
are set aside by the wise.

Especially these days, a great deal of unrestrained merriment can be seen to occur among Dharma friends. Though you may not intend harm by teasing others and calling people names, there is still heavy fault in this. Long ago, a novice called another novice a monkey. Because he regretted this later and confessed the offense, he was not reborn in hell, but he took five hundred births as a monkey.

Again, there was once a Mānava named Kapila who, due to having called a group of Brahmins many bad names, was reborn as a sea monster with eighteen different heads and underwent great suffering. It is said that even after that birth he was born in the lower hells. Again, a monk in China, having composed a treatise that compared others to snakes, had his body transformed into that of a snake, and, in accord with what he had written, disappeared into a deep forest. Thus it is very important not to accumulate the sin of senseless speech.

### *Stop all negative thinking about others.*

People in general, and especially those who have entered the door of the Dharma, should never be regarded as engaging in any sort of wrongdoing. If you see conduct that seems to be wrong, say to yourself, "This is due to the impurity of my own sight. What is happening may be totally different than what it appears to be." Even the Lord Buddha was made to look corrupt in stories spread by Devadatta and Legpay Karma.

The second Buddha, Padmasambhava, was considered by some of the evil ministers of Tibet to be a master of diabolical spells, a teacher who would bring disaster to Tibet. There are also accounts of Panchen Śākyaśrī and others that depict them as spiritual teachers with ordinary desires. Moreover, the great siddha masters, Tilopa and Shavari and others, were seen by most people as being just ordinary and prosperous men of India. Many great teachers appeared

to be of the lowest castes, such as fishermen and huntsmen. How could anyone realize the extent of their inner qualities?

It is said that because the Lord Buddha appears to be just like us, people do not comprehend what kind of being a Buddha really is. We therefore do not know what sort of person may actually be just like him. And if we were to think any bad thoughts at all about someone who is actually a saintly person, we will end up in hell for a kalpa.

It is a general principle that nothing but great harm arises from belittling others or, in fact, disparaging anything at all. When attachment to your own beliefs makes you despise the beliefs of others or even think about the faults of others, you at once debase yourself and obscure your pure perception. After thinking about how such thoughts and actions may mean that you will not be able to escape bad states of being in future lives, make sure that you do not cultivate such karmic transgressions or destructive actions, and rid yourself of harmful thoughts. Regarding this, the Great One of Oḍḍiyāna has stated:

Do not revile other people or anything at all. Just as sea water
is inseparable from its saltiness, the result and the initial objective
are inseparable. Thus, do not despise any spiritual vehicle:
They all have one objective, like the steps of a ladder.
As you lack omniscience, you have no way to know the true stature
of another. Lacking such knowledge, never disparage anyone.

The essential nature of all sentient beings is the spontaneous Buddha-nature, the innate heart or potential for enlightenment. Therefore, do not dwell on the wrongdoing of others or on their mistakes. Rather, think of the vast possibilities of others, and think of their path as your own. Do not think about the faults of others; think about your own faults. Again, the greatest wrongdoing comes from bragging about your knowledge of the Dharma or from despising other people.

The protector Atīśa has stated:

When you do not look for the faults of others but see your own faults,
you purify the perception of the Teacher in everything.
The heirs of the Jina, entering the door of the Dharma,
concentrate on applying such a mind.

And again:

Never feel that you are being harmed
or look for faults in others.

And again:

Never show partiality toward any Dharma teaching:
With admiration, cherish them all.

The All-Knowing Lord of Dharma stated:

If your consciousness is pure, you will see everything as pure:
Seeing impurity in anything, your sight is faulty.
Just as jaundice makes you see a white conch as yellow,
seeing faults in others is completely your own error.

Again, in Entering the Bodhisattva Path, we find:

The masters of compassion see themselves
as having the nature of all beings . . . .
Why do I not honor beings as does the Protector? [6.126–27]

*Purify the strongest of your emotional attachments first.*

Look within yourself for your greatest emotional disturbance and
gather to yourself all the teachings that can serve as an antidote.
Subdue the strongest emotion at the start. During a great battle, if
you first slay all those who are brave and strong, you will not have to
kill the rest. It is the same when you use your inner strength for self-
discipline. Atīśa has said:

If you subdue the mind within,
no outer enemy can harm you.
If your inner mind is unsteady,
the outer enemy will cause misfortune.

Your inner foe will consume your own nature:
Therefore, conquer this inner adversary!
Once you have subdued the inner enemy,
various methods have been taught to rid yourself of it completely.

Again, Śāntideva has stated:

Those who, abhorring all suffering,
conquer the enemies such as hatred
are the true heroes.
Others kill only corpses.
—*Entering the Bodhisattva Path, 6.20*

And again:

Truly, I must never retreat
from conquering the kleśas. [4.42]

*Give up all hope of getting anywhere.*

Through the practice of self-mastery, you may hope for results such as being able to subdue evil forces. Or, when you return help for harm, you may hope to be regarded as someone special. This is hypocritical: Give up such thoughts! In brief, give up all hopes for attaining your own selfish goals—both the goals of this life such as happiness, praise, renown, respect and the like, and the goals for a future life, such as taking birth joyfully in the heavenly or human realms or nirvana for yourself alone. In The Seventy Resolves, we find:

May I never be attracted to the states of being
of those possessing the supreme wealth
of the most powerful of the gods or the chakravartin kings,
for such states of being are tainted by desire.

As this is the cause for existence which is
like the burning house of iron, there is no joy for me there.
Rather, guided by compassion, may I produce
everything that could be of benefit to others.

Truly, you must abandon your own desires and strongly develop the one desire to benefit others. A Jātaka states:

All my efforts have not been made to obtain the Bodhisattva stages;
nor to gain the higher realms or some great kingdom.
Nor were they made to gain great holiness for myself.
Rather, by this merit, I would see all things as they are.

This vision obtained, I will have conquered evil
through the desire to free all beings from the ocean of samsara,
churned by the waves of birth, old age, and death.

*Stop poisoning yourself.*

Action that seems virtuous but is mixed with selfish aims and is actually ego-driven is like food mixed with poison: Give it up! Atīśa has stated:

Just as food is ruined when placed in a vessel
filled with poison, so the inner defilements ruin virtue.
Having washed these away with the water of the antidotes,
the pure obtain great bliss.

And again, in The Verse Summary of the Prajñāpāramitā, we find:

The Buddhas have taught that focusing on the pristine Dharma
when you have inner defilements is like mixing profoundly good
food with poison. [6.7]

And again, the Great One of Oḍḍiyāna has stated:

Of those who commit themselves to the Dharma, some are led
by pride and self-complacency to great attachment. Others see
themselves as having great wisdom because they have studied
and explained the teachings. Some see themselves as being most
devout due to their Dharma activities. Still others see themselves
as great meditators because they have visited a few monasteries
or retreats. Still others see themselves as having great powers
and ability. When they finally see the error of such vanity,
they grow deranged, like wild beasts in the presence of blood.
They see the harm that they did not mean to do and turn away,
as if they saw the path blocked before them.

Pride in your own qualities is like the pride of a peacock
in his feathers. Envy at the good qualities of others is like
the jealous watchfulness of a guard dog over his master's wealth.
Followers of the Dharma who are complacent are foolish servants
of that devil, their own ego. Truly, ignorance is the mode of action
of these demons, and we must think of them with compassion.

*Do not tie yourself to a rigid sense of right and wrong.*

A worldly person with a rigid sense of right and wrong would never forget anyone who had helped him, no matter how great the time or

distance that separated them. But this same sense of justice causes people, when harmed by others, to let enmity fester and not to give it up. Consider it to be like a drawing made in water: Let it subside and disharmony will disappear.

In cultivating peace, you abandon rigid attitudes: When any harm is done to you, rather than wishing to retaliate in kind, the inclination to return benefit for harm arises. In the Instructions from a Spiritual Friend, we find:

Know that the mind can be like
a painting on the water, on earth, or on stone:
Truly, the disturbed mind is like the first.
The last and best is the desire for the Dharma. [17]

Entering the Bodhisattva Path states:

Under the influence of the emotions,
people will kill themselves—
harming the one they cherish most.
Since that is so, they will surely be prepared
to cause physical harm to others.

If I cannot feel compassion for those
who, giving birth to such emotionality,
attempt to kill me,
at least I should not respond with anger! [6.36–37]

*Never get caught up in cycles of retaliation.*

Never take delight in finding faults in others. More particularly, never vilify others in retaliation for bad things they have said about you. Even if you are hurt by such words, strive to praise the good qualities of those who have said the bad things about you. We find in The Seventy Resolves:

Even if I must bear the brunt of anger and hatred—
abuse, fault-finding, and beatings—
I will not give up patience.
To reach the level of activity of the heirs of the Jinas,
I will take on the responsibility to purify all suffering.

Again, we find in Entering the Bodhisattva Path:

When becoming abusive or quarrelsome,
Stop! Stay as still as a tree. [5.50]

Atīśa has stated:

Proclaim your own wrongdoing
and never look for others' faults.
Proclaim the good qualities of others
and hide your own virtues.
  —*Jewel-Garland of Bodhisattvas, 3*

Again in the same text:

When hearing harsh words,
look upon them as an echo. [16]

### Do not lie in ambush.

The memory of harm done to us by others tends to fester and not be forgotten even after the passage of many years. But when the time comes that you can retaliate, do not do so. Instead, do whatever you can to help. Even if the harm done to you was the most evil imaginable, meditate only on love and compassion, and do not act in any way to harm those who harmed you. We find in Entering the Bodhisattva Path:

Harming others in return for harm
offers you no protection;
instead, you undermine your own practice.
Thus is ascetic practice destroyed. [6.51]

And again:

I must rejoice in my enemies,
who help me to perform enlightened action. [6.107]

### Do not strike at the heart.

When you expose the faults of others, your hurtful words strike at the very heart. Do not use words that cause pain to others, or even say mantras meant to affect the lives of nonhumans. Gyalsay Rinpoche states:

Harsh words bring distress to the minds of others
and undermine the conduct of the Bodhisattva.

Since that is so, abandon harsh words that disturb others:
This is the Bodhisattva's practice.
                    —*The Thirty-Seven Bodhisattva Practices, 35*

We find in Entering the Bodhisattva Path:

Why do I not see that glory, fame, and happiness
in this life, and also, look!
becoming a Buddha in the future—
come from honoring sentient beings! [6.133]

*Do not place the load of a dzo on an ox.*[18]

Do not take the difficult burdens that are your responsibility and try to shift them onto others. When you manipulate others to take on your responsibilities, it is like taking a load from the back of the very strong dzo and placing it on the much weaker ox. This is wrong.

At one time, there lived a Kashmiri monk named Ramapati who possessed great spiritual abilities and knowledge and had many disciples. One day in his forest retreat, as he was boiling his saffron-colored robes in a large pot, he was approached by a neighboring householder who had entered the forest in search of a lost calf and had seen the smoke from the fire.

The householder came up to the monk as he was tending the fire and asked, "What are you doing?"

"I am boiling my robes," the monk replied.

The householder opened the pot, and said, "This is meat!" The monk also looked into the pot and saw what did indeed look like meat. The furious householder then hauled the monk off to the ruling magistrate, and said, "This man has stolen my calf! You must punish him!" In response, the magistrate at once ordered the monk to be placed in a pit.

A few days later, the householder found the calf and realized that Ramapati had not stolen it after all. He thus asked for the monk to be released. However the magistrate was distracted and six months went by without Ramapati being freed.

At that point, the monk's disciples, who had also obtained extensive spiritual power, went before the magistrate. They displayed their powers and then requested the release of their teacher, stating, "This monk is a good man! Please free him!"

The magistrate went at once to free Ramapati, and seeing the great suffering the monk had undergone, expressed deep remorse: "Due to my forgetfulness I have accumulated great sin!"

Ramapati, however, replied, "This is the repayment for my own actions."

"What karma could have caused this?" asked the magistrate.

"In a previous life I was a thief. Having stolen a calf, I ran into a forest, where I came upon a Pratyekabuddha in meditation. Knowing I was being followed, I threw the remains of the calf in front of him. The Pratyekabuddha was seized in my stead and placed into a pit for six days. The maturation of that action has caused me to experience the suffering of bad states of being for many lifetimes. Even in this lifetime I have undergone such suffering, but now the karma has fully matured and my misery has ended."

From this story, know that appearances can lie, that karma has great force, and that deceitfulness is a very great sin: These three things can have great impact. Thus in Entering the Bodhisattva Path, we find:

If you harm others for your own sake,
you will experience the suffering of the myriad hells. [8.186]

*Do not practice magic.*

If you practice self-mastery out of desire to gain your own inner satisfaction, to gain the upper hand, or in hopes of curing illnesses and reversing adverse circumstances, your practice is as repellant as that of those who perform magic rites. You must not practice in such a way. Rather, give up doubt, hope, fear, and pride. Meditate without regard for whether happiness or suffering will come to pass.

Our Omniscient Lama taught that self-mastery practiced selfishly is similar to the practices that serve evil forces—no different from

practicing magic. Real Dharma activity acts as an antidote to emotionality and disruptive thinking.

It is also said that wrong teachings make themselves known by certain signs. These include incorrect views such as eternalism, wrong meditations such as those that aim at attaining higher states, and wrong action that does not accord with the three vows. Anything contrary to the view and conduct taught in the sacred scriptures is said to be a wrong teaching. Whether it comes from one considered great or lowly, whether it comes from you or someone else, it will propel the one who acts into samsara and bad states of being. Such teachings are like taking the wrong medicine to cure an illness.

Certain people claim that texts by specific authors or specific treasure teachings (terma) are "mistaken teachings," without ever examining even a single passage to see if the meaning of the text is correct or not, or whether the text is newly composed or actual treasure text. They seem to make these claims based on their own personal preference or from some partiality for specific tenets. But it is said that only the Buddhas can measure the consciousness of others. Although you may not like or respect someone, that person may still have correct views and action. Your own dislike does not make a teaching or teacher wrong. For example, a merchant may deal in fine gold or in costume jewelry that just looks like gold: It is the merchandise, not the merchant, that is good or bad. Therefore, the Buddha has stated:

Rely on the Dharma, not on individuals.

The Buddha taught this repeatedly. It is clearly very important to understand this, and so I emphasize this point.

### *Do not aim to finish first.*

Give up any ambitions that call for using material resources for personal gain. True self-mastery means giving others the best of everything. If you are unable to do that, of what use is your virtue? Thus Atīśa has stated:

Do not wish for anything for yourself. All ways apart from this only produce karma. Just relax, and accept whatever happens.

*Do not bring a god down to the level of a demon.*

When ordinary people come to harm, they tend to say, "God is angry and is punishing me." In this way, gods are brought down to the level of demons.

Similarly, if you become self-satisfied and proud in the process of gaining self-mastery, you grow inflexible. This brings your spiritual practice down to a non-spiritual level. Self-mastery means to transform your consciousness, while pride leads to a rigidity that prevents you from getting to the heart of the Dharma. It is like lying in wait at the western gate to subdue the troublemakers at the eastern gate. Therefore, just as you would take medicine to cure an illness, use the teachings to help you stop cherishing yourself, and learn to be like a servant to all. As Entering the Bodhisattva Path states:

My arrogance, brought on by the emotion of pride,
leads me to lower states of being.
The table bearing the joyous feast of being human is overturned,
and I am condemned to eat the food of others.
Stupid, ugly, and weak, I am despised everywhere. [7.57]

And again:

Some there are who, for the sake of others,
pay their own body no heed.
Why do I act so foolishly towards them?
Why do I act with such pride, and not as their servant? [6.121]

It is also said: "Pride is the root of all carelessness."

In The Verse Summary of the Prajñāpāramitā, we find: "Understand that a proud mind is a small mind." [21.1]

*Do not seek pleasure at the expense of another's pain.*

If a benefactor or patron becomes sick and dies, you look forward to a share of his wealth and possessions. If a Dharma brother or close friend dies, you look forward to receiving a favorite painting or other such item. If a co-worker dies, you prepare to take full credit for the work you have done together. If an enemy dies, you feel pleasure at his absence.

Rid yourself of all such hopes for happiness that comes at the expense of the misery or distress of others! Take great care, for great harm comes from such selfish concern.

For humble Dharma practitioners, the actual enemy is to take sides: to take a stand that proclaims someone friend or enemy. 'Friend' and 'enemy' are postures that depend on your own mind: You distinguish 'your Lama', 'your teacher,' 'your country', and so on, dividing everything into 'your side' and 'the other side'. But 'the other side' does not harm you in the least, and 'your side' does not help you at all. Still, in hopes of gaining power or status, some people maliciously jump at the chance to put others down.

Long ago, there were two celibate geshes who were rivals. One heard that the other had broken his vows and taken a wife. He at once said to his disciple, "Boil up the finest tea! I have heard the greatest news!"

The disciple prepared the tea and brought it to his teacher. "What is this good news?" he asked. The geshe replied, "They say that our rival is living with a woman!"

This remark was later passed on to the master Kunpang Drag Gyal. His face grew somber, and he asked: "Of the two geshes, which one has committed the greater sin?"

Entering the Bodhisattva Path states:

If an enemy of yours is unhappy,
why should this delight you?
Your wish for that to happen
was not the cause of his coming to harm.

Even if you achieve your desire,
and he comes to harm,
why should this delight you?
What could come of this other than wretchedness? [6.87–88]

Householders in general, and those who gain their livelihood from farming, money-lending and so forth, all depend on miserable and harm-producing ways to support their happiness. Give up all such destructive ways of supporting yourself! Always delight in the happiness of all sentient beings, and you will never be estranged from goodness or from joy and a happy mind.

## *The Jewel of Undefiled Moral Practice*

The source of all good qualities and the finest virtue
is the jewel of noble undefiled moral practice:
This is the true crown of beings, even for the gods.
Wearing this ornament, you naturally
bring about all benefit for both yourself and others.

It supports renunciation and upholds
the pure moral practice of the Prātimokṣa rules.
On this ground grows the wish-granting tree
of the enlightened mind that aims to help others.
It nourishes the meditative stages of development and completion,
the many fruits of mantra, and the desire for liberation;
it is the bases of all to be honored, of all to be done and not done.

If you do not subdue your own mind, your uncouth actions
will disturb everyone, like monkeys in the jungle.
Shamed by the pure gods, you will go to lower states of being.
Therefore, be peaceful and subdued, and take the greatest care.

Those who are not impartial are faulty in self-mastery,
so always praise the gentle moderation of abiding in impartiality.
On the highest peaks, in the forefront of those who engage
in helping others, are those who shine impartially like the sun.

The base inclinations that formerly were so attractive are refined
and transformed into elixir by the two aspects of Bodhicitta:
By the practice of cherishing others, the sublime essence
that purifies gold, you firmly embrace this way of being,
unchanging forever.

The poisonous arrow of abusive speech sears the consciousness
and severs the living root of virtue in both self and others.
But speech concordant with the teaching is suitable to offer,
for its healing moisture always falls like an elixir on the mind.

Just as those with faulty vision see as yellow the white conch shell,
through the filter of our faults we see good qualities as tainted.
Though we try subjectively to determine purity or impurity,
there is no way: Only through abandoning false thinking
is appearance purified.

Those who never hesitate to use the most effective antidotes
to subdue the destructive emotions rampant in their mind
are the true and unexcelled heroes of the three worlds:
far greater than those whose arrows pierce the flesh of others.

Under the sway of compassion, the mind that helps others
gives up all hope for personal results. The understanding
behind the effort that aims to free all beings is the disposition
natural to the Holy Ones, unoppressed by any circumstances.

Those who desire to actually grasp the truth,
who apply themselves to virtue,
are said by the Jina to be like peacocks that thrive on poison.
Henceforth strive for the root of virtue of the Mahāyāna path,
never corrupted by the disruptive thinking of the three realms.

Malice that swells and festers in the heart
is certain to devour the life of liberation.
The power of the antidotes is the key to giving up the self—
of vanishing, like writing on water.

If you do not water your own consciousness
with the stream of patience, the kindling of your virtue
will be consumed by the fire of hatred.
Therefore, never repay abuse in kind:
This is the practice of virtue as followed by the Jina.

Never prompt agitation in the minds of others;
make sure that honors granted you are never bad for others.
To gain what you desire, reject the hypocritical pretense
of doing good, and using various methods,
stop nurturing your own desires.

When you continue to nurture the emotions of pride and all the rest,
self-centered desires draw suffering down on others.
Let the ills that go counter to the mind of enlightenment fall away,
and having examined, looked, and questioned,
abandon all harmfulness now!

> This finishes the section
> on the commitments of self-mastery.

ཀོང་སྤྲུལ་བློ་གྲོས་མཐའ་ཡས་ལ་ན་མོ།

*Kongtrul Lodro Tayay*

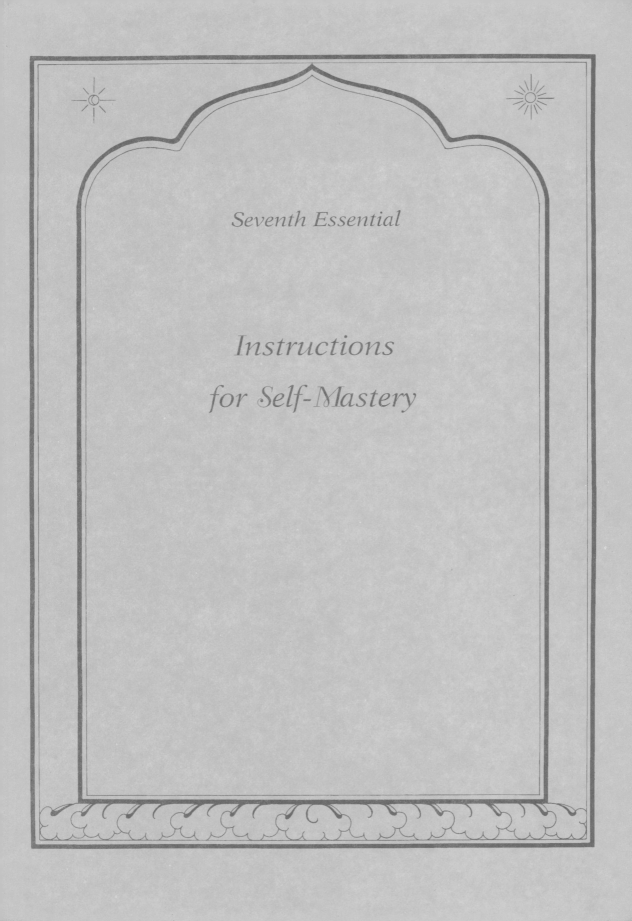

*Seventh Essential*

*Instructions*

*for Self-Mastery*

# Practice of the Seventh Essential

*Unify all that you do as practice.*

*Overcome all difficulties with this one remedy.*

*At both start and finish, do the two practices.*

*Whether good or bad arises, practice patience.*

*Guard the two, though it cost you your life.*

*Master the three challenges.*

*Take up the three principal resources.*

*Meditate on the three things that must not weaken.*

*Make sure to maintain the three as inseparable.*

*Train impartially in every sphere.*

*Cherish the depth and breadth of practice.*

*Always meditate on the most volatile situations.*

*Do not depend on external conditions.*

*Right now, practice what matters.*

*Do not misdirect your concern.*

*Do not vacillate.*

*Practice with determination.*

*Free yourself through both investigation and analysis.*

*Do not be complacent.*

*Do not give in to irritation.*

*Never be temperamental.*

*Do not look for thanks.*

# Reflections

## Guidelines for Self-Mastery

*T*he practice of self-mastery is the practice of yoga or unification, where every aspect of life becomes a manifestation of enlightened action. For those who can focus the mind solely on the Dharma, enlightenment may manifest even through the practice of the most mundane daily activities, as demonstrated in the biographies of the great siddhas.

While study of the Buddha's teachings is very helpful for gaining understanding of the true nature of existence, with the guidance of a spiritual teacher, scholarly study of the teachings may not be necessary or even helpful in traveling the path to enlightenment. Atīśa, one of the greatest Buddhist scholars of his time, directed those intent on enlightenment to follow the instructions of the lama rather than to concentrate on studying the teachings, for the pride that comes from intellectual understanding may even prove to be a drawback on the path.

On the other hand, these days many consider that they can attain enlightenment on their own: While they view the study of Buddhist philosophy as too intellectual, they also feel that following a teacher's directives is too limiting. However, trying to penetrate the mazes of the mind without a guide or trying to go 'beyond' the established path can unwittingly lead people much deeper into suffering.

In fascination, people read of the powers gained through practicing Tantra or the Vajrayāna and imagine they can gain enlightenment by giving full reign to their emotions. They imagine there is no need to make any effort on the path towards enlightenment, as many texts state that we are already enlightened. This may be true on one level, but it must be taken in the context of the teachings as a whole: The water of a cesspool may be pure in itself, but if you drink the water without first purifying it, you will get very sick.

Although quick answers are popular and appealing, they are distracting and can even be dangerous. Thus the Buddha and the great masters who came after him emphasized the importance of following a responsible guide, a teacher who can help point out the way. Without the directives of a teacher, the inner voice of self-interest will often gain ascendency.

The enlightened masters of the past prophesied that in the future, twisted teachings would appear, creating fascination and confusion. They also foretold that people who professed to be enlightened teachers would assert that the basic teachings of the Buddha were subject to dispute. To counter such forces of ignorance, they presented the path of self-mastery, which leads us away from all possible harmful directions directly onto the path of enlightenment. We can learn from our mistakes and discover the underlying patterns of samsara. Here is available a body of knowledge that gives us the ability to cease being victimized by samsara.

Bodhicitta activates the twin powers of samādhi and realization: samādhi or contemplation clears away confusion and all destructive tendencies, and realization cuts through the very root of samsara, opening the mind to the beautiful, joyful states beyond this realm of illusion and suffering. But 'going beyond' samsara does not mean that we leave it to go somewhere else, to a mystic land or unknown place. Instead, we discover within samsara a new beauty and freedom. Like skilled athletes or artists, we find fresh joy in our abilities, appreciating the display of appearance, glorying in the challenge that samsara presents, rejecting nothing, and participating with delight in the whole of existence.

# Guidelines for
# Developing Self-Mastery

*I* bow to the feet of the incomparable Lama,
Master of the Nāgas of Lake Manasarowar,
source of the hundred thousand rivers
of the teaching of enlightened mind,[19]
that clears away the anguish
of the many troubles of the world.

The following section presents the teachings that develop the seventh essential of self-mastery: ways to expand this training and prevent its decline. Regarding this the root text states:

*Unify all that you do as practice.*

Unify all your activities through the single intention to benefit others. Whether eating, dressing, sleeping, moving about, or so on, make all that you do a meditation. Concerning this, we find in Entering the Bodhisattva Path:

Whether openly or indirectly,
never do anything that is not in accord
with the welfare of others. [5.101]

*Overcome all difficulties with this one remedy.*

Just as analysis is used to counter mistakes in analysis, use self-mastery to counter any difficulties you may confront when you are practicing self-mastery. When others demean your practice; when evil forces, quarrelsome folk, or enemies try to harm you; when increasing emotionality begins to disturb you greatly; when meditation itself is making you uncomfortable: Use self-mastery to deal with all such obstacles.

Concentrate on how sad it is that so many sentient beings with problems similar to our own exist in the myriad universes. Meditate solely on removing the obstacles to exchanging self for others, thinking, "May I gather to myself all the miseries and undesirable things oppressing all sentient beings, adding them to everything I myself do not desire."

Many kinds of mental or physical imbalances may cause your meditation to falter. While you are concentrating on compassion, the energy-currents of the inner channels may reverse, causing anger or attachment to arise. With this, your meditation falls apart. To clear away such obstacles, meditate on both aspects of enlightened mind. Accordingly, we find in Entering the Bodhisattva Path:

Those who desire to overcome the hundreds of miseries of samsara, those who desire to clear away the unhappiness of sentient beings, and those who desire to enjoy multifold delights, must never give up the two aspects of enlightened mind. [1.8]

Again, it is said: "This is the way to clear away fear and suffering."

After going for refuge to the Lama and the Three Jewels, meditate on openness or on seeing all appearance as an illusion. At the same time, meditate with love and compassion on cherishing others. This is said to be the best way to clear away obstacles.

*At both start and finish, do the two practices.*

As soon as you get up in the morning, concentrate strongly on the thought, "Today I will never forget the two aspects of enlightened mind." At the end of the day before going to sleep, review your day, remembering in sequence all of your actions. Consider everything you thought or did, and if anything is contrary to enlightened mind,

enumerate such faults and confess them. Then resolve never to let such actions happen again. Do this periodically during the night as well. The Legs-grub states:

Having been negligent during the day,
you must confess well at night.
Confess the next day what you have done at night.
In doing this well, you will manifest delight.

In Entering the Bodhisattva Path, we find:

Each and every time a wrong arises
I must do what I can to humble myself.
I must reflect at length:
"In the future this will not happen again." [7.72]

If you have not done anything wrong, meditate joyfully, praying that in the future both you and all others will be able to surpass even this achievement, as you learn to continually practice both aspects of Bodhicitta. Concentrate your attention on the importance of never falling into any sort of wrongdoing, and henceforth act accordingly. In short, as Śāntideva stated:

I must examine again and again
the condition of my body and mind.
Put briefly, this alone
is the sign of mindfulness well guarded.
　—*Entering the Bodhisattva Path, 5.108*

The Instructions from a Spiritual Friend states:

The Buddha taught that taking care
is the foundation of immortality,
and carelessness the foundation of death.
Therefore, for the sake of increasing the virtuous Dharma,
always act with care and devotion. [13]

　　　*Whether good or bad arises, practice patience.*

If great suffering or wretchedness occurs in your life, contemplate your previous karma. Do not be angry or disheartened, but take upon yourself all the wrongs and sufferings of others, and strongly apply the methods for clearing away evil and obscuration. If great delight

and happiness occur in your life and you are surrounded by wealth and servants, do not be careless or complacent: Devote your wealth to virtue. Concentrate your energy on transforming everything into virtue, and pray for the delight and happiness of all sentient beings.

In short, whether you experience happiness or misery, understand that both are like an illusion and realize that everything that occurs is a part of the path. Gyalsay Rinpoche has stated:

The cause giving rise to both self and others
is the collection of skandhas comprising the body.
If you have aches and illnesses, rejoice!
They are expressions of your bad karma previously amassed.

All your various acts of Dharma practice
are for the sake of purifying the two obscurations.
If you are without pain, there is nothing to delight in;
if you are happy in body and mind,
increase your application to virtue!

If you devote yourself to helping mankind,
continue to apply yourself to the virtues
of body, speech, and mind.
If you have no wealth, delight in its lack—
maintaining and guarding what you have is a waste.

Whatever anger or disruption arises
comes from the error of attachment to things.
If you have wealth, rejoice that its existence
enables you to increase the virtues of merit.

Whatever happiness or benefit you have
in the present and the future
is certainly the fruit of merit.
Should you soon come to die, rejoice at death;
do not avoid adversity.

Assisted by good intentions at the time of taking birth again,
you will certainly enter the path without error.
But even should you find yourself butchered, rejoice,
as this too produces the fruit of experience.

Relying on the life-giving moisture
of the precepts that never disappear,
you will mature if you give them your trust.
Whatever you do, rejoice and meditate!

In summary, we find in The Precious Garland:

Though you have the perfections of the gods,
do not be proud; though you have the frailties
of the hungry ghosts, do not be disheartened. [273]

*Guard the two, though it cost you your life.*

All present and future happiness comes from guarding your commitments: both the general Dharma commitment (the vows of the three ordinations) and the specific commitments for guarding the samaya vows and teachings of self-mastery as presented above. Protecting these vows correctly gives rise to complete bliss later on. Guard both sets of commitments even at the risk of your life.

Again, whatever you do, never let yourself be led by thoughts of your own benefit. Value only the ambition to benefit others. The Great One of Oḍḍiyāna has stated:

Five hundred years from now, during the age of degeneration, there will be people who will lack all insight concerning the true nature of self and thus will fail to counteract the process of disruptive thinking. They will act crudely due to their disturbing emotions, and they will mouth opinions such as, "The view maintaining the cause and effect of virtuous and evil karma is a lower teaching." They will despise the effects of karma, saying, "This is just an idea the Buddha was playing with." These people will be rash in their actions, making everything a cause of contention. Their twisted way of life will undermine both their own welfare and the welfare of others. Following such a way for even a single instant is totally unacceptable.

In Entering the Bodhisattva Path, we find:

Whatever you do in any circumstance,
whether done for yourself or for another,

strive to put into practice
whatever you have learned for such a situation. [5.99]

In Letter to a Disciple, we find:

The best of mothers acts with modest restraint,
personifying the qualities suffused with unwavering
and perfect love. Just so, those with the radiant joy
that illuminates through truth and honesty
easily give up their life, but never their vows. [15]

Again, we find in Instructions from a Spiritual Friend:

Someone who has status, beauty, and learning
but lacks wisdom and moral practice is not to be respected.
Those who have these two qualities
are to be honored even if they lack all other virtues. [28]

### *Master the three challenges.*

Firstly, because we are born full of emotionality, it is difficult at the outset to recognize emotionality for what it is. Secondly, it is difficult to counteract the emotions. Thirdly, it is difficult to stop their flow.

As to the first, you must be able to recognize the harmful emotions as soon as they appear. Then you must put an end to them by generating the power of the antidotes. Finally, adopt the resolve never to allow these emotions to arise again. These are the three things to master. Regarding this Gyalsay Rinpoche stated:

Being so accustomed to the emotions,
it is difficult to use the antidotes to counter them.
But with alertness and mindfulness, having taken hold
of the weapons of the antidotes, the very moment emotions
such as attachment first arise, you can conquer them at once:
This is the Bodhisattva's practice.
                    —*The Thirty-Seven Bodhisattva Practices, 36*

### *Take up the three principal resources.*

The chief resource for successful Dharma practice is introduced in The Verse Summary of the Prajñāpāramitā:

The Jina, the Lord of supreme qualities, has taught:
"The Buddhadharma depends upon
the spiritual friend of virtue." [15.2]

Atīśa has stated:

The wellspring of all good qualities,
as praised in the Mahāyāna scriptures,
is the spiritual teacher, ever dependable
like the water in the great ocean.
On that basis, the wise gather good qualities
until they can perform the deeds of Bodhisattvas.

Thus make sure to meet with a good Lama who teaches the way of the Mahāyāna. In the Instructions from a Spiritual Friend, we find:

"Control your mind!" The Bhagavan has said:
"The mind is the root of the Dharma." [117]

Thus, the second principal resource for successful Dharma practice is to use the mind well. We find in Entering the Bodhisattva Path:

The advent of a Tathāgata, the attainment of faith, a human form, and the ability to cultivate virtue are rare events indeed.
When will you ever obtain them again? [4.15]

The third principal resource for successful Dharma practice involves assembling everything you need to support your Dharma practice, such as food and clothing and the like. Once you have done this, meditate in delight, and pray that others may obtain these three factors for successful practice as well.

If you have not activated these three resources, think of what a pity it is that so many others in the world also lack these three things that together make possible sustained practice of the Dharma. Take upon yourself the responsibility for producing these factors for all sentient beings. Pray that everyone, both you and all others, should gain these conditions for practice.

*Meditate on the three things that must not weaken.*

All the qualities of the teachings of the Mahāyāna depend on the Lama; therefore you must learn not to weaken in your devotion to the Lama. We find in The Flower Ornament Sūtra:[20]

He has come here with this one thought in mind:
"Our spiritual teachers who teach the Dharma
demonstrate all the wondrous qualities of truth;
they demonstrate the mode of action of Bodhisattvas.

"By giving birth to virtue, they are like my mother,
offering the milk of virtue for me to drink.
They cleanse the limbs of enlightenment—
these spiritual teachers who keep me from all harm.

"They are like physicians who free me from old age and death,
and like Indra, Lord of Gods, who lets falls the rain of nectar.
They are like the full moon as they intensify the wholesome
Dharma, and like the shining sun
as they teach the perspective of peace.

"They are like a mountain, there for both enemy and friend;
in mind unshakable as the ocean.
They are like gentle defenders to protect us."
With such thoughts has Sudhana come hither.

"They generate the mind of the Bodhisattvas,
children of the Buddhas, who have generated
the enlightened mind. My dear friends,
they are praised by the Buddha."
With such a mind of virtue has Sudhana come hither.

"They are like great heroes, protectors of the world;
leaders who provide protection and refuge.
They are my eyes of strength and happiness."
With such a mind, he honors the spiritual friend.

Again, we find in Entering the Bodhisattva Path:

I will learn how to respect the Lama
from the biography of Śrīsambhava.[21] [5.103]

Second, as self-mastery is the heart of the Mahāyāna teachings,
you must never let your delight in its practice diminish. The Verse
Summary of the Prajñāpāramitā states:

This vehicle is a palace great as the sky;
it is the sublime vehicle

for reaching true pleasure and manifest joy.
Whoever mounts this vehicle
carries all sentient beings to nirvana. [1.21]

Atīśa has also stated:

The spiritual teacher frames all instructions
and every undertaking to accord
with the scriptures of the Mahāyāna—
with innermost mind intent on the Dharma.

You must never let your practice of the teachings of either the Greater or the Lesser Vehicle waver, even those teachings that may seem insignificant. In Entering the Bodhisattva Path, we find:

Strive to never waver,
and never stray from your practice. [4.1]

*Make sure to maintain the three as inseparable.*

Always avoid any wrongdoing of body, speech, or mind, and never allow body, speech, or mind to stray from the root of virtue. The Great One of Oḍḍiyāna, Padmasambhava, has stated:

Even if you realize your own mind as being the Buddha,
never reject the Lama. Even if you realize all appearance
as being mind, do not sever the stream of the virtuous activity
of conditioned existence. Even if you have given up all hope
and expectations of becoming a Buddha, honor the divine nature
of the Three Jewels. Even if you do not fear samsara, abandon
even the most inconsequential wrongdoing. Even if you are sure
of the immutable nature of dharmatā, do nothing to disparage
the Dharma. Even if the qualities of samādhi and omniscience
arise within you, give up all arrogance and pride. Even if you
realize the inseparability of samsara and nirvana, never stop
the stream of compassion for sentient beings.

If you practice in such a way, you proceed as did Zhang Gomripa. Having received guidance from the Lord of Dharma, Godtsangpa, Zhang Gom was living and meditating in the cave called Lingway Drag. The ruling family of that area, greatly impressed by his demeanor, invited him into their presence. Desiring the initiation of

the Black Yamāri, they said to him, "Please give us the devotions necessary to undertake this practice. We will adhere to the vows!"

"Well then," Zhang Gom began, "there are three things you must
practice at all times. If you can do these three things I can give you
the practice. But I don't think you can do them."

Thinking he meant the three elements of the tantric teachings of
the Yamāri cycle—the Yamārirakta or Red Yamāri, the Kṛṣṇayamāri
or Black Yamāri, and the Bhairava or Formidable cycle, they said to
Zhang Gom, "Please give us the practices. We can do them! You must
give them to us!"

"Well then," he replied, "here they are. Of course you must abandon all attachment and hatred as you perform these pure Dharma
practices.

"First of all, you must give up all the things you find desirable.
Even though I have never had a fraction of the wealth and power you
have, at one time I lived at Samling Monastery, where I had many attendants and disciples. I turned them all away, and having freed
myself from those responsibilities, I was able to practice. But I don't
think you can do this.

"Secondly, you must be at the service of your enemies until they
are appeased. I went to the land of my rivals and offered them gifts.
They were very impressed at this, and said to me, "In return for your
actions, henceforth we will show you the greatest respect." They then
invited me in and showed me the greatest esteem. We must make our
enemies joyful in such a way, calming our own feelings of hatred and
the hatred of others. But I don't think you can do this practice.

"Thirdly, having abandoned attachment and hatred you must go into
retreat. Having gone to a place of solitude, I lived quietly and restfully,
working diligently. There I applied myself to the practice of virtue, not
letting myself be lax even for an instant in any of the three gates of
body, speech, and mind. But I don't think you can do this practice."

And indeed, they were most surprised at these directives. Moreover, the Great One of Oḍḍiyāna taught:

If you would genuinely practice the Dharma, you must reverse
your way of life in fourteen ways. In a forest retreat where

wild animals roam, practice self-discipline. Eat sparingly
and act with humility. Stay away from places where there are
powerful and self-important people. Cut off connections
with anyone who might delight in hostile activity.
Like a beggar, wear loathsome clothes.
Cultivate revulsion for your friends and loved ones.

Strive to compare with the Buddha in your practice.
After reflecting on the precepts, practice the Dharma.
Chant your yidam's mantra with perseverance.
Turn away from the evils of bad counsel.
Give whatever good things you have to the Lama.
Turn your back on samsara and generate heartfelt remorse.
Give others every advantage and never support contention.
Calculate the many faults you must abandon.
When you do these things, the Dharma passes into the Dharma.
This way will turn aside samsara!

Even if you are not able to practice in this way, Atīśa states:

If you cultivate meditative balance, your external actions
of body and speech do not matter.
If you do not cultivate such balance,
your actions of body and speech may seem virtuous,
but your affairs will accord with common worldly concerns.

When the mind is virtuous, both body and speech will naturally be
virtuous. Even if they seem otherwise on the surface, they will be
faultless. But if the mind is not virtuous, even when body and speech
appear to be virtuous, their goodness is far from certain. Therefore
strive for mental virtue. Thus Śāntideva stated:

Let all other virtues decline,
but may I never lose the virtues of the mind.
        —*Entering the Bodhisattva Path, 5.22*

*Train impartially in every sphere.*

*Cherish the depth and breadth of practice.*

Self-mastery should be practiced with complete impartiality toward everything. This includes both the animate and inanimate—all sentient life as well as the elements. When you understand that self-mastery relates to whatever arises as a mental object, whether good or bad, whether concerning human beings or not, this is breadth of practice. Do not just pay lip service to this practice, but cherish it from the depth of your heart.

In Entering the Bodhisattva Path, we find:

Due to their skill in thus abiding,
there is nothing that the heirs
of the Victorious One do not learn;
there is nothing that they do not turn to merit. [5.100]

And again:

I will practice these teachings in my actions,
for what can I accomplish by merely reading the words?
How can the sick be helped by reading medical texts? [5.109]

*Always meditate on the most volatile situations.*

Make the object of your meditation those who cause you the most difficulty: those hostile to you and full of hatred, those who create obstacles for you, and especially those who, perversely, seek to harm you in return for your help. Meditate on those who compete with you; those you must live with but find annoying; those who just naturally seem to create trouble for you even though they are not malicious; those who are innately bad-natured due to the power of their karma, and so forth. Meditate intently on love and compassion, and direct it especially toward such people.

In The Four Hundred, we find:

Like a mother who shows
special kindness to her sick child,
Bodhisattvas show the greatest kindness
to those who are unrighteous.

We find in The Seventy Resolves:

"May I never find fault in anyone—
even those who cut off my head
and chop it into a hundred pieces.
May such beings be as dear to me as my own child,
and may I stand by them always!"

Beginners may think that there is no way they can show compassion that even approaches the loving-kindness shown by the holy ones, but if you meditate again and again, such compassion will arise. Thus Śāntideva has stated:

Do not turn away from what is difficult:
With the force of practice, those whose very name
now frightens you, even when they are not present,
will no longer cause you misery.
                    —*Entering the Bodhisattva Path, 8.119*

If you do not generate compassion for those who cause you difficulty, you will never become a Bodhisattva, for you are not purifying your mind.

Also make it a special point never to do anything that could harm others who are close to you: your parents, your teachers, and so forth. Thus, the Prophecy of Mañjuśrī states:

In the future, some will disdain Vajradhara
and thus disdain sentient beings.
Doing so, they disdain me.
Thus I must ever abandon disdaining others.

The Fifty Verses on Devotion to the Lama states:

Should you despise the spiritual masters,
you will die in great delusion,
from leprosy or other infectious diseases,
or from the evil forces of illness, plague, or poison.

Kings or fire or poisonous snakes,
floods or missiles or thieves,
evil forces or bad leaders will cause your death
and you will go to hell.

Never cause the mind
of a spiritual master to be agitated.
If you should act with such neglect,
you will certainly boil in hell.

Avīci and the other hells—
places certain to terrify:
It is taught that those who disparage the masters
will surely end up there. [11–14]

It is said elsewhere:

Having listened to just a single passage of the teaching,
should you fail to uphold the one who taught it,
you will take repeated births as a dog
and then be born as a butcher.

### *Do not depend on external conditions.*

In practicing self-mastery, do not let your practice hinge on whether or not your circumstances are favorable to practice. Practice whether you are in good health or not; whether your living conditions are comfortable or not; whether or not you are given support in your practice; and whether or not you are beset by troubles. If circumstances are favorable, practice above and beyond what would be expected. If conditions are not favorable, use that circumstance to unfold your practice of both aspects of enlightened mind. In short, always involve yourself in the practice of self-mastery, not depending on your own state of mind or outside circumstances.

Gyalsay Rinpoche has said:

To take up dauntlessly the sins and sufferings of all beings,
though they be destitute and despised by all,
diseased and possessed by demons:
Such is the Bodhisattva's practice.

Though praised by many with heads bowed at their feet
or endowed with the riches of the God of Wealth,
they see the senselessness of the glories of samsara
but never show disdain: Such is the Bodhisattva's practice.
            —*The Thirty-Seven Bodhisattva Practices, 20–21*

*Right now, practice what matters.*

In all the countless forms we have assumed from beginningless time, what have we done of real significance? Finally we have obtained a human life in which we have met with the genuine Dharma. As none of us can expect such a favorable conjunction of circumstances to come about again, we must practice what is most important for making our existence meaningful.

What will benefit us in future lives is more important than what will benefit us in this. For the future, liberation is more important than samsara, and the welfare of others is more important than our own welfare. The All-Knowing Lama has stated:

From among the six types of beings, it is rare
to obtain a human life and rare to obtain a body
with which to practice the Dharma.
Having gained the perfect path of freedom
and good fortune, how could it be right to achieve
my own enlightenment alone?

Not striving every minute to aspire to the path of liberation,
we are buffeted by the agitation of worldly commotion.
What am I doing in this lifetime of illusory appearances?
Right now I must seek to achieve the meaning of existence.

The enjoyments of this lifetime
are like the appearances in a dream;
whatever they may be, they cannot help us
and are certain to desert us. What use to me
are my wealth and provisions? Now I will seek
to achieve the profound meaning of the Dharma.

Like shoppers in a crowded market,
we are separate even when together.
We hamper each other, though we aspire to closeness and love.
What use do I have for these many companions?
Now I will seek to achieve the meaning of union.

Amazing! Fame, renown, praise, and respect are like a dream;
yet fools in their confusion let these phantoms feed their pride.

Why should I ask for the esteem of others?
Now I will seek to achieve the meaning of clear light.

Whatever we do to support our lives,
all these senseless actions cause us to suffer.
What use is such irrational conduct?
Now I will seek to achieve the meaning of non-action.

When it is time to depart alone from all we have,
no one can give us the slightest help.
What use to me are this lifetime's reflections?
Now I will seek to achieve the benefit of careful counsel.

Whoever is close to us, whatever wealth we have—
nothing will go with us: Only our vice and our virtue.
What use are my many friends and wealth?
Now I will seek to achieve the sacred Dharma that benefits all beings.

The many pleasures of faraway lands,
even the vast array of pleasures of body and mind—
at the time of death, what can we do with them?
As body and mind are sure to part, I will seek true benefit.

No anguish at sickness, no lament at death:
With no regrets at the time of dying,
I seek the Dharma, the profound meaning, the heart of being,
in the sky of dharmatā, attunement of self-knowing,
the stronghold of the meaning of the natural mode of being.

And further:

When the seeds and root of enlightenment are sustained
by compassion, the many fruits of happiness come forth,
and finally the wish-granting treasure of inconceivable virtue.
Thus I must generate the perfect enlightened mind,
for the welfare of others.

This inconceivable mountain of merit
is extolled by the Victorious Ones and praised by the three worlds.
Just as the Dharmadhātu overarches the expanse of space,
the enlightened mind embraces perfect and boundless qualities.

We find in the Sūtra of the Questions of Ratnacūḍa:

Noble son, to achieve the roots of virtue for your own welfare
is to be like a firefly, but to achieve the roots of virtue for others'
welfare is to be like the orb of the sun.

In the Sūtra of the Questions of Sāgara, we find:

The difference in merit achieved when the roots of virtue
are practiced for the welfare of self or for the welfare
of others is like the difference in expanse
between the footprint of an ox and the wide ocean.

Comparing the merits of study to practicing the Dharma, practice
is by far the more important. In the Sūtra of the Ornamental Array,
we find:

The teaching of the perfect Buddha
is not achieved just by study.
Swept away by a great river,
it is still possible to die from thirst:
The Dharma without meditation is like this.

Even though you give food and drink
to a great many beings,
you yourself may die from hunger:
The Dharma without meditation is like this.

A physician who possesses
every kind of medicine
may die from indigestion:
The Dharma without meditation is like this.

A treasure house of wealth
is filled with any number of gems,
but you yourself may not obtain a single one:
The Dharma without meditation is like this.

Imagine finding yourself in the palace of a king
with all kinds of pleasures at your beck and call
yet lacking food or drink:
The Dharma without meditation is like this.

An artist gone blind who still
tries to paint in the middle of a market place
will not see even himself:
The Dharma without meditation is like this.

The riverboatman
who saves many beings
may himself die in the river's rushing currents:
The Dharma without meditation is like this.

Being able to explain
perfectly and fully all the four paths
but not having attained them yourself:
The Dharma without meditation is like this.

And again, in the Sūtra called King of Samādhis, we find:

If you do not meditate on the Dharma
you will not see the nature of existence, dharmatā.
You may listen to the water and gaze at it,
but if you do not drink it, you will clearly go thirsty.

In the Appeal for Open-Minded Caring, we find:

The sugar cane plant has no real core,
but the taste that delights is to be found within.
Just eating the rind will not give you the sweet taste of sugar.
The words of the Dharma are like the outer shell;
for the meaningful taste, look to the mind.

The same Sūtra states:

Kumāra, Bodhisattva Mahāsattvas find ten benefits
that come through their efforts in meditative introspection:
Their minds are untroubled; they abide in carefulness;
they are mindful of the Buddha; they have faith in enlightened
action; and they are never perplexed with respect to pristine
awareness. They remember the Buddha in all that they do;
they never depart from Dharma; they are highly committed;
they are self-disciplined; and they manifest the four analytical
knowledges. Kumāra, these are the ten benefits arising from the
Bodhisattva Mahāsattvas' efforts in meditative introspection.

In summary, the Sūtra of the Magnificent Crown states:

There is greater merit for one who meditates on dharmatā
for one day than for one who listens to the Dharma and studies it
for many kalpas. Why is this so? Because through such meditation
you are able to put the path of birth and death far behind you.

To develop the two aspects of the enlightened mind matters more
than to develop other attainments, for the two aspects of Bodhicitta
are the actual basis of all the Dharma of the Mahāyāna. As Entering
the Bodhisattva Path states:

Through giving and the other perfections,
your activities proceed from high to higher.
Never forsake the greater for the lesser—
consider above all what will benefit others. [5.83]

The above teachings have been expressed in great detail. Clearly,
earnest practice based on the Lama's instructions is more important
than practice centered on learning the scriptures and their commentaries. When you are able to calm the mind to some extent, the
Lama's instructions alone will be enough for your mind to be at once
refreshed. When you question your Lama and meditate accordingly,
you will never be perplexed by the basic teachings as found in the
seven texts of logic, the four principal grammars, the seven texts of
the Abhidharma, the Yogācārabhūmi, and so on.[22]

Even if you have felt drained and weary for inconceivable eons, the
harmony gained through such practice will be lasting, leading to
consummate fulfillment in this lifetime. The Lord Atīśa has stated:

In the course of a single short life many things must be learned,
and you have no way to know just how long this life will be.
Eager to fulfill your own desires
you are like a goose attempting to strain milk from water.

Looking to externals, being occupied with worldly concerns,
only means that what you do will lead to senseless suffering.
As such worldly thoughts do not help you,
attune yourself to looking at your own mind!

The seven texts of logic, the four of grammar,
the śāstras of the Abhidharma and the Yogācārabhūmi;

the Sūtras, the Vinaya, the Abhidharma,
and all the established scriptures—
regarding all of these, it is said: "Do not look,
do not listen, do not explain, do not transcribe."

Those of fine demeanor thus do not perplex themselves:
Rather, they taste the nectar called Instruction of the Lama.
For those who settle the mind in meditation,
what need is there for many scriptures?
Their profusion completely confuses the mind.

This state of samsara being so uncertain,
you cannot even be sure who are your parents:
So abandon attachment to those you hold so dear.
Abandon hatred as well, for how can you be sure
who your enemies are?

The nature of the glories of youth and health
and the five objects of desire are also uncertain:
Abandon attachment to them. Give up gain and respect,
fame, lineage and class, and all pontificating;
give up connections to students and to teaching!

The things of the world are as dangerous
as tigers or snakes, fire or poison.
Having considered this deeply, abandon society
and stay in solitude. Examine the characteristics
of women and men, of medicine, elephants, astrology,
and weapons; consider horses; imagine jewels:
Then give them all up. Abandon as well
all reading and learning of senseless commentaries.

Concerning this, Lord Gyalsay stated:

The teachings and their explanations are not what is most
important; what you do is important. Through misunderstanding,
many people do not practice in accord with the teachings, or their
practice is meaningless, or it is sidetracked. So basically, although
your practice must accord with the teachings and their
explanations, rather than reciting many scriptures and teachings,
it is far more to the point to follow the instructions of the Lama.

Putowa and Geshe Chogyi Odzer, a very learned Lama, both had many students in common. These students said to Geshe Chogyi Odzer, "When Putowa explains the Dharma, we clearly understand what he is teaching; when you explain the teachings, we don't gain the same degree of understanding."

Geshe Chogyi Odzer pondered this. "How can it be? I am more learned than he is! Well then, he must have teachings that I do not have." And so he proceeded to listen to Putowa teach the Dharma, and he also came to understand the teachings more clearly. Having gained this understanding, he said to Putowa, "Listening to you teach the Dharma, I did not learn anything I did not know before, but I came to clearly comprehend what I had not truly understood."

To this, Putowa replied, "This is true. I did not teach you anything you did not already know: You are more learned! I led you to clearly comprehend what you had not understood. I have internalized the meaning of all the Dharma, and having done so, I then explain it."

When Geshe Chogyi Odzer spoke of this he would say, "How very true this is. My teaching was empowered by discerning knowledge. Putowa's teaching is empowered by practice and is joined to his very nature."

Sitting practice is thus more important than other modes of practice. The Great One of Oḍḍiyāna has stated:

Continue sitting until death!
Cultivate the meditation of the Great Perfection.

We find in Entering the Bodhisattva Path:

With body and mind in solitude,
distractions do not arise. [8.2]

Gyalsay Rinpoche expressed this in the following way:

Through giving up bad objectives,
you will diminish the fetters by stages.
Through being unswerving,
you will gradually increase your devotion to virtue.
Through clearing up your mental quality,
you will generate clear knowledge of the Dharma:

This is the practice of Bodhisattvas who rely on solitude.
           —*The Thirty-Seven Bodhisattva Practices, 8*

Further, Yang Gonpa has stated:

In grass huts, at home with hunger and cold
are the intrepid who fear suffering:
Zealously they stay rooted to their seats.

Sharawa has said:

All my allies are with me on my meditation seat.

At one time Milarepa said to Gampopa, "I have the most profound instruction to give you! I will give it to you now!" But he said no more.

Later, when Gampopa was about to return home, he asked Milarepa to give him the instruction he had been offered. Milarepa replied, "In a while!" But still he did not give it.

When Gampopa finally set out, Milarepa accompanied him a short distance along the way. After many farewells and pleasantries, Gampopa went on alone.

After he had proceeded some ways, Milarepa shouted to him, "Come back!" And then he added, "Going away is not going to help you."

Milarepa then went on to say, "Wear a coat of lambskin, and seated on a meditation cushion, practice intently until sores form on your posterior. That is called the most profound of teachings. That is the most wonderful instruction."

For those who would abandon worldly ways, it is most important to depend on the antidotes. In Entering the Bodhisattva Path, we find:

Where could you find enough leather
to cover all of the earth?
But you can cover all of the earth
with the leather of the soles of your shoes. It is the same.

Likewise, though you cannot actually alter external events,
you can alter your own mind.

What need is there
to try to change others? [5.13–14]

It is vital to practice these principal teachings.

*Do not misdirect your concern.*

Give up the six misdirected concerns:

Misdirected patience is to patiently endure the difficulties of worldly life such as arise in making money, getting even with your enemies, and protecting your friends, while being impatient at the difficulties of practicing the Dharma.

Misdirected craving is to crave wealth and happiness in this lifetime rather than desiring to practice the pure Dharma.

Misdirected enjoyment is to enjoy material goods rather than to find enjoyment in hearing, thinking upon, and meditating on the Dharma.

Misdirected compassion is to feel compassion for those who undergo hardships for the sake of the Dharma, while not feeling compassion for those whose actions are harmful.

Misdirected helpfulness is to help those who rely on you to be successful in worldly ways instead of bringing them into contact with the Dharma.

Misdirected delight is to reflect joyfully on the suffering of your enemies, rather than meditating joyfully on the virtues and happiness that transcend samsaric concerns.

These misdirected concerns have been discussed in many previous texts. Yet I mention them here as they must be totally rejected. You must always take great care to rid yourself of them as soon as they arise.

The Great One of Oḍḍiyāna, Padmasambhava, has stated:

To be miserable when those who are close to you die
is not the way of those who follow the Dharma.
For the Dharma practitioner, five things need to be done
when faced with bereavement: In the case of being separated
from your Dharma teacher, to pass through the stage of mourning,
you need to make offerings. When separated from your dear

Dharma friends, mourn by accumulating merit and wisdom.
When falling prey to weakness and breaking your practice,
mourn by purifying your faults and confessing. When unable
to practice due to a long spell of illness, mourn by depending
on the Lama. When allowing your mind to get trapped
in the eight worldly concerns, mourn by turning away from
attachment from the depth of your being.

*Do not vacillate.*

Those who practice only sporadically have not generated clear
understanding of the Dharma. It is very important to practice self-
mastery single-pointedly and not to be restless. Thus we find in
Entering the Bodhisattva Path:

Whatever spiritual practice you set out to do,
do not let your thoughts drift away.
Direct your thoughts toward your practice
and accomplish just that very thing.
Acting in such a way, all will be well:
There can be no other outcome. [5.43]

The Great One of Oḍḍiyāna has stated:

Dharma practitioners must be endowed with five aspects of greatness. They must have the greatness of the Lama's instructions.
Along with the instructions, they must have the greatness gained
through skillful means. They must have greatness in their capacity
for difficult meditations. They must have great admiration for all
aspects of the Dharma, and they must have great decisiveness in
practice. If you are not endowed with these five, you will not be
able to travel far towards liberation from samsara.

*Practice with determination.*

Practice only self-mastery, giving up everything else that might
distract you. Thus we find in the Crown of Sūtras:

Be devout and train yourself. [15.10]

The Great One of Oḍḍiyāna, Padmasambhava, has stated:

When you are single-minded and decisive,
you will cast off all hardship.

*Free yourself through both investigation and analysis.*

You need to free yourself from self-grasping and the emotional fetters by investigating and then examining the course of your consciousness. Concentrate on the objects that give birth to the emotions in your consciousness. Carefully investigate: Are the destructive emotions arising in your consciousness? If so, apply their antidotes.

Again, look at how self-grasping operates. If no self-grasping seems to be in operation, investigate again, focusing on an object of attachment or hatred. If at this point self-grasping arises, concentrate on its lack of self-nature. You can also instantly rid yourself of self-grasping through the antidote of exchanging self for others. Strive in this way until finally self-grasping no longer arises. The Great One of Oḍḍiyāna, Padmasambhava, has stated:

Dharma practitioners seldom acknowledge being tempted
by demons. Yet those with powers are tempted by the demons
of pride and arrogance; the mighty are tempted by the demons
of flattery and manipulation; the undiscerning are tempted
by the demons of ignorant thinking; and the rich are tempted
by the demons of wealth and possessions.

All are tempted by the demonic wish to increase their resources
for practicing the Dharma. Many experience the demonic
temptation to propagate their genes. Others are tempted
by the demonic admiration of disciples and attendants.
Many are tempted by the demonic love of friends and intimates.
Some are tempted by the demon of revenge
in the face of hated enemies.

There is temptation by the demons of admiring relatives;
temptation by the demons of sweet words and smooth talk;
temptation by the demons of the mind's hankering
and attachment. There is the temptation of demonic yearning
for love and beauty. There is the demonic temptation
to expend great effort in senseless activities.

When the five poisons abide in you, that is the demon of mind.
When you are predisposed towards the six objects of the senses,
those are outer demons. Attachment to the experience of samādhi
is an inner demon. Hope for the fruit of the Great Perfection

is a demon of view. Magnificent qualities can also be demons,
and ignorance is a demon as well. But the greatest demon
is that of holding to a self. This demon is not some other person,
but arises within you yourself. If you destroy this inner demon,
the demons that come from without will not arise.
But so many people do not recognize the inner demon!

Dharma practitioners must cut off the root of the five poisons.
Hatred causes people to suffer greatly. Delusion causes people
to become like animals, so that they cannot even comprehend
the Dharma. Pride causes people to have many enemies,
even if their other qualities are untainted. Attachment
causes people to go through periods of great elation
and depression, so that they are unable to control themselves.
Jealousy causes people to have strong ambition and to delight
in suspicion. Do not let yourself be swayed by these five poisons;
seek to destroy them from within as you seek to liberate beings.
People who delight in the activities of the five poisons
attain only misery for themselves.

Dharma practitioners must tame their consciousness.
They must put out the fire of hatred with the water of love.
They must cross over the river of attachment on the bridge
built with the strength of the antidotes. They must light up
the darkness of ignorance with the lamp of awareness.
They must overturn the rocky mountain of pride with the lever
of effort. They must escape from the red tide of jealousy
by donning the lifejacket of patience. Remember: If you lose
yourself in the delights of the five poisons, your consciousness
will be corrupted. Exult in not giving in to any of the five poisons.

*Do not be complacent.*

When you show kindness to your opponents, do not feel smug
about it: To cherish others is your meditation. Even if you have been
practicing the Dharma with skill and reverence for years, it is senseless to brag about the time you have spent and the hardships you
have undergone for others. That is your purpose for practicing. Do
not trade boasts with others. In the words of Radrengpa: "Do not set
great hopes on human beings; pray to the holy ones."

Śāntideva stated:

Truly, even while acting for the welfare of others,
do not become proud or think yourself special.
Delight in the welfare of others alone—
and have no expectations for the fruit of your actions.
    —*Entering the Bodhisattva Path, 8.109*

*Do not give in to irritation.*

Do not harbor jealous thoughts towards others. Should others humiliate you publicly or cause you harm, do not retaliate in kind— you need to give up such mental agitation. Thus, Entering the Bodhisattva Path states:

There is no evil like hatred,
no challenge like patience.
Therefore you must meditate in myriad ways,
striving constantly for patience.

Bearing the painful thoughts of hatred,
the mind never experiences peace.
You find no joy or happiness:
When you feel so unstable, even sleep will elude you.

Even a master depended on
for profit and prosperity
will always find his life in jeopardy
if he is full of hatred.

When you are filled with hatred,
friends and loved ones have misgivings;
they will not trust you, even if you give them gifts.
In short, for one full of anger, no joy exists.

The enemy, anger,
gives rise to actions that lead to suffering.
Those who steadfastly conquer anger
will be happy in this life and in all lives to come. [6.2–6]

Putowa stated:

When those of us who follow the Dharma do not activate
the antidotes to self-grasping, we are as easily inflamed

as the tender flesh of a healing wound. Annoyance flares up
as readily as sparks on tinder. As this mental state is ineffective
for Dharma practice, we need to practice the antidotes
to counter self-grasping.

*Never be temperamental.*

Do not upset your friends by showing pleasure or displeasure at
every little thing. Regarding this, Śāntideva states:

Stop being gloomy, stop frowning;
always show a smiling face.
Be sincere and a friend to all.

Do not be inconsiderate and make loud noises;
do not toss chairs and things about;
do not slam doors or open them loudly.
Always delight in peace and quiet.

The stork, the cat, the thief
slip silently about
to achieve whatever they desire.
The Muni also acts in such a way.

Humbly accept
even unsolicited help from
those skilled in advising others;
always act like a student of all.

To all who speak the Dharma well,
give credit: "How fine your words!"
When you see virtuous actions,
be pleased and give great praise.

Quietly speak of the good qualities of others,
and hearing such qualities expressed, agree at once.
If your own good qualities are spoken of, do not take it personally,
but hear it as praise of good qualities alone.

Virtue commenced is indeed a joy,
rare even if it could be bought.
Truly there is joy in being happy
for the good done by others.

Acting in this way, I will lose nothing in this life,
and will have great happiness in the next.
　　　—*Entering the Bodhisattva Path*, 5.71–78

*Do not look for thanks.*

Do not hope for words of thanks from others for your help, for your practice of the Dharma, for your virtuous actions, or for anything at all. Thus, Śāntideva states:

Having acted for the benefit of others in some way,
do not consider it so wonderful.
When you feed yourself food,
do you hope for anything in return?
　　　—*Entering the Bodhisattva Path*, 8.116

In short, give up hoping for any honor or admiration. The Great One of Oḍḍiyāna, Padmasambhava, said about this:

To think you can generate the enlightened mind
without abandoning harm to sentient beings is senseless.
To consider taking initiations when unable to live up
to other commitments is senseless. To listen to teachings
that do not benefit your own mind is senseless. To perform
virtuous actions polluted by wickedness is senseless.
To follow a Lama but always associate with sinful people
is senseless. To perform work that promotes the eight worldly
concerns is senseless. To rely on your inner spiritual development
yet feel hatred towards your parents is senseless. To speak of
the horrors of hell when your actions are exceedingly non-virtuous
is senseless. To give gifts that are unsustained by faith
and the enlightened mind is senseless. To guard your moral
practice when you are not sustained by thoughts of renunciation
is senseless. To trust a thin veneer of patience unsupported
by the strength of the antidotes is senseless. To depend on
meditation when you are always overwhelmed by either
sluggishness or excitement is senseless. To take great pains
when you are not on the path of enlightenment is senseless.
To attempt to generate wisdom when you direct
your actions towards extending the five poisons is senseless.

To attempt to follow the Great Vehicle and yet set yourself apart
from the path of compassion is senseless.

To practice meditation that is not realized as mind itself
is senseless. To learn instructions that you do not practice
is senseless. To attempt to act for the welfare of beings
without the support of the enlightened mind is senseless.
There are many senseless activities that no one needs to do,
yet foolish people do not hear this.

Again he stated:

A Dharma practitioner must practice restraint or four things
will never come to be. Unless you keep death in mind, the time
will never come when you obtain the Dharma. Unless you
believe in cause and effect and thus give up non-virtue, the time
will never come for you to gain liberation and the higher states
of being. Unless you generate Bodhicitta for the sake of sentient
beings—seeking instead to gain liberation and freedom
for yourself alone—the time will never come for you
to gain the perfection of a Buddha. Unless you turn your mind
away from activities of this life, the time will never come
for you to abide in the genuine Dharma.
Thus do not give in even a little to the worldly mind.

As a Dharma practitioner, you must put your heart into whatever
you do. A body without a heart is useless; to give it heart, guard
pure moral practice. Enjoyments that lack heart are senseless;
to give your actions heart, perform true sacrifice by generating
the mind of giving. Right conduct without heart is worthless;
to give your attempts at virtue heart, accumulate merit
as the cause and wisdom as the result. Learning without a heart
is worthless; to give it heart, strive to apply what you learn
in your practice. Truly, if you do not know how to put your heart
into what you do, your conduct is only the action of this world.

A Dharma practitioner must be faultless in five ways.
You must protect yourself by being faultless in the moral practices
you take up and in guarding your commitments. Be faultless
at all times in meditating on the mind of enlightenment, love,
and compassion. Avoid even the most minute wrongdoing

by faultless contemplation on the cause and effect of karma.
Be faultless in your meditation on the Lama as the Buddha,
and always visualize your Lama on the crown of your head.
Be faultless in your meditation of all dharmas as śūnyatā:
Realize everything as being unified.

A Dharma practitioner must practice from the standpoint
of the Six Pāramitās. When you are never tempted
to fall sway to greed, that is the pāramitā of giving.
When you dismiss all emotionality through skillful means,
that is the pāramitā of moral practice. When you are never angry
or spiteful, that is the pāramitā of patience. When you are never
lazy or lethargic, that is the pāramitā of effort. When you are
unattached to the taste of either mental distraction or meditation,
that is the pāramitā of meditation. When you are free
from conceptual confusion, that is the pāramitā of wisdom.

Dharma practitioners adhere to spiritual practice in three ways.
The lower type of practitioners adhere to practice for the purpose
of gaining a high state of being in a future life. As they never strive
for anything else, they are sure to obtain that high state of being.
The middling type of practitioners adhere to the practice of virtue
due to their disillusionment with all samsara: They are sure
to attain liberation. The highest type of practitioners
adhere to the practice of the enlightened mind for the purpose
of all sentient beings: They thus obtain perfect enlightenment.

I have quoted these teachings extensively, for they are vital for understanding the meaning of the scriptures. Through these teachings,
practitioners can increase the effectiveness of their self-mastery and
prevent its degeneration.

In summary, Gyalsay Rinpoche has stated:

For as long as you live, develop confident practice.
Purify yourself from the standpoint of the two aspects
of enlightened mind, both during practice and in its aftermath.

Always strive to follow such instructions.

## Knowing the Path of Openness and Compassion

The eye of the skilled physician sees whether
a substance is useful as a medication.
Similarly, if you know the path of openness and compassion,
you know which paths of action assist in virtue and which do not.

Whatever is produced by various actions and conditions
formed by inharmonious factors is like a heap of burning embers.
To extinguish this fire, the lucid peace
of the precepts for self-mastery rains down.
No other antidote equals this.

For those attentive and mindful, circumspect and diligent,
this peace is a true companion, the best of teachers:
With it you will never again be subject
to the downfall of the defilements,
and you will come to hold in your hand
all the virtuous dharmas.

Whoever realizes well that all dharmas are like an illusion,
though wealthy, will never be proud;
though enmeshed in difficulties, will never be disheartened.
Those with such a mind are suitable to be praised by all.

The ornament of precious modesty and restraint,
supreme in this world, is as exquisite as the face of the sun.
The noble-minded will never support views
that contradict their commitments;
they will even sacrifice their life to keep their vows.

Though you are accustomed to the emotions,
difficult to reverse by the antidotes,
see the emotions as your enemy
and take up the antidotes as weapons.
From the first, generate the strength of the antidotes:
You will then defeat the emotions,
for they will have no way to advance.

The true spiritual friend, teaching the finest path,
is the enlightened mind of self-discipline,
the basis of all the best qualities.

It produces the finest actions, assists in virtue,
and is the cause for the holy
proceeding to the highest liberation.

Powered by the sun of spiritual longing,
drawn by the golden horse Devotion,
it will carry you along the path of the Great Vehicle
to the palace whose battlements are the three vows.

There, in the radiant, blossoming lotus garden of liberation,
beneath a sky free from the dark clouds of hindrances,
you will always be attuned to the enlightened mind:
like the sky, vast and overarching;
like the great ocean, unfathomable in depth;
like the sun and moon, shining down impartially on all.

There you naturally feel sympathy for the wayward,
like a mother for her sick child.
This is the highest service of the Holy Ones:
their natural engagement and their vital duty.

Riding the steed of the light rays of this sun,
you need not ever again depend on other conditions.
Accordingly, those who are wise abide in enlightenment
and are never agitated by good or bad situations.

But those who do not apply themselves continually in the present,
who are careless, agitated, giving no time to practice,
will find their conduct dwindling into meaningless activities.
Right now it is imperative: Practice profound one-pointedness!

Those who do not strive for the Dharma that endures
will increasingly rush into the anguish of certain destruction.
Thus you must abandon forever the six mistakes
that lead to misplaced concentration and application.

Whoever wastes time, dallying with flighty mind
and touching on too many things, has cause to be wearied.
Best to carry to completion whatever you commence:
To do this, diligently direct yourself
one-pointedly through all hardships.

Bring into your stream of consciousness
the minute investigation of all things.
If you do not now subdue self-grasping and emotionality,
everything needful will be scattered and lost.
The ivy that grows from the root of samsara
must be destroyed to keep from spreading.

In order to obtain the finest fruit of liberation, you must
undergo hardships to help the Dharma benefit others.
These efforts are for your own benefit as well:
Whoever you are, stop thinking of yourself!

The fire of anger consumes the fuel of virtue,
while the rain of patience helps the shoots of liberation grow.
Therefore, confronted by whatever others do in error,
let your consciousness be happy and peaceful and never disturbed.

Like the movements of a dancer, naturally flowing,
hundreds of changes occur in each moment.
They cause agitation to arise; they bring distress to friends.
Therefore, be full of inner calm and peace.

Desire for the demonic offerings of gain, fame, and praise
lead you to fall away from the genuine Dharma.
Therefore, never long for the appreciation of others:
It is crucial not to undermine the Bodhisattva conduct.

Called by the drumbeat of lofty exhortations,
let the youthful peacocks,
close friends with a common interest, gather.
Well satisfied with the brilliant display,
shining expression of pure action,
they transmute all into the great drama
of benefiting self and other.

This completes the section
on the main practice of self-mastery.

## Conclusion

The karmic energy of previous practice, awakened,
led me to be greatly inspired.
Disregarding suffering and insults,
I requested the precepts for subduing self-grasping.
Now when I die, I will have no regrets.

These instructions are the quintessence of nectar,
the heritage of Serlingpa.
Through them, the five degenerations,
ever intensifying in this degenerate age,
are transformed into the path of enlightenment.

Due to the degeneration of these times, physical resources decline. People have little chance to savor the fruits of the earth, for harvests do not ripen in a timely fashion, and vast numbers of people are wretched and impoverished. Due to the degeneration of sentient beings, the physical body declines: People are prone to many illnesses and have little strength. Due to the degeneration of the life-force, life grows short: The length of life declines in stages from one hundred years to ten. Due to the degeneration into emotionality, the virtue of householders declines: The five poisons spread and increase. Due to the degeneration of view, the virtue of monks declines: Monks are attracted to the extremes of eternalism and nihilism.

As these five degenerations intensify, everything conducive to happiness grows weak, and everything that works against humanity and is disagreeable proliferates and grows strong. Under these conditions, antidotes based on other teachings are ineffective. But those who wisely practice self-mastery can strengthen their virtuous activity even as they encounter adverse circumstances, like a fire whose flames increase as more fuel is added.

All adverse conditions and emotions can be transformed into the path of enlightenment. No other teaching so specifically benefits everyone: those of greater or lesser abilities alike. Because these instructions touch your very nature, they are like the essence of nectar. Such are the profound teachings transmitted in the lineage of Lord Serlingpa, the kindest of Lord Atīśa's principal Lamas.

It is said that if you understand self-mastery, the City of Happiness arises. And that City is said to be the body attuned to self-mastery. Self-mastery brings with it all the benefits of samsara and of nirvana, for both self and others. Mingling together all practices, it joins the Dharma with the mind, and in so doing, it is certain in the end to purify the mind. You will then quickly bring to completion the perfect benefit of both self and others.

The karmic energy of previous practice, awakened,
led me to be greatly inspired.
Disregarding suffering and insults,
I requested the precepts for subduing self-grasping.
Now when I die, I will have no regrets.

When the most virtuous of spiritual teachers, Chekhawa himself, awakened the energy of his previous karma, he was wholly inspired by this teaching. He underwent great hardships for this root of all the Dharma, these precepts that subdue the self-grasping of the mind. Having requested the transmission of the father-son lineage of Lord Atīśa, he practiced these teachings well, taking them to heart. Thus he was able to develop complete disregard for his own welfare, so that his only desire was to cherish others more than himself. By achieving the final fruit, the objective of entering the door of the Dharma, he obtained true confidence, and was truly without regrets.

This great spiritual friend, Chekhawa, bastion of the Nyingma lineage, was called Yeshe Dorje, Diamond of Wisdom. He embodied knowledge of both Old and New lineages and their qualities, and drew out the deep meaning of the teachings.

One day, while visiting the lodgings of Geshe Chagshingpa, Chekhawa saw a small book on a pillow. He saw it but once: a teaching that said, "Give every gain and victory to others; take upon yourself all their troubles and difficulties."

Having understood immediately the wonderful implications of this teaching, he asked Geshe Chagshingpa for its source. "This book is the Eight Verses of Self-Mastery by Lang Tangpa," he was told.

"Well then, who has these teachings?"

"Only Geshe Lang Tangpa has them."

Chekhawa realized that he must go in search of that master, and went at once to Lhasa. After circumambulating the main temple for some days, he came upon a leper who told him where Lang Tangpa could be found. But when he went there and inquired, he was told, "Lang Tangpa has passed away."

"Who then holds the seat of his main teaching?" he asked.

"There are two claimants," he was told. "One is a practitioner of the Sūtrayāna, a Dodaypa, and the other is a Zhang Zhungpa. They are not in agreement as to the teachings or as to who has the correct lineage."

Chekhawa then overheard the two pretenders talking together. The Zhang Zhungpa was saying to the Dodaypa, "As you are the elder, I ask you to give me the seat. For I am the only one who can provide teachings identical to those of Lang Tangpa."

The Dodaypa also requested to be given the seat. "Due to your great virtue, I ask you to give the seat to me. I am no different from Lang Tangpa, and carry on his teachings."

Even though both men otherwise appeared to be faultless, Chekhawa realized that their disagreement as to who should hold the seat of the teachings showed that neither of them possessed the teachings he was searching for. He then asked the monks in the area which of Lang Tangpa's disciples was the strongest in practice, and was told that it was Sharawa. And so he went to meet him.

Chekhawa found Sharawa teaching thousands of monks. Every day he would read from the scriptural texts and then explain the teachings. For some days Chekhawa listened to the teachings, but not a single phrase did he hear concerning the teachings he was searching for. As he had no way to tell whether or not Sharawa had this teaching, he decided to question him personally. If he had the teaching he would stay; if not, he would leave.

Early the next day he went to where Sharawa was circumambulating a stupa. He spread his robe as a seat for the teacher, and then asked Sharawa to sit a while, indicating that he had some questions to ask. Sharawa said to him, "What more do you want? What don't you understand in the teachings I have given?"

Chekhawa replied, "I have seen a teaching that states: 'Give every gain and victory to others; take upon yourself all their troubles and difficulties.' This struck a chord in me. Just how deep does this teaching go?"

"Whether you find this teaching captivating or not, if you wish to become a Buddha, following this teaching is the only way: There is no other."

"What is the scriptural source of this teaching?" Chekhawa asked again.

"The source is found in Nāgārjuna's teachings: the teachings that are not concerned with dialectics." And Sharawa quoted, "'May all wrongdoing ripen upon me; may all my virtues ripen upon others!' This must be practiced," Sharawa went on. "The lord Asaṅga also wrote:

If you do not actually exchange the suffering of others
for your own happiness,
you will not become a Buddha,
and you will be joyless in samsara as well.

"This point has been very clearly made."

"Well then," Chekhawa replied, "please give me the full instructions!"

Sharawa agreed to his request, stating, "You must remain with me for some time and not allow any adversity to get in your way."

And so Chekhawa stayed with Sharawa for six years, practicing only the teachings of self-mastery. Meditating on these teachings, a deep understanding of the destructive embrace of self-grasping arose.

Gyalsay Togmed said of Chekhawa, "He definitely obtained the path of seeing, and he was without even the smallest attachment to the individual path of liberation."

Chekhawa delighted all those who had the good fortune to listen to him with his teachings given in stages. By providing all who came before him what they requested, it is said that he illuminated the whole world like the sun and moon.

## Closing Verses

I prostrate myself with humility
at the feet of the Lama, Master of Siddhis.
In the sky of the Dharmadhātu, encompassing
the cloud of Omniscience and Mercy,
Khyentse radiates lightning flashes of joy
and benefit for beings.
He calls out in sweet, thunderous sounds
that pervade space in all directions,
and the cool rain of the Dharma
of the Supreme Vehicle streams down
to quicken the numberless seeds
in the realms of those to be trained,
sustaining the sprouts of liberation.

Ah! To have found such a friend,
as well as the marvelous foundation of freedom
and good fortune so difficult to attain!
This life is short and unpredictable;
through its sudden changes, nothing is certain.
Struck by the barrage of hundreds of afflictions
brought on by wrongdoing, I have been
perpetually anxious and in turmoil.
Now, making heartfelt effort to obtain emancipation,
I will achieve enlightenment!

From the beginningless beginning, all the dharmas
of samsara and nirvana are free from intellectualization,
radiant, balanced and compassionate;
yet through the error of ignorantly maintaining
subject and object, beings, like wild animals, enter a trap.
All these beings, their minds so wretched, are my parents,
who have shown boundless kindness.
To repay their kindness, I must gain understanding
of their actions, and with love and compassion,
I must learn to equalize self and other.

Giving to beings unstintingly all the virtues
of the three times and all enjoyments of my body;

fearlessly dealing with the source of their suffering,
taking it upon myself: This is indeed the cherished key
to the path of the Great Vehicle. There is no means
of gaining omniscience other than this.
Thus I must constantly attune myself
to the many ways of skillful means.

Renouncing the harmful intention that would delight
in my own welfare, I will cultivate great kindness for all.
Holding others more dear than myself, I will rely on generating
the relative mind of enlightenment and the ultimate mind as well,
through which illusory appearance displays itself as the Four Kāyas.
Through the matchless method of the four applications,
I will turn all detrimental circumstances
into aids for the path of genuine enlightenment.

From the ground of genuine determination, I will grow
this taproot into the branches and leaves of supreme practice,
until it matures into the great flowers and fruit
of the path of purification and accumulation.
Depending on the fruitful practice of the five powers
that extend outward the cooling canopy of prayer,
until I die I will overflow with the yield of the two purposes,
never sounding even a single disheartening word.

I will gather all understanding of the Dharma so well taught,
and expel from the land the evil spirit of self-grasping.
Many among the gods, though considered great,
have no shame. They believe in themselves as the ultimate—
as the creators of all life. But though their rapture flows,
they do not merge mind with the Dharma.
Even when distracted, may I devote myself
to the final measure of realization,
attuned to the supreme Muni.

Purified by the ketaka gem of alertness and mindfulness,
blemishes of wrongdoing are removed through the Three
Trainings. Undisturbed by the impressions made by evil deeds
brought about by carelessness and disruption, the impartial ocean
of the enlightened mind, moving with the hundred-thousand waves
of self-mastery, only benefits others.

Having given up the wretched mind that grasps at this existence,
I will guard with my life these commitments. Having given up
the desire for the eight worldly concerns—
gain and fame and the rest—I will attune myself
to only helping others, whether rich or poor, eminent or lowly.
Never giving up the teachings of the Bodhisattvas,
I will assist virtue however it appears.
In short, I will transform all my meditative action
into the path of the genuine Great Vehicle.

Here, where the earth burns with the fire of evil,
auspicious clouds will gather and pour down healing rain.
Watered by this refreshing rain of awe-inspiring virtues,
the mandarava flower of the gods will grow on the Isle of Peace,
untainted liberation. Traveling to that isle, the magnificent boat
of the Supreme Vehicle, made of precious gems,
churns the Ocean of Milk so that ghee is drawn forth.

Even if you have not truly trained your mind
and the fruit of spiritual experience has had no chance
to spring forth, the sound of thatness—no-mind—
will produce joy in all with minds, just as they are.
Thus I have gathered here, in condensed form,
the meaning of the teachings, based on the Lama's
instructions and the scriptures of sound reasoning.
Confessing to the wise all my faults in practice,
I have attempted to communicate the meaning of the teachings.

Alas! Though I have obtained a human body, free and fortunate,
meaningless worldly concerns toss me about.
Though the Holy Protector embraces me,
my lack of good qualities leaves me desolate.
Though I hear the deep and profound precepts,
my consciousness is like a stone on the ocean floor.
Alas! Will there ever come a time
when one such as I will gain freedom from all this?

White-haired, drooling like Yama but without his strength,
I can make only senseless whistling sounds.
My face reveals the violence of the Lord of Death in each wrinkle.
Swiftly, swiftly my life is passing, like water over a waterfall:

I cannot expect to stay more than a moment.
Not thinking to rest for an instant,
let me now quickly quickly withdraw into the forest!

In the forest, the fine phrases of the Victorious One
calm all quarrels, disturbance, and turmoil.
The birds and beasts, saying not a single disturbing word,
are my delightful companions. There in the forest,
free and joyous, my actions are unimpeded like the wind.
Even those with the wealth and power of the gods
rarely obtain such joy at life's end.
How could an ordinary being such as I see such bliss?

Self-evolved, an unchanging mountain cave
is as wondrous as the palaces of the gods—
a garden of joy, captivating as an abode of goddesses,
scarcely touched by the whirlwind of time:
There, surrounded by the sweet sound of waterfalls,
I will be strengthened by the food of joyful samādhi.
In such a place of hardships lies much satisfaction
and good fortune. Having proclaimed this,
may I take my body there!

With my own consciousness untrained, now is not the time
to train others. Alone in a place of solitude, when I have practiced
the essential meaning of the Great Vehicle, a time will come
when I can help beings throughout all the ages. May I then,
in each instant of life, liberate all beings from samsara!

May all that anyone could desire radiate from the peak
of the victory banner of explanation and practice,
crowned with the pristine doctrine of the Muni—
a fertile rain of happiness and benefit,
sparkling with millions of glorious virtues.
May this sign of virtue never fail: May it be always on the side
of goodness, guarded by the sheltering gods and nāgas,
protected by the glorious riches of the Dharma,
like the earthly city of hundreds of joys.

Unheralded by humanity so troubled by fear and suffering,
may I liberate all beings. May the glorious ocean of bliss

awaken even the beings in the highest realms
to the lineage of the supreme vehicle.

Generously upheld by the true spiritual friend,
mounted on the steed of both method and wisdom,
may I reach the supreme city of beginningless omniscience,
filled with joyous ease.

# Notes to Volume II

## Second Essential

1  These are the six preparatory practices described in the first volume. There is also a set of five practices known as the special preliminaries, usually presented as prerequisites for Vajrayāna practice. The five are as follows: 100,000 prostrations; 100,000 prayers for taking refuge and cultivating Bodhicitta; 100,000 prayers of Vajrasattva purification; 100,000 mandala offerings; and 100,000 prayers of Guru Yoga. *Jamgon Kongtrul's Retreat Manual*, translated by Ngawang Zangpo (Ithaca, NY: Snow Lion, 1994), links the special preliminaries to the practice of the Seven Essentials of Self-Mastery (the topics of this text), suggesting that the seven essentials should be taken up at the time of performing the 100,000 repetitions of refuge and Bodhicitta and should thereafter continue to form the basis for all practice.

2  The posture referred to here is known as the Seven Gestures. Seated on a cushion with legs crossed, place your hands together with the back of your left hand resting on your right palm, thumbs slightly touching, and hold them above your lap and just under the navel. (Or place hands lightly on the knees, palms down.) Keep the back straight, with the neck drawn back a bit. Allow the eyes to relax, about half open; let the mouth be slightly open, with the tip of your tongue lightly touching the palate.

3  For more information on the teachings of blo-rigs (teachings concerning the mind) see *Mind in Tibetan Buddhism* by Lati Rinbochey and

Elizabeth Napper (Ithaca, NY: Snow Lion, 1980). For more information on the teachings of khams-rigs and dus-tshod, see *Ways of Enlightenment* (Berkeley: Dharma Publishing, 1993), 130–31, 200–4.

4 Spiritual warmth comes in the second of the Five Paths, the Path of Linking. When it has developed, the practitioner attains the Path of Seeing that corresponds to the first of the Ten Stages of the Bodhisattva. See *Ways of Enlightenment*, chapter 42.

5 For a more detailed explanation of Buddhist cosmology, see chapter three of *Abhidharmakośabhāṣyam* (Berkeley: Asian Humanities Press, 1988–1990) and *Ways of Enlightenment*, chapter 29.

6 These lines are an amalgam of verses 91 and 93 of Letter to a Disciple.

7 The precious wheel is one of the seven treasures of the chakravartin king. This wheel is described in *The Voice of the Buddha* (Berkeley: Dharma Publishing, 1983), p. 30: ". . . the chakravartin king . . . having received royal consecration . . . sees the treasure of the divine wheel appear in the East, emitting a thousand rays, seven tāla trees in height, with circumference and hub all of gold . . . and the consecrated king reaches out his right hand to turn this divine wheel, proclaiming: 'Turn with the Dharma. . . .'"

8 Thirty-four Jātaka, or birth stories, can be found in *The Marvelous Companion* (Berkeley: Dharma Publishing, 1983).

9 "Place all blame on one source . . ." is the third element of the third essential.

10 Rlung, mkhris, and bad-gan correspond roughly to the early Western medical terms of wind, bile, and phlegm, indicating certain physical types and diseases.

11 The channels (rtsa, nāḍī) are the pathways along which the currents of the life-force (rlung, prāṇa) move. The main channels are the central channel (dbu-ma, avadhūti) and the right and left channels (ro, ida, and rkyang, piṅgala).

## *Third Essential*

12 The Buddha, in his previous lives as a Bodhisattva, sacrificed himself many times to help others. See *The Marvelous Companion*, pp. 241–47 for the story of the Sharabha deer who rescued a king trapped in a ravine.

13  Here a non-returner refers to a Bodhisattva on the path of seeing, the third of the five paths (mārga) and the level where the Bodhisattva enters the first of the ten stages (bhūmi), rather than to a practitioner on the third of the four paths of the Śrāvaka.

14  Development and completion (skyed-rim and rdzogs-rim) are the two main aspects of Vajrayāna practice. Uniting the skillful means of the development stage with the wisdom of the completion stage, one obtains complete enlightenment.

## Fourth Essential

15  See pp. 323–24 for more on this great Lama.

16  Ring-bsrel are small round objects, often white but also of other colors, found in the ashes of great practitioners. gDung relics are similar, but unlike ring-bsrel, are bonelike and unbreakable. Both types of relics are a sign of great spiritual realization.

## Sixth Essential

17  This is the story of the Nāga Elāpatra. In a former life as a bhikṣu at the time of the Buddha Kāśyapa, he cut down an Elāpatra tree, a variety of tree beloved by the Nāgas. For this act he was reborn as a Nāga named Elāpatra. When the Buddha Śākyamuni was teaching at Sārnāth, the Nāga Elāpatra stretched his body from his home in Taxila across the breadth of India to pay homage to the Buddha and ask how long he must remain a Nāga before regaining a human birth.

18  A dzo (mdzo) is the offspring of a yak bull and a common cow. This type of hybrid is known for its strength.

19  This refers to the great Master Nāgārjuna who received the teachings of the Prajñāpāramitā from the Nāgas.

20  This passage is found in the Gaṇḍavyūha, the final chapter of the Avataṁsaka Sūtra. Here Maitreya, the future Buddha, is praising the youth Sudhana, who has been seeking the practice leading to supreme enlightenment.

21  In the Śrīsambhava-vimokṣa-sūtra section of the Gaṇḍavyūha, Śrīsambhava speaks in detail of the characteristics required of both a teacher and a student.

22 Formal study of Buddhist philosophy in Tibet develops within five major topics: the Vinaya, based on the Prātimokṣa as explicated in the commentaries of Guṇaprabha; Abhidharma, based on the Abhidharmakoṣa of Vasubandhu and the Abhidharmasamuccaya of Asaṅga; Prajñāpāramitā, as systematized in the Abhisamayālaṁkāra of Maitreya, its commentaries, and the work of Haribhadra; Mādhyamika, based on texts by Nāgārjuna and Candrakīrti; and Logic, based on the Pramāṇasamuccaya of Dignāga and the Seven Treatises of Dharmakīrti, primarily the Pramāṇavārttika.

Study in the Nyingma tradition begins with instruction in the sDom-gsum, the Three Commitments of the Vinaya, the Bodhisattva-yāna, and the Mantrayāna. The practices of this training include meditation to develop inner calm and clarity. Specific meditative practices involve visualization and mantra, analytic practice, and awareness of the breath. Students then study the Bodhicaryāvatāra (Entering the Path of Enlightenment), the renowned work by Śāntideva that focuses on Bodhicitta and practice of the six pāramitās as the foundation of the Bodhisattva path. In *Path of Heroes,* Zhechen Gyaltsab quotes extensively from this important Mahāyāna teaching.

# Tibetan References

# Tibetan Text List

ༀ།། ཐེག་པ་ཆེན་པོའི་བློ་སྦྱོང་གི་དཀར་ཆག།

ༀ། །ཁམས་པ་ཆེན་པོ་གཡོན་རུ་རྒྱལ་མཚོག་པ་དང་། གྱུས་པ་ཆེན་པོ་དཀོན་
མཆོག་རྒྱལ་མཚན་པ་དཔོན་སློབ་གཉིས་ཀྱིས་ཐེག་པ་ཆེན་པོ་བློ་སྦྱོང་གི་རྒྱ་གཞུང་བོ་
གཉེན་ཞིན་ཏུ་གཅེས་པ་རྣམས་ཕྱོགས་ག་ཅིག་ཏུ་བསྐྲིགས་པའི་བུ་སྟེ་འཛིན་པ་ལེགས་པའི་
དཔེ་ཚན་གྱི་རྣམ་གྲངས་ལ།། རྗེ་བོ་རྗེ་རྒྱལ་གྱི་དངུལ་རྟེ་ཐར་བསྐུལ་པའི་རྣམ་ཐར་
འགྲོ་མགོན་གྱི་གམ་མཛད་པ། རྗེ་བོ་བཅུག་མེད་གསེར་སྦྱིང་པ་དང་ཨཱལ་བའི་རྣམ་ཐར།
བློ་སྦྱོང་དོན་བདུན་མའི་གཞུང་མཚན་ཡོང་པ་གཅིག མེད་པ་གཅིག བློ་སྦྱོང་དོན་
བདུན་མའི་གྲེལ་པ། བློ་སྦྱོང་མཚན་ཚན་འོར་གོ། བློ་སྦྱོང་ཚིག་དགའ་འཛོམས།
གྲུར་སྐྱམ་རྗེ་རྗེའི་སྐུ། བྱམས་པའི་རྣམ་འཕོར་བཔའི་བློ་སྦྱོང་། བློ་སྦྱོང་ཤེམས་དཔའི་
རིམ་པ། ཤེམས་དཔའི་རིམ་པ་ལས་རང་རྒྱུན་དན་པ་སྐྲ་དབབ་པ། ཤེམས་དཔའི

རིམ་པ་ལས་ཟག་བཅས་དགེ་བའི་སྟོབས་བསྐྱེད་པ། གསེར་གླིང་པས་ཇོ་བོ་ལ་མཐའ་འཁོབ་འདུལ་བའི་ཆེད་དུ་གནང་བའི་བློ་སྦྱོང་། ཉོན་མོངས་ལམ་དུ་སློང་བའི་མན་ངག བླ་མའི་རྣལ་འབྱོར། ཐེག་ཆེན་མཁོན་སྦྱོང་། ཇོ་བོ་ལ་རྣལ་འབྱོར་མ་གཉིས་ཀྱིས་སེམས་སྦྱོངས་ཤིག་ཅེས་གནང་བའི་བློ་སྦྱོང་། ཀུ་སུ་ལུའི་ཚོགས་གསོག སྐྱིད་སྡུག་ལམ་ཁྱེར། སུམ་པ་ལོ་ཙཱ་བ་ལ་མཁའ་འགྲོ་མས་གནང་བའི་བློ་སྦྱོང་། །ཀུན་ཏུ་བཟང་པོའི་བློ་སྦྱོང་། བློ་སྦྱོང་ཤུན་བརྒྱད་མ། ཟས་ལ་བརྟེན་པའི་བློ་སྦྱོང་། དབུགས་ལ་བརྟེན་པའི་བློ་སྦྱོང་། ལུས་གང་གཱ་ཀླུང་གི་བྱེ་མ་སྙེད་དུ་སྤྲུལ་ནས་རིགས་དྲུག་གི་སྡུག་བསྔལ་དང་དུ་ལེན་པའི་བློ་སྦྱོང་། ཤ་ཁྲག་ལ་བརྟེན་པའི་བློ་སྦྱོང་། གཏོར་མ་ལ་བརྟེན་པའི་བློ་སྦྱོང་། འབྱུང་བ་ལ་བརྟེན་པའི་བློ་སྦྱོང་། ལུས་ཡིད་བཞིན་ནོར་བུར་བསྒྱུར་བའི་བློ་སྦྱོང་། འཆི་ཁ་མའི་བློ་སྦྱོང་། གེགས་སེལ་བློ་སྦྱོང་། མ་འོངས་པའི་འགལ་རྐྱེན་སྔོང་བའི་བློ་སྦྱོང་། ཇོ་བོའི་བློ་སྦྱོང་དོན་བདུན་མ། མཆིམས་ཀྱི་བློ་སྦྱོང་། བི་རཱུ་པའི་བློ་སྦྱོང་། རྣམ་དག་གཙུག་གི་ནོར་བུལ་གནང་བའི་བློ་སྦྱོང་། བློ་སྦྱོང་ཚིག་རྐང་བརྒྱད་མ་ལོ་རྒྱུས་དང་བཅས་པ། གླང་ཐང་པའི་ཚིག་རྐང་བརྒྱད་མའི་འགྲེལ་པ། ཨ་ཏི་ཤ་ལ་གསེར་གླིང་པས་མཐའ་འཁོབ་འདུལ་བའི་ཆེད་དུ་གནང་བའི་བློ་སྦྱོང་། ཐེག་པ་ཆེན་པོའི་བློ་སྦྱོང་ཞེས་པའི་དཔེ་ཚན་གཅིག ཞང་རཏྣ་གུ་རུའི་ཚོགས་ཆོས་ཆེན་མོ། ཡང་དགོན་པའི་བློ་སྦྱོང་། རྟེན་འབྲེལ་སྙིང་པོའི་ཁྲིད་ཡིག་རྣམས་བཞུགས་སོ།། །སརྦ་མངྒ་ལཾ།

# Tibetan Text Outline

༄༅།། །།དཔལ་སྟོན་འགྲོ་རྗེ་ཀྱི་ཆོས་བསྐན་པ། འདི་ལས་ཚུར་ནད་སྒྲོས་ཏེ་

བ་ཁད་པ་ལ་གསུམ། །དཔལ་ལ་མ་ཀྱི་ཅུ་བ་བཤེས་གཉེན་བསྟེན་ཚུལ་དང་། །

གཉིས་པ་ལ་ལམ་ཀྱི་སྟོན་འགྲོ་དྲོས་ཉིད་བ་ཁད་པོ། །དེ་ལ་དཔོ་དཔལ་འབྲར་རྗེང་པར་

དགའ་བར་བསམ་པ། །འདི་ལ་ཁྲུས་པར་བྱེན་བཞི། །ལམ་བྱོར་ཆོས་བསྒན་བ། །

དེ་རྗེང་པར་དགའ་བའི་ཚུལ། །རྗེང་ན་དོན་ཆེ་བའི་ཚུལ། །རྗེང་དུས་ཐན་པ་སྐྱབ

བགོས་པར་བསམ་པ། །གཉིས་པ་ཚོ་མི་རྟག་པར་བསམ་པ། །འདི་ལ་གཉིས།

ཇི་ལྟར་བསྐོམ་པའི་ཚུལ། །དང་པོ་ལ་གཉིས། །སྐྱེར་འདུས་ཐམས་ཀྱི་རང་བཞིན་

བསམ་པ། །བྱེ་བྲག་ཏུ་འཆ་མི་རྟག་པ་ཉིད་བསྒོམ་པ། །གཉིས་པ་ལ་གཉིས། །

འཆི་བ་དགོ་ཕུགས་ས་བསྒོམ་པ། །དང་པོ་ལ་གསུམ། །ཁ་དག་རེས་པར་འཆི་བ་ལ་ཁྲུ

མཆན་གསུམ། །སྐྲ་མ་ཤི་བར་ཁུས་པ་མེད་བས་རང་ཡང་ངེས་པར་འཆི། །ལུས

འདུས་བྱས་ཡིན་པའི་ཕྱིར་ངེས་པར་འཆི། །ཚོལ་བསྒོན་པ་མེད་ཅི་དུས་སྐྲ་ཅི་གས་ཤོ

ཚིག་གིས་འཛིན་པའི་ཕྱིར་ན་ཡང་དོ ས་པར་འཆི༔    །གཉིས་པ་ནམ་འཆི་ཆ་མེད་པའི་

ཚུལ་ཀྱིས་འཆ ་བ་ལ་རྒྱ་མཚན་གསུམ༔    །ཚོལ་དོས་པ་མེད་པའི་ཕྱིར་འཆི བ༔    །

ལུས་ལ་སྙིང་པོ་མེད་པའི་ཕྱིར་འཆི བ༔    །འཆི་བའི་ཀྱེན་མང་བའི་ཕྱིར་འཆི བ༔

གསུམ་པ་ཚེ ས་ཀུ ་མི་སྟོ ས་པར་འཆ ་བ་ལ་རྒྱ་མཚན་གསུམ་པ༔    །ནས་ནོ ་ཀྱིས་མི་

སྟོ ས་པ༔    །གཉེན་བཤེས་ཀྱིས་མི་སྟོ ས་པ༔    །ད་གི་ལུས་ཀྱིས་མི་སྟོ ས་པ༔    །

མན་ངག་ཚོ ་ལུ་ལ་བརྟེ ་ནས་ནྱོ་སྟོ ་བ༔    །དེ་ལྟ ་བརྒྱ ས་པའི་ཐན་ཡོ ༔    །རྩ་བའི་

གསུམ་པ་ལས་རྒྱ འ་བས་སྐྱི ་ན་ཆ ་ལ་བསམ་པ༔    །བཞི་པ་འཁོ ་བའི་ཉེ ་ད མི གས་ལ་

བསམ་པ༔    །ཕྱི ་འཁོ ་བའི་སྱུ ་བསྟ ལ་ལ་བསམ་པ༔    །ད ་པོ ་ད ག་གཉེ ་ག ས་

ལུས་པོ ས་སྟོ ་ཐ མས ་ཅ ་དོ ས་མེ ་ད ་འགྱུ ་བས་སྱུ ་བསྟ ལ་བའི་ཉེ ས་ད མི གས

གཉེ ས་པ་མཐོ ་ ོ ས་ད ་ད ན་ ོ ་ལ་ ོ གས་པའི་བ ེ་སྱུ ་གི་ ན ་པ་ ེ་ཚ ་ ྱྱུ ་ཡ ༔

ོ ས་བ ་ད ་སྱུ ་སྱུ ་མེ ་བ འི་ཉེ ས་བ༔    །གསུམ་པ་ལུས་ཡ ་ཡ ་འ ོ ་བའི་ཉེ ས་ བ༔    །

བཞི་བ་ཡ ་ཡ ་ཉི ་མ ཆ མས་སྟོ ་བའི་ཉེ ས་བ༔    །ལྔ་བ་ཡ ་ད ་ཡ ་ད ་མ ོ ་

ད མ ་ད ་འགྱུ ་བའི་ཉེ ས་བ༔    །ད ག་བ་ག ཅི ག་ ུ ་ ོ ག ས་མེ ་ བ ས་སྱུ ་བ ྱུ ལ་ བའི་

ཉེ ས་པ༔    །གཉི ས་པ་ ི་ བ ག་ ུ ་ དོ ག ས་ད ག་ ོ ་ བོ འི་སྱུ ་བ ྱུ ལ་ལ་བསམ་པ༔    །

ད ་བོ ་ད མྱ ལ་བའི་སྱུ ་བ ྱུ ལ་ལ་བསམ་པ༔    །གཉི ས་པ་ཡི ་ད ག ས་ཀྱི་སྱུ ་བ ྱུ ལ་ལ་

བསམ་པ༔    །གསུམ་པ་ད ད ་འ ོ འི་སྱུ ་བ ྱུ ལ་ལ་བསམ་པ༔    །བཞི་བ་མ ོ ་རི ས་མི ་

ཡི ་སྱུ ག ་བ ྱུ ལ་ལ་བསམ་པ༔    །ལྔ་བ་ལྷ ་མི ན ་ཡི ན ་ཀྱི ་སྱུ ག ་བ ྱུ ལ་ལ་བསམ་པ༔    །

ད ག ་པ་ལྷ ་ཡི ་སྱུ ག ་བ ྱུ ལ་ལ་བསམ་པ༔    །གསུམ་པ་ཁ ར་ བ ྱུ ང ་ ུ ་ ཏེ ་ལྟ ར་སྱུ ན ་པའི་

ཐབས་ཀྱི ་ཡ ན ་ལ ག ་འ ག ་འ ག ་འ ཤི ག ་བ ད ་ པ༔    །ཚ ་བའི ས་བ ཅ ད ་གཉི ས་པ་ད ོ ས་ག ཞི ་ བ ྱུ ང

ཆུབ་ཀྱི་སེམས་གཉིས་ལ་བློ་སྦྱོང་བ། དེའི་ཆལ་བཤད་པ་ལ་གཉིས། །དོན་དམ་

སེམས་བསྐྱེད་བསྒོམ་པ། །ཀུན་རྫོབ་ལ་སྦྱོར་དངོས་རྗེས་གསུམ། །ཀུན་རྫོབ་ལ་སྦྱོར་བ་ནི།།

ཝི་གནས་བསྐྱེད་པའི་དོན་དུ་རྟོག་པའི་གཉེན་པོར་བསྒོམ་པ། །ཀུན་རྫོབ་ལ། སྣང་ཁྱ

དང་པོ་ལ་འད། །གཟུང་བའི་ཡུལ་གཏན་ལ་དབབ་པ། །འཛིན་པའི་སེམས...

གཏན་ལ་དབབ་པ། །གཉིས་པ་གཉེན་པོ་ཉིད་གཏན་ལ་དབབ་པ། །གཉིས་པ

དངོས་གཞི་ལ། །ལུག་མཐོན་བསྐྱེད་པའི་དོན་དུ་གནས་ལུགས་གཏན་ལ་དབབ་པ། །

གཉིས་པ་ཝི་ལུག་རྲང་འཕྲེལ་བསྐྱེད་པའི་དོན་དུ་སྒོམ་མེད་ལ་འཛིན་མེད་དུ་བཞག་པ། །

གསུམ་པ་རྗེས། །གཉིས་པ་རྒྱུན་ཏོབ་བྱང་སེམས་བདག་གཞན་བརྗེ་བ་བསྒོམ་པ། །

དེ་ལ་གསུམ། །སྟོན་འགྲོ་ཁྱམས་སྐྱེད་རྗེ་བསྒོམ་པ། །དངོས་གཞི་བདག་གཞན་

བརྗེ་བ་བསྒོམ་པ། །རྗེས་དག་གསུམ་འགྲེཔར་བསྐུར་བ། །དངོས་གཞི་བྱང་ཆུབ་ཀྱི་

སེམས་ལ་བློ་སྦྱོང་བའི་རིམ་པ་བཤད་ཟིན། །རྒྱ་བཞིས་བཅད་གསུམ་པ་སྐྱེན་འན་བྱང་

ཆུབ་ལམ་དུ་བསྒྱུར་བ་ལ། །བསམ་སྦྱོར་གཉིས། །དང་པོ་བསམ་པ་ལ་ཡང་ཀུན་

འཛོབ་དང་། དོན་དམ་བྱང་ཆུབ་སེམས་ཀྱིས་སྐྱེན་འན་བྱང་ཆུབ་ཀྱི་ལམ་ལ་བསྒྱུར་བ། །

དང་པོ་ནི། །ཀུན་རྫོབ། །དོན་དམ་བྱང་ཆུབ་སེམས་སྒྲུས་པ་ལ་བརྟེན་ནས་སྐྱེན་འན་

བྱང་ཆུབ་ཀྱི་ལམ་ལ་བསྒྱུར་བ། །སྦྱོར་བ་ཁྱད་པར་ཅན་བསགས་སྲུང་གཉིས་ཀྱིས་སྐྱེན་

འན་ལམ་དུ་བསྒྱུར་བ། །རྒྱ་བཞིས་བཅད་བཞི་པ་ཚོ་གཅིག་གི་ཉམས་ལེན་རྟིལ་ནས་

བསྟན་པ་ལ་གཉིས། །ཚེའདིར་རྗེ་ཤུར་བྱ་བ། །འཆི་ཁར་རྗེ་ཤུར་བྱ་བ། །རྒྱ་བཞི

ས་བཅད་ལྔ་བ་བློའ་འཕྲོས་པའི་ཆད་བསྟན་པ། །རྒྱ་བཞིས་བཅད་དྲུག་པ་བློ་སྦྱོང་གི་

དམ་ཚིག་བསྟན་པ། །རྒྱ་བཞིས་བཅད་བདུན་པ་བློ་སྦྱོང་གི་བསླབ་བྱ་བསྟན་པ།། ॥

༄༅། བློ་སྦྱོང་དོན་བདུན་མ།

།དད་པོ་སྦྱོན་པ་ཁྲོ་དག་ལ་བསླབ་པ།

།དངོས་གནས་བུད་ཆུབ་ཀྱི་སེམས་སྐྱོང་བ།

།ཚོས་རྣམས་སྒྱུ་ལ་གཉུ་བུར་བསམ།

།ཨ་སྐྱེས་རིག་པའི་གཞིས་ལ་དཔུད་པ།

།གཉེན་པོ་ཉིད་ཀྱང་རང་སར་གྲོལ།

།དོ་པོ་གུན་གཞིའི་དང་ལ་བཞག

།ཐུན་མཚམས་སྒྱུ་མའི་སྐྱེས་བུར་བྱ།

།གཏོང་ལེན་གཉིས་པོ་སྤེལ་མར་སྦྱངས།

།དེ་གཉིས་རླུང་ལ་བསྐྱོན་པར་བྱ།

།ཡུལ་གསུམ་དུག་གསུམ་དགེ་རྩ་གསུམ།

།དེ་ལ་དྲན་པ་བསྐྱེལ་བའི་ཕྱིར།

།སྐྱིད་ལམ་ཀུན་ཏུ་ཚིག་གིས་སྤྲུངས།

།ལེན་པའི་གོ་རིམ་རང་ནས་བཅུག

༺

།སྐྱེན་ནས་བྱང་ཆུབ་ཀྱི་ལམ་དུ་བསྒྱུར་བ།

།སྒོང་བཅུད་སྲིག་ལས་གདང་བའི་ཚོ།

།སྐྱེན་ནས་བྱང་ཆུབ་ལམ་དུ་བསྒྱུར།

།ཡི་ལན་ཕབས་ཚད་ག་ཅིག་ལ་བདའ།

།གང་ལ་བསམ་པ་དེ་ཡོང་བ།

།དེ་ནི་དེ་ལ་དོན་ཀྱིས་ཞུགས།

།འཁྱལ་སྲུང་སྐྱ་བཞིར་བསྟུ་བ་ཡི།

།སྒོང་ཅིང་དསྲུང་བ་བླན་མེད།

།སྒྱིར་བ་བཞི་ལྡན་ཕབས་ཀྱི་མཚོ།

།འཁྱལ་ལ་གང་ཕབ་སྒོམ་དུ་སྒྱུར།

།ཆོག་ཅིག་གི་ཉམས་ལེན་རྩོལ་ནས་བསྐྲུན་པ།

།མན་ངག་སྙིང་པོ་མངོར་བསྒྲུབས་པ།

།སྟོབས་ལྔ་དག་དང་སྒྱུར་བར་བྱ།

།ཕྱག་ཆེན་འཕོ་བའི་གདམས་ངག་ནི།

།སྟོབས་ལྔ་ཉིད་ཡིན་སྒྱུད་ལམ་གཅེས།


།བློ་འབྱོངས་པའི་ཚད།

།ཆོས་རྣམས་དགོས་པ་གཅིག་ཏུ་འདུས།

།དཔང་པོ་གཉིས་ཀྱི་གཙོ་བོ་གཟུངས།

།ཡིད་བདེ་འབའ་ཞིག་རྒྱུན་དུ་བསྟེན།

།ཡེངས་ཀྱང་ཐུབ་ན་འབྱོངས་པ་ཡིན།

།བློ་སྦྱོང་གི་དམ་ཚིག

།སྐྱི་འོན་གསུམ་ལ་ཏ་ག་ཏུ་བསླབ།

།འདུན་པ་བསྒྱུར་ལ་རང་སོར་བཞག

།ཡན་ལག་ཉམས་པ་རྣམས་མི་བརྗོད།

།གཞན་ཕྱོགས་གང་ཡང་མི་བསམ་མོ།

།ཉིན་མོངས་གང་ཆེ་སྙོན་ལ་སྦྱང་།

།འབྲས་བུའི་བཐབས་ཅང་སྤང་།

།དུག་ཅན་གྱི་ཟས་སྤང་།

།གཞུང་བཟང་པོལ་བརྟེན།

།ཕག་དན་མ་སྒོམ།

།འཕྲང་མ་སྒྲུགས།

།གནད་ལ་མི་དབབ།

།མཆོ་ཞལ་སྐྱང་ལ་མི་འགྱོ།

།ཕྱི་ཕོག་མི་བྱ།

།མཆོག་གསུམ་ཀྱི་ཙེ་ལ་གཏོད།

།ཁྱེ་བ་དང་དུ་མི་དབབ།

།སྐྱིད་ཀྱི་ཡིན་ལ་གཤ་སྲུག་མཆོ།

།བློ་སྦྱོང་གི་བསླབ་བྱ་བསྟན་པའོ།

།ནལ་འབྱོར་ཐམས་ཅད་གཅིག་གིས་བྱ།

།ལོག་ནོན་ཐམས་ཅད་གཅིག་གིས་བྱ།

།ཐོག་མཐའ་གཉིས་ལ་བྱ་བ་གཉིས།

།གཉིས་པོ་གང་བྱུང་བཟོད་པར་བྱ།

།གཉིས་པོ་སྲོག་དང་བསྡོས་ནས་བསྲུང་།

།དགའ་བ་གསུམ་ལ་བསླབ་པར་བྱ།

།རྒྱུ་ཡི་གཏོ་བོ་རྣམ་གསུམ་བླངས།

།ཉམས་པ་མེད་པ་རྣམ་གསུམ་བསྒོམ།

།འབྲལ་མེད་གསུམ་དང་ལྡན་པར་བྱ།

།ཡུལ་ལ་ཕྱོགས་མེད་བགྲོད་སློང་ས།

།ཁྱབ་དང་གཏིང་འབྱུངས་ཀུན་ལ་གཅེས།

།བཀོལ་བ་རྣམས་ལ་ཏུག་ཏུ་བསྐོམ།

།ཀྲུན་གཞན་དགལ་འཕྱིས་མི་བྱ།

།དངེས་གཏུ་བོ་ཆུམས་སུ་བླང་།

།གོ་ཡོག་མི་བྱ།

།ཐེས་འཛོག་མི་བྱ།

།དོལ་ཆོད་དུ་བླང་།

།ཇོག་དགྱོད་གཉིས་ཀྱིས་ཐར་བར་བྱ།

།ཡུས་མ་བསྐོམ།

།ཁོ་ཡོང་མི་སྟོམ།

།ཡུད་ཚག་པ་མི་བྱ།

།འིར་ཆེ་བ་འདོད།

།སྟོན་སྣུངས་ལས་ཀྱི་འཕྲོ་སད་པས།

།རང་གི་མོས་པ་མང་བའི་རྒྱུས།

།སྒྲུབ་བསྒྲལ་གཏམ་དང་ཞེན་བསད་ནས།

།བདག་འཛིན་འདུལ་བའི་གདམས་ངག་ཞུས།

།དངེ་ཤི་ཡང་མི་འགྱུད་དོ།


།དབེ་དེ་དག་གི་མཐག་སྟུང་ཀྱི་ཚལ་དུ།

།སྤྲིགས་མལུ་པོ་བདོ་བའི།

།ཞུང་ཆུབ་ལས་དུ་བསྒྱུར་པ་ཡིན།

།མན་ངག་བདུད་ཙིའི་སྲིང་པོ་འདི།

།གསེར་སྒྱིང་པ་ནས་བརྒྱུད་པ་ཡིན།

# Four-Month Program

# A Four-Month Program
# for Study and Practice

*T*his program is designed to provide a flexible approach for those who wish to investigate the way of self-mastery but do not necessarily have access to a teacher. For this program, *Path of Heroes* will be your guide.

While this program will prove most effective if you follow a traditional schedule for practice, dividing the day into four or more practice sessions of two to three hours each, it can also be adapted for shorter periods. Try to allow at least four hours a day for meditation practice and one hour each day for reading and contemplation.

Take sixteen weeks in all to go through the text. However, if that is not possible, an hour of meditation a day can be effective, and even a week-long retreat that follows this model can have great benefit. Whatever your practice, between sessions reflect on the teachings and allow your meditation to extend into all your experience.

The program has been divided into eight sections: Four topics relate to the first two essentials, and four topics relate to the remaining five. This is in keeping with Zhechen Gyaltsab's advice that the beginner should focus primarily on the first two essentials.

To review the seven essentials:

1. The preliminary teachings: the foundation of Dharma practice
2. The actual practice of self-mastery: training in enlightened mind
3. Transforming adversity into the path of enlightenment
4. Making self-mastery your way of life
5. Measuring your progress in self-mastery
6. The commitments of practice
7. Basic teachings for self-mastery.

A list of suggested readings has been provided for each topic. It is not necessary to read all of the books suggested. Begin with readings that you find most appealing, and gradually broaden your reading into less familiar subjects. Incorporating readings from one of the Crystal Mirrors (*Light of Liberation, Lineage of Diamond Light*, or *Crystal Mirror VI*) into your daily or weekly program of study will help you develop a fuller perspective on the scope of the Buddhist traditions.

Full bibliographic information on books listed under Suggested Readings is given on pp. 598–601. Other fine books are available for many of these subjects, and you may find additional translations for specific Sūtras and śāstras. For the books suggested here you may wish to substitute readings on the same topics from books you already have at hand.

# Topic One:
# The Prerequisites

## Week One

### *Readings from Path of Heroes*

"Introduction," "Lineage of Compassion," "Overview of Meditation: Preparation," xv–19.

### *Contemplation*

The process of self-mastery begins with turning away from the ordinary samsaric preoccupations described in the text as the eight worldly concerns. Awakening the motivation to change priorities and to turn the mind toward enlightenment is the focus of the initial topic for practice.

Zhechen Gyaltsab suggests focusing on three topics to develop a new sense of the possibilities we have as human beings: the life of the Buddha, the scope of the teachings in time and space, and the availability of the Path of Heroes to us today.

Let the sweep of the possibility for enlightenment catch you up: Read the life of the Buddha and the history of the Sangha; remind yourself that you are the beneficiary of a tradition that has been handed down for more than 2,500 years. The great masters who have carried on this lineage have each overcome the inertia that typically channels human beings toward the repeating patterns of samsara. Each one of these masters, true heroes, rejected the dulling security of familiar patterns and generated the resolve to discover what has real and lasting value. You can do likewise.

## Suggested Readings

On the life of the Buddha: *Ways of Enlightenment*, 1–22; *Light of Liberation*, 37–147; *The Voice of the Buddha* (Lalitavistara Sūtra); *The Marvelous Companion* (a collection of Jātakas or birth stories).

On the history of the Dharma in India: *Light of Liberation*, 149–253, 278–413.

On the Three Turnings of the Wheel of the Dharma: *Ways of Enlightenment*, 23–100; *Crystal Mirror VI*, 27–36, 50–52; "The Questions of Paramārthasamudgata," in *Wisdom of Buddha*, 93–145; *The Nyingma School of Tibetan Buddhism*, 23–24, 28, 76, 151–55, 187.

On Bodhicitta: chapters 1–3 in the Bodhicaryāvatāra (see p. 598 for titles of specific translations); chapters 2, 7, 9, and 10 in *The Jewel Ornament of Liberation*, 14–29, 91–98, 112–49; chapter 8 in *Kindly Bent To Ease Us, Part One: Mind*, 123–47.

## Meditation

Meditation is essential for cultivating the sense of new possibilities. Basic meditative practices will help you to calm the mind and develop mental clarity, making it possible to relax the hold on samsaric ways of being and create favorable conditions for unfolding inner potential.

The text suggests how to prepare for meditation by creating a suitable place and time for practice. You will also want to become familiar with the meditation posture known as the Seven Gestures:

Sit on a cushion with your legs crossed, your hands held above your lap, just under the navel, with the left hand above the right, the thumbs slightly touching. If you prefer, the hands can also be placed lightly on the knees with palms down. Your back should be straight, with your neck drawn back a bit. Your eyes should be half open, and your mouth slightly open, with the tip of your tongue lightly touching the palate.

If sitting on a cushion is not comfortable, you may begin by sitting on a chair, making sure that your back is very straight. Sitting on a

cushion is preferable, however, as it is easier to develop stability in a seated position.

After a few minutes of sitting quietly, concentrate on relaxing every part of your body, including your eyes and the muscles of your face. When you feel relaxed, let your senses open; with each breath sink more deeply into relaxation until you begin to feel a warm and gentle flow of feeling coursing through your body. Let this feeling expand into the breath and into your thoughts.

Be aware of your breath as it flows in and out of your body.

Approach your meditation lightly, gradually extending the period of time that you sit in the meditation posture. When you grow restless or physically uncomfortable, you can vary the schedule by doing movement exercises such as those found in *Kum Nye Relaxation*. You may wish to try all of the exercises in Part One, including massage. The exercises done standing can be a good way to relieve the physical discomfort that can develop during long periods of sitting practice.

For the first week, focus on developing relaxation as a normal state of being. Indications of a shift toward relaxation include a sense of lightness in both mind and body and a feeling that awareness is settling deeper in the body. You may also notice your breath slowing down, or a sense of well-being or energy.

Initially, as you relax the mind and let go of ordinary mental activities, you may experience bouts of restlessness or anxiety. Whatever feelings arise, let them pass through you. Simply relax into the feelings and remain relaxed as long as possible, without letting this peaceful state become a source of attachment.

## Suggested Readings

On the Seven Gestures: *Kum Nye Relaxation, Part 1,* 26–28.

On relaxation: "Relaxation," in *Gesture of Balance,* 47–65; Exercises 1–8 and 20–24, in *Kum Nye Relaxation, Part 1*; Exercise A, in *Mastering Successful Work,* 243–47; "Relaxation," in *Skillful Means,* 19–22.

On beginning meditation: *Hidden Mind of Freedom,* 3–26; "Concentration," in *Skillful Means,* 29–33; *Gesture of Balance,* 69–77.

# Topic One:
# The Prerequisites

## Week Two

*Readings from Path of Heroes*

"The Spiritual Teacher," "Traits of the Spiritual Teacher,"
"Practicing Guru Yoga," 24–51.

*Contemplation*

Having considered your innate potential for enlightenment, contemplate the Buddhas and Bodhisattvas. Zhechen Gyaltsab urges us to reflect on the spiritual teacher. He also provides traditional forms for taking refuge and generating devotion to the guru.

In the Vajrayāna, formal devotional and ritual practices expressing appreciation for the Enlightened Ones play an essential role in opening the heart and mind. For Westerners, however, particularly those who have rejected organized religion, these practices can be difficult to understand or accept. It may be helpful to look at these practices as a way of opening the mind to the infinite possibilities lying within seemingly static outer forms.

The Bodhisattva, the Hero of Enlightenment, takes refuge placing foremost in mind the wish that all beings become enlightened. Refuge is fourfold: refuge in the Lama, as the embodiment of all the Three Jewels; refuge in the Buddha, as the principle of enlightenment; refuge in the Dharma, as the teachings that open the path to enlightenment; and refuge in the Sangha, as the community of those who travel the path with us.

To keep in mind the goal and purpose of enlightenment, those on the path of self-mastery begin every meditation session with the practice of taking refuge:

I take refuge in the Lama.
I take refuge in the Buddha.
I take refuge in the Dharma.
I take refuge in the Sangha.

Refuge may be followed by the Seven-Limbed Practice, a traditional way of creating and strengthening attitudes that nurture the development of enlightened mind. The seven limbs are:

1. Prostrations
2. Offerings
3. Confession
4. Rejoicing in virtue
5. Requesting the Buddha to turn the Wheel of Dharma
6. Requesting the Teacher to remain in the world
7. Dedicating merit.

The opening stanzas of Samantabhadra's Prayer for Enlightened Practice convey the spirit and significance of these practices. You may wish to begin each session of practice by reading or reciting these inspiring verses:

In all the worlds of the ten directions,
all the Buddhas, the lions of mankind,
course throughout the tides of time:
I bow to them all, with pure body, speech, and mind.

The powerful prayer of enlightened practice
presents all these Victorious Ones before my mind:
Reverently, with bodies as many as atoms of the Buddha-fields,
I respectfully bow to all these Victorious Beings.

Upon each single atom, Buddhas as numerous as atoms
are seated in the midst of the Buddha's offspring:
I envision the entire expanse of space
filled with Victorious Beings in this way.

With oceans of sound and rivers of melody,
with oceans of inexhaustible praise,
I celebrate the qualities of all the Victorious Ones—
and praise those gone to bliss.

Exquisite flowers and garlands,
sweet-sounding cymbals and scented oils,
the finest parasols and lamps, and fragrant incense,
I offer to those Victorious Ones.

Splendid robes and sweet-smelling perfumes,
medicinal powders piled high as Mt. Meru,
all the finest, rarest, and most exceptional arrays,
I offer as well to these Victorious Ones.

I offer these vast and incomparable gifts
to all the Buddhas, as I bow before them
in devotion to all the Victorious Ones
and with the force of my faith in enlightened practice.

Whatever wrongdoings I have done
with body, speech, or even mind,
through desire, hatred, or ignorance,
all these I separately confess.

Rejoicing in the merit of all beings,
I rejoice in the merit of all Buddhas of the ten directions;
of the Bodhisattvas; Pratyekabuddhas;
those on the stage of Learning
and on the stage of No More To Learn.

I implore all the Protectors illumining
the worlds of the ten directions
upon attainment of the non-attachment of the Buddha
through the stages of enlightenment,
to turn the incomparable Dharma Wheel.

To those who intend to demonstrate Nirvana,
I humbly beseech you with folded palms:
Stay for as many eons as there are atoms in the universe
for the sake of the happiness and benefit of all beings!

Even the slightest merit amassed
from my prostrations and offerings,
my confessions and rejoicing,
my entreaties and prayers,
I dedicate to the enlightenment of all beings.

Having honored all the Buddhas of the past,
and those who now abide in the worlds of the ten directions,
may those who have not yet come,
come swiftly to fulfill their aims,
and passing through the stages of enlightenment,
become Buddhas!

Each of the traditional seven limbs also has a basis in at least one of the Sūtras. Reading the Buddha's Sūtras also gives focus to practice. A partial list of Sūtras in translation can be found in the Bibliography (Appendix, 604–11).

## Suggested Readings

On the Guru: "Introduction," in *The Wish-Fulfilling Jewel*, 3–16; "Trusting the Inner Teacher," in *Gesture of Balance*, 163–70; chapter 6 of *Kun-zang La-may Zhal-lung, Part 1*, 189–228; chapter 3 of *The Jewel Ornament of Liberation*, 30–40; *Fifty Verses of Guru-Devotion*, 3–32.

On refuge: "Refuge," in *Openness Mind*, 141–45; chapter 6 in *Kindly Bent to Ease Us, Part One: Mind*, 90–105; "On Taking Refuge," in *Kun-zang La-may Zhal-lung, Part 2 and Part 3*, 231–64; chapter 8 of *The Jewel Ornament of Liberation*, 99–111; *Dakini Teachings*, 10–28.

On the Seven-Limbed Practice: footnote 54 and appendices in *The Great Path of Awakening*, 65, 77–84; *Kun-zang La-may Zhal-lung Part 2 and Part 3*, 265–366; chapter 2 of Part 2 of *The Tantric Mysticism of Tibet*, 147–68; Part 2 of *A Lamp for the Path*; *The Excellent Path to Enlightenment, Short Preliminary Practice*.

## Meditation

Once you are familiar with the traditional forms of refuge and the Seven-Limbed Practice, you may decide to begin your formal meditation sessions with these two practices.

Continue to incorporate relaxation exercises into your meditation until you become able to develop a balanced, relaxed state of mind. This will let you deepen your practice no matter what form it takes.

Do not be surprised if you experience periods of dullness, restlessness, or agitation. As you learn to relax and open the mind and body, a part of you may be reluctant to let go of what feels comfortable and familiar. Initial discomfort may simply be the result of focusing attention on a previously overlooked aspect of your experience; while engaging the unfamiliar in this intimate way can be disconcerting at first, you will soon note a new freshness and vitality emerging within your meditation.

As you continue with this practice, you will develop a sense of a shift that takes place when customary patterns of the mind slip away, signaling that you can go deeper with your practice. The more you practice, the more easily you will be able to enter this focused, concentrated, and quiet place, where the mind is more flexible and ready to take up specific meditative topics.

## Suggested Readings

On meditation: *Gesture of Balance,* 91–119; *Mahāmudrā,* 19ff.; *Openness Mind,* 40–64.

On simple devotional practices: "Prayer to Śākyamuni Buddha," in *Footsteps on the Diamond Path,* 144–47.

On Vajrayāna practices: "Ritual Practice: Entering the Mandala," in *Footsteps on the Diamond Path,* 168–74; commentary on Paltrul Rinpoche's Practice of View, Meditation, and Action in *Heart Treasure of the Enlightened Ones,* 56–146; chapters 2–5 in *The Torch of Certainty,* 29–132; *The Great Path to Awakening,* 3–9.

# Topic Two:
# Turning the Mind toward the Dharma

## Weeks Three and Four

### Readings from Path of Heroes

"Awakening to Freedom and Good Fortune," "Awakening to Impermanence," "Awakening to the Significance of Karma," "Awakening to Suffering in Samsara," 54–180.

### Contemplation

The preliminary practices are divided into two types: General Preliminaries and Special Preliminaries. The General Preliminaries are the Four Thoughts that turn the mind toward the Dharma: a precious human birth, impermanence, karma, and suffering in samsara.

In the light of the possibility of enlightenment and inspired by the presence of the Buddhas, Bodhisattvas, and teachers, focusing on these four thoughts develops determination to find a new way of being.

For weeks three and four, concentrate on these four themes of awakening. Contemplate each of these themes, after first settling the mind through basic meditative relaxation, taking refuge, and practicing guru yoga. (If you have no connection to a particular teacher or lineage, you may wish to visualize Śākyamuni Buddha or Guru Padmasambhava before you.)

Reflection on each of the four themes is intended to encourage you to make greater efforts in your practice. The quality of making effort is itself a practice that cultivates a steady mindfulness and alertness. Bring this alertness into every aspect of your practice, catching yourself each time your attention starts to wander.

## Suggested Readings

On the four preliminaries: chapters 1–6 in *The Jewel Ornament of Liberation*, 1–90; chapters 1–5 in *Kindly Bent to Ease Us, Part One: Mind*, 3–89; *The Excellent Path to Enlightenment;* chapter 1 in *The Torch of Certainty*, 29–52.

## Meditation

Awakening to freedom and good fortune:

In discussing this topic, Zhechen Gyaltsab includes cultivating faith in the Dharma. It is important to understand that this faith grows out of seeing with greater clarity. Here is a practice for developing such clarity, which you can repeat throughout the day:

1. Listen to sounds as they arise, without judgment and as much as possible without naming. Let the sounds penetrate deep inside you.

2. After relaxing the eyes, move the eyes gently across your field of vision, from left to right and then back, appreciating all that you see.

3. Move your awareness slowly through all parts of your body, starting at the crown of the head. Expand and deepen any feelings and sensations you encounter, without judging them as good or bad, pleasant or unpleasant.

Awakening to impermanence:

1. Developing a sense of time: As you sit in meditation, see if you can poise yourself at the edge of the present, welcoming each future moment as it arises. Let yourself awaken to the rhythm of the flow of time.

2. Awareness of a sense of self: The self is the one that thinks it is immortal, the one that denies the reality of death. As you practice, see if you can be aware of the sense of self, the one that is "doing" the practice. What does the self rely on to establish its own existence?

3. Awareness of the compounded nature of existence: Look at how situations in your own life, in the lives of others, and in your surrounding environment have come to be; consider how the circumstances that brought them about will also bring about their decay and dissolution. Include in these reflections the situations that you care about and rely on: your own existence, your possessions, the

presence of friends and loved ones, your status, your health, and so on. Reflect as well upon your childhood and consider the process by which you gradually reached your present age; play that process out in time until your imagined death. As the text advises: Think over all the periods of happiness and misery you have undergone up until the present time and how death approaches closer and closer. Meditate clearly and with deep feelings of regret over any of your thoughts or actions that have not been beneficial.

Awakening to karma:

1.  Review your actions for a day or longer, or your actions during a typical day in your life. How many of your actions are directed to unselfish purposes? How many are dedicated to self-centered aims? What is the outcome of such actions?

2.  Again review your actions for a day, this time looking at actions to determine whether they are generated by any of the three poisons: desire, hatred, and ignorance. Looking at times in the past when such motivations were dominant, see if you can trace the consequences.

Awakening to suffering:

1.  Contemplation of desire: a) Let your deepest desire come to mind, and imagine that it has been fulfilled. Let the feeling of fulfillment be rich and powerful. What happens then? b) In the flow of thoughts from moment to moment, see if you can trace very subtle overtones or undertones of desire that may initially escape your notice.

2.  Contemplation of suffering: At those times in meditation when you feel especially alive and well, be sensitive to the subtle shifts away from that feeling, as well as your attempts to hold on to the initial feeling. Without judging, look at how this cycle plays itself out.

3.  Exploration of nihilism: If you have any doubts about the value of Dharma practice, the truth of Dharma teachings, or your own ability to attain realization, bring those feelings to the fore. Go into them as fully as possible; insist to yourself that they are true. What is the feeling tone of this experience?

4.  Contemplation of non-human states: a) Even though the teachings on the six realms of being cannot be dismissed as "simply"

psychological, psychological experiences corresponding to the six realms are a part of everyone's experience. Experiment with such states of feeling. For example, let the hungry-ghost feeling of desire unfulfilled build up within you; explore it as fully as you can. Again, let the narrow focus and fear of the animal realm build up until it is almost overwhelming. b) Build up feelings as before. When they are quite strong, rapidly switch to another feeling. This can be the opposite of the feeling you were just exploring, or else a feeling linked to another non-human realm. As you grow more familiar with this process, you can speed up the process of switching from one state to another.

5. Making connections. In the last two days for this topic, review all four themes that you have been exploring, and go more deeply into the meaning of taking refuge, discussed in the text on pp. 185–95. Finally, explore the antidotes to suffering and samsara: the Three Jewels, the Lama, and Bodhicitta. Look honestly at your own sense of commitment to practice, and cultivate it as much as you can.

## Suggested Readings

On faith: chapters 15–16 in *Ways of Enlightenment,* 113–24; "Attaining Inner Confidence," in *Gesture of Balance,* 84–90.

On the sense of self and the belief in self: chapter 10 in *Ways of Enlightenment,* 77–82; chapters 13–25 in *Love of Knowledge,* 99–208.

On impermanence: chapter 5 in *Tantric Practice in Nying-ma,* 57–63; chapter 2 in *Kindly Bent to Ease Us, Part One: Mind,* 13–20.

On karma: chapters 25, 31, and 32 in *Ways of Enlightenment,* 183–90, 226–37; "Publisher's Introduction," in *The Marvelous Companion,* xv–xx; chapter 6 in *The Jewel Ornament of Liberation,* 74–90; *The Torch of Certainty,* 38–43.

# Topic Three:
# Developing Bodhicitta

## Weeks Five and Six

### *Readings from Path of Heroes*

"The Importance of Taking Refuge" and the following eight chapters, ending with "After Meditation: Play of Illusion," 182–295.

### *Contemplation*

The starting point for developing compassion is to draw on your own experience with samsara, penetrating the depths of suffering that come from samsaric attachment. Developing the feelings that arise into Great Compassion is the work of the Bodhisattva, the Hero of Enlightenment.

Rather than concentrating on your own escape from suffering, now is the time to concentrate on all other beings. Compassion for others underlies Bodhicitta, and is based on the desire to rescue all sentient beings from suffering. This becomes the aspiration for the perfect enlightenment of the Buddha.

To become a Buddha, one must generate both aspects of enlightened mind: the relative enlightened mind of great compassion for all beings and the ultimate enlightened mind which views all existence as śūnyatā, or openness. Bodhicitta is the essence of compassion and openness which are developed through skillful means and wisdom.

Skillful means includes the practice of compassion which is developed by the Four Immeasurables of love, joy, compassion, and equanimity and by the perfections of giving, moral practice, patience, effort, meditation, and wisdom.

Wisdom appears as a pure understanding of the openness of all existence as well as of the cause and effect of karma. Bodhisattvas join this wisdom with compassion to happily give up everything they have to help others; their practice of wisdom heightens their skill in means, empowering their efforts to benefit beings. As stated in the Gayaśīrṣa-sutra (The Sūtra Delivered on Mt. Gayā): "Skillful means accompanying wisdom and wisdom accompanying skillful means is liberation."

Reflect with complete honesty on your life and on the patterns that characterize it. Do not try to make yourself more or less than you are, and be ready to go into all your emotions, including feelings of loss and disappointment as well as hope and fear.

## Suggested Readings

On compassion and wisdom: *Compassion in Tibetan Buddhism,* 81–92, 101–25; "Meditation on Compassion," in *Kun-zang La-may Zhal-lung, Part 2 and Part 3,* 274–90; "The Questions of Suvikrānta-vikrāmin," in *Perfect Wisdom, The Short Prajñāpāramitā Texts,* 1–78.

## Meditation

Meditation practices are generally designed to develop tranquility (śamatha) and awakened awareness (vipaśyanā) (also translated as insight or wider seeing) and the unity of the two.

1. Counting the breath (a basic śamatha practice). Directions for this practice are on p. 271.

2. No coming or going. Watch how thoughts arise in the mind. Can you see where they come from? Can you see where they go?

3. Equality of arising. Look at whatever arises in the stream of thought and sensation as being fundamentally equal. For example, although there is clearly a difference between a house that you imagine, a house that you remember, and a house that you see across the street, consider this difference as having to do with the quality of these experiences rather than with their substance or "reality." Apply this fundamental sense of equality to whatever arises, making no

attempt to distinguish between sense experience and imagination, between thoughts and images, or between good and bad.

4.  Dream world. Consider that all appearance is like a dream, as suggested in the text. What is the quality of this experience? Go into it again and again, never settling for a previous answer or description.

5.  Unborn awareness. What is the quality of mind that allows awareness to arise? Instead of asking this question in a conceptual way, look at your own experience. As before, do not expect to arrive at a single answer. The question itself is the practice. A good starting point is the observation in the text: "The mind has no color or form or the like. The mind is not located either inside the body or outside it; no nature at all for the mind can be established."

6.  Clear light. Consider the nature of all appearance as composed of pure light or energy. This same perception can be extended to the emotions, to thoughts, and to everything else that arises, in accord with the quote in the text: "The mind itself is the Buddha—no other Buddha should be sought."

7.  Ground of being. When the mind is settled and calm, look within experience as it arises for a level that is more fundamental, more stable, as the bottom of the ocean is more fundamental and stable (though not inseparable from) the waves at the surface. As the text suggests (pp. 281–82), rest in this nature.

## Suggested Readings

On tranquility and awakened awareness: *Hidden Mind of Freedom*, 3–26; chapters 2–4 in *Mahāmudrā*, 39–88; *Openness Mind*, 111–24.

On meditation and the six perfections: *Calm and Clear*, 29–41.

On the seven consciousnesses and the ground of being: *Tibetan Buddhism in Western Perspective*, 115–30, 142–47.

On the obstacles to meditation and their antidotes: chapter 1 in *Mahāmudrā*, 19–26; *Calm and Clear*, 38–41.

# Topic Four:
# Exchanging Self and Other

## Weeks Seven and Eight

### Readings from Path of Heroes

"Exchanging Self for Others," "Preparation: Cultivating Love and Compassion," "Practice: The Actual Exchange of Self for Others," "After Meditation: Transforming the Emotions," 296–353.

The practice of exchanging self for others is central to the development of Bodhicitta. As a principal means for cultivating Bodhicitta, it is also central to all Mahāyāna practice. In this two-week period, focus first on cultivating thoughts of love and compassion. Then begin to move on to the main practice.

### Contemplation

1. Cultivating love. Consider times that others have shown you love and kindness, helped you, cared for you, or met your needs in some way. Imagine that at one time or another all beings have been kind to you, and form the thought to repay this kindness. With that motivation, generate the wish for all beings to attain happiness. Let this wish expand as much as possible, pervading your whole being.

2. Cultivating compassion. Look back into your own history for times when you have felt discouraged or frustrated or have had to face great loss. Go into these feelings deeply, letting them build and intensify. Now imagine how often others have the same feelings.

Everyone you meet—as well as the billions of people you will never meet—will undergo similar kinds of pain and dissatisfaction. Bearing that in mind, let feelings of compassion for all beings take form within your heart. Let your experience of suffering guide you, without being attached to your experience or considering it more important than anyone else's. The feelings of compassion that develop in this way can expand outward, filling your whole body and radiating beyond it to embrace the whole universe.

3. Dream-like compassion. For this practice, return to the "dream world" practice presented in connection with the previous topic. Apply this sense of reality as dream-like to the suffering of others, being sensitive to the way that people consider their existence and suffering to be real. Hold both these contradictory ways of seeing in your mind at once, letting the contradiction itself fuel the quality of compassion born of so much needless suffering.

4. Sky-born compassion. Consider all beings as insubstantial. From this awareness, allow appreciation for all manifestations—for their beauty, their splendor, and their boundless capacity—to arise within you. These feelings have an ecstatic quality to them which can flower into an open-ended love and compassion, unbound by any concepts or any clinging to self-concern.

## Suggested Readings

On the insubstantiality of existence: chapters 1, 3–8 in *Kindly Bent To Ease Us, Part Three: Wonderment,* 33–49, 63–108.

On understanding the nature of compassion: *Gesture of Balance,* 37–44; *Hidden Mind of Freedom,* 56–63; *Skillful Means,* 112–26; *Openness Mind,* 134–40, 146–51;

On the Bodhisattva's compassion: chapter 5 in *The Holy Teachings of Vimalakīrti,* 42–49.

## *Meditation*

1. Sending and receiving on the breath. As you breathe in, imagine that you are gathering into your being all the wrongdoing and all the suffering of others and all the negative karma that results from it. As you do so, others are freed from the burden of this suffering, which now becomes yours. As you breathe out, imagine that all your merit and well-being are flowing out to others, nourishing them and relieving them of all unhappiness. Let this practice build on itself, so that with each breath in you take on increasingly subtle forms of pain and with each breath out you broadcast more refined forms of virtue and merit. Continue this practice as the breath itself grows more subtle.

2. Starting with yourself. The following description is taken directly from the text, p. 348:

*Start the process of taking on suffering with yourself.*

When your mind has not yet been purified through hearing and studying the teachings, so that you still think basically of yourself and are afraid to take on the suffering of others, you must first learn to accept your own suffering.

Concentrate on the thought: "In all my future births, may I never again have to experience the maturation of karma or the kleśas, or the suffering that is their result. May they ripen upon my mind and body in this birth. May I never again experience negativities that will mature later in this lifetime: May they ripen this year. May I bring to fruition in this month what would otherwise ripen this year; may I ripen today what would otherwise ripen this month. May I take on in this instant what would otherwise ripen sometime today."

3. Preparation. Integrate the practice of Tong Len, unconditional giving and taking on all suffering, with other practices, including the practice of taking refuge and the practice of prayer.

4. Perfect transfer. Reflect on some wrong that someone has done to you or to someone else. Imagine this wrong and the negative karma that results from it as a dense, dark ball in that person's heart. Now imagine yourself taking this ball and placing it in your own heart, freely and willingly taking on all this wrongdoing and the pain that

results from it as your own. Do not be afraid of the consequences; just let yourself accept the pain and suffering as fully as you can.

5.  Perfect giving. Imagine that you are giving someone dear to you all that is valuable or delightful; as the text says, "all the immeasurable resources that exist in this world as well as in all other realms, including the transworldly ground of the perfect Buddhas." Let yourself be deeply delighted that you can make such an offering. Once you are able to do this, imagine that you extend the field of giving to include other beings: friends, acquaintances, people you admire, and eventually all beings, including those you do not know, those you dislike, and those you would normally take no notice of whatsoever.

## Suggested Readings

On the Four Immeasurables: chapter 7 in *Kindly Bent To Ease Us, Part One: Mind,* 108–22; *Kun-zang La-may Zhal-lung, Part 2 and Part 3,* 266–96.

On awakening Bodhicitta: chapters 1–5 in the Bodhicaryāvatāra; *The Jewel Ladder,* 50–66; *Kun-zang La-may Zhal-lung, Part 2 and Part 3,* 296–304.

On the Bodhisattva's love for beings: chapter 7 in *The Holy Teachings of Vimalakīrti,* 56–63.

On coursing in the path of the Bodhisattva: chapters 6 and 7 in *Illuminations,* 81–100; chapter 30 in *The Perfection of Wisdom in Eight Thousand Lines and its Verse Summary,* 277–90; chapters 5–8 in the Bodhicaryāvatāra.

On exchanging self for others: *Kun-zang La-may Zhal-lung, Part 2 and Part 3,* 304–319.

On the perfection of giving: chapter 9 in *Compassion in Tibetan Buddhism,* 182–91; *Kun-zang La-may Zhal-lung, Part 2 and Part 3,* 319–27; the story of Prince Maṇicūḍa in *Joy for the World,* 3–135.

# Topic Five:
# Transforming Emotionality

## Weeks Nine and Ten

### *Readings from Path of Heroes*

"Meditative Action," "Motivated Concentration on Relative Enlightened Mind," 356–96.

The remaining topics in this program of practice can all be considered to grow out of the basic practice of cultivating Bodhicitta by exchanging self for others. They deal with how to carry out this practice in the various aspects of life, and how to let it guide your conduct in the face of obstacles such as emotionality or great suffering.

Continue to focus on the core practices presented in the previous topic. The additional practices given over the next several weeks can be considered as supplements or refinements of the basic practice.

### *Suggested Readings*

On the three poisons: "Emotional Afflictions," chapter 33, and "Deadly Influences," chapter 34 in *Ways of Enlightenment*, 238–50.

### *Contemplation*

1. Transmuting the three poisons. Look within your experience for the arising of the three poisons of desire, hatred, and ignorance. As your investigation grows more subtle, you may well notice that these

poisons are present much more often than you initially imagined, perhaps to some extent in every thought. As you continue with this analysis, let the wish form to transmute each of the three poisons into compassionate action for yourself and for others.

## Meditation

1.  Cleansing breath. While holding the right nostril closed with your right forefinger, breathe out, imagining that you are blowing out from your left nostril all the emotions that you try to push away from you, such as hatred and fear. When breathing in, imagine that you are breathing in love and compassion. While holding the left nostril closed with your left forefinger, breathe out, imagining that you are blowing out from your right nostril all the emotions you hold on to, such as desire and anger.

2. Open compassion. As feelings of love and compassion arise in your practice, let these feelings themselves be without substance. In this way you can move toward the Bodhisattva practice of love and compassion which is inseparable from the open nature of all appearance and all that claims to be real.

## Suggested Readings

Cleansing breath: Exercise 13 in *Kum Nye Relaxation, Part 1*, 52–53.

On the openness of existence: "Reality and Illusion," in *Openness Mind*, 70–73; *Hidden Mind of Freedom*, 81–94.

On the nature, attitudes, and view of Buddhas and Bodhisattvas: "The Diamond Sūtra" and "The Heart of Perfect Wisdom" in *Perfect Wisdom: The Short Prajñāpāramitā Texts*, 122–43.

On how the Bodhisattva helps beings: *The Perfection of Wisdom in Eight Thousand Lines and its Verse Summary*, 188–90; "The Four Social Means," in *Illuminations*, 76–80.

# Topic Six:
# Transforming Adversity

## Weeks Eleven and Twelve

### *Readings from Path of Heroes*

"Dealing with Demonic Forces," "Motivated Concentration on Ultimate Enlightened Mind," 397–418.

### *Contemplation*

As the basic practice of exchanging self for others deepens, it becomes increasingly central to your reality. As the text says, "If you practice the Dharma, the Dharma itself emerges through the force of great blessings as your reality." It is possible to cultivate and encourage this deepening of your practice, transforming the nature of the world that you inhabit for your own sake and for the sake of others.

1. Thinking only of others. Allow the thinking mind to operate freely, but direct your thoughts entirely to benefiting and bringing joy to others. Be alert to subtle shifts in focus toward your own pleasure. ("How they will admire me; how grateful they will be; how good I will feel!") Combining this practice with observing the three poisons can help guard against this kind of self-deception.

2. Bring to mind individuals with whom you have had difficulties or with whom you have had disputes or disagreements. Following the analysis in the text, consider how such beings are causing themselves great pain and sorrow through their wrongful actions, and cultivate with all your heart feelings of compassion, wishing them well. Finally, in your thoughts, invite them to make use of your resources or

whatever else they desire to accomplish their own desires and aims. Let this thought and wish be as heartfelt as possible.

## Suggested Readings

On thinking only of others: chapter 7 in *Kindly Bent to Ease Us, Part One: Mind*, 106–22; chapter 10 of the Bodhicaryāvatāra (see p. 598 for specific translations of this text).

## Meditation

1. Cultivating joy. As you settle into meditation, let feelings of joy arise. Encourage and develop these feelings, allowing all worry, doubt, or concern based on thoughts of the self to slip away. Let these joyful feelings suffuse your body and mind, and let the energy that develops in this way support and sustain your practice.

2. Investigating the self. Look at the concept of self and the thought or assumption 'I am' as they arise in your experience. What is their basis? Who is their guarantor? Do not ask these questions conceptually; rather look at what is actually happening in the stream of your experience. What is the basis of the distinction you make between self and other?

3. As a refinement of the inquiry into self, investigate the five skandhas. Can you find any 'self' in any part of the body?

4. Cutting thought. This is a refinement of the practice of observing the three poisons in your own mindstream. Watch the flow of thoughts for any kind of emotionality, including daydreams, longing, anger, confusion, dullness, and laziness. As soon as they arise, cut them off, and turn your thoughts instead to the welfare and happiness of others. Do this again and again, at first for short periods of time, then gradually extending the practice into all activities.

5. Perfect mandala. Introduce yourself to the purity of Bodhisattva perception by practicing with this inspiration from the Song of Tselay Natsog Rangdrol, p. 416:

"The whole of the visible world is the mandala of the Lama:
The purity of appearance demonstrates complete compassion.

"All that happens in the world is a manifestation of the Lama:
All actions benefit beings with what they need.

"All beings born in the world are the manifestation of the Lama:
The Dharmakāya, as the heart of the Sugata, pervades everything.

"All joy and happiness are a manifestation of the Lama:
a gift of siddhi, granting whatever the mind could wish for.

"All the distressing conditions of illness are also
manifestations of the Lama,
for the experience of suffering purifies wrongdoing."

## Suggested Readings

On investigating the self and the skandhas: *Calm and Clear*, 43–49,
55–80; *Heart Treasure of the Enlightened Ones*, 125–40; *The Perfection
of Wisdom in Eight Thousand Lines and its Verse Summary*, 97–98.

On the openness of meditative freedom: "Instructions on Vision in
the Middle Way," in *Calm and Clear*, 93–106.

On seeing all appearance as mandala: chapter 9 in *Kindly Bent to
Ease Us, Part One: Mind*, 148–66.

On expressions of enlightened vision: chapter 12 in *The Holy
Teachings of Vimalakīrti*, 91–95; "Prashantarutasagaravati," and "The
Vow of Practice of Universal Good," in *Entry into the Realm of
Reality*, 205–14, 379–94.

# Topic Seven:
# Accumulation and Purification

## Weeks Thirteen and Fourteen

### Readings from Path of Heroes

"Application: Accumulation and Purification," "Practice as a Way of Life," "Evaluating your Practice," 421–67.

### Contemplation

Read from the traditional texts that describe making offerings, such as Samantabhadra's Prayer for Enlightened Practice given on pp. 574–76. If you do not feel able to carry out visualizations as described in the texts, practice offering every moment and every experience—whatever happens—to the Three Jewels for the sake of your own realization and the liberation of all beings.

### Suggested Readings

On offering the mandala: chapter 4 in *Kun-zang La-may Zhal-lung, Part 2 and Part 3,* 395–414; chapter 4 in *The Torch of Certainty,* 93–117; chapter 13 in *Tantric Practice in Nying-ma,* 154–60.

### Practice

1. Boundless offering. Throughout this program, you have followed the practice of making offerings and taking refuge as a preliminary to other meditations. Now concentrate on these two practices in their own right. Develop as fully as you can the wish to offer all that has value to the Three Jewels and to the Lama.

2. Boundless renunciation. Allow images or thoughts about what you desire to arise in the mind, building them up until they are very real. Then mentally renounce this cherished object completely, abandoning it for the sake of all beings.

3. Boundless resolve. Let the wish to benefit all beings sink deep into your mind and your body. Imagine that this wish is pervading every cell of your physical being and every thought that arises in the mind, until the wish is inseparable from your being. There is no one to do the wishing and no one to receive the benefit: simply the wish itself.

## Suggested Readings

To evoke and strengthen the aspiration for enlightenment: recite daily the entire Samantabhadra-praṇidhāna-rāja, "Samantabhadra's Prayer for Enlightened Practice," in *World Peace Ceremonies, Bodh Gayā,* 162–74; (another translation) in *Entry into the Realm of Reality,* 387–94.

On the culmination of the Bodhisattva path: Reread daily chapter 10 of the Bodhicaryāvatāra.

# Topic Eight:
# Self-Mastery

## Weeks Fifteen and Sixteen

### *Readings from Path of Heroes*

"Keeping Your Commitments," "Guidelines for Self-Mastery," 471–547.

### *Contemplation*

1. Investigation and analysis. Look carefully at the workings of the mind, being particularly sensitive to the motivation with which you act, evaluating the degree to which your conduct of body, speech, and mind conforms to the practice of Bodhicitta. Look with special clarity at moments when you feel restless or when negative emotions arise. When negativity grows strong enough to prevent you from carrying out such practice, cultivate feelings of joy until you are once again able to look with a clear mind at what is happening. As you cultivate clarity, greater joy will arise naturally, further enhancing clarity in a positive cycle of awakening. Resolve to apply the antidote for any emotion or obstacle the moment it arises and to put that resolve into practice. No matter what arises, stay with your practice.

2. Confession. Confession is one of the Seven-Limbed Practices. Now practice it more intensively, in accord with these instructions from the text:

> As soon as you get up in the morning, concentrate strongly on the thought: "Today I will never forget the two aspects of enlightened mind." At the end of the day before going to sleep, review your day, remembering in

sequence all of your actions. Consider everything you thought or did, and if anything is contrary to enlightened mind, enumerate such faults and confess them. Then resolve never to let such actions happen again.

## Suggested Readings

On the value of adhering to the Bodhisattva vow: Review "The Ethical Impulse," chapter 8 in *Kindly Bent to Ease Us, Part One: Mind*, 123–47.

## Meditation

1. Origins. Let the mind rest in stillness, relaxing and opening completely. Without losing a sense of clarity and lightness, let awareness settle low in the body, where all is at peace. From there, watch to see how the impulse to act arises and how perceptions and emotional reactivity take form.

2. Self-grasping. Drawing on all the previous practices, look at how self-grasping arises in the stream of your consciousness. If no self-grasping seems to be in operation, investigate again, bringing up latent feelings linked to objects of attachment or hatred. If at this point self-grasping arises, concentrate on its lack of self-nature.

## Suggested Readings

A summary on utilizing the practice of self-mastery in daily life: *The Great Path of Awakening*, 23–50.

On awakening from interpretation: "Expressions and Preconceptions," chapter 43, and "Light of Understanding," chapter 44, in *Ways of Enlightenment*, 298–308.

## Bibliography: Readings for the Four-Month Program

Bodhicaryāvatāra, by Śāntideva. *Entering the Path of Enlightenment*, translated by Marion L. Matics. New York: Macmillan, 1970.

————. *A Guide to the Bodhisattva's Way of Life*, translated by Stephen Batchelor and Sherpa Tulku. Dharamsala: Library of Tibetan Works and Archives, 1979.

*Calm and Clear,* by Mi-pham 'Jam-dbyangs-rnam-rgyal-rgya-mtsho, translated by Tarthang Tulku. Berkeley: Dharma Publishing, 1973.

*Compassion in Tibetan Buddhism, by Tsong-ka-pa, with Kensur Lekden's Meditations of a Tantric Abbot,* edited and translated by Jeffrey Hopkins. Valois, NY: Gabriel / Snow Lion, 1980.

*Crystal Mirror, Volume VI.* Berkeley: Dharma Publishing, 1984.

*Dakini Teachings, Padmasambhava's Oral Instructions to Lady Tsogyal, Revealed by Nyang Ral Nyima Oser and Sangye Lingpa,* translated by Eric Pema Kunsang. Boston: Shambhala, 1990.

*Dhammapada, Translation of Dharma Verses with the Tibetan Text.* Berkeley: Dharma Publishing, 1985.

*Entry into the Realm of Reality, The Text, a translation of the Gandavyuha, the final book of the Avatamsaka Sutra,* by Thomas Cleary. Boston: Shambhala, 1989.

*The Excellent Path to Enlightenment: Short Preliminary Practice,* by Jamyang Khyentse Wangpo, explained by H. H. Dilgo Khyentse Rinpoche. Kathmandu: Rangjung Yeshey Kanying Shedrup Ling, 1987.

*Fifty Verses of Guru-Devotion ("Gurupañcaśikā," "La-ma nga-chu-pa"),* by Aśvaghoṣa. Prepared by the Translation Bureau of the Library of Tibetan Works and Archives. Dharamsala: Library of Tibetan Works and Archives, 1975.

*Footsteps on the Diamond Path.* Berkeley: Dharma Publishing, 1992. (Crystal Mirror Vols. I–III, revised and expanded.)

*Gesture of Balance,* by Tarthang Tulku. Berkeley: Dharma Publishing, 1976.

*The Great Path of Awakening, a Commentary on the Mahayana Teaching of the Seven Points of Mind Training*, by Jamgon Kongtrul, translated by Ken McLeod. Boston: Shambhala, 1987.

*The Heart Treasure of the Enlightened Ones, The Practice of View, Meditation, and Action*, by Paltrul Rinpoche, with commentary by Dilgo Khyentse. Translated from the Tibetan by The Padmākara Translation Group. Boston: Shambhala, 1992.

*Hidden Mind of Freedom*, by Tarthang Tulku. Berkeley: Dharma Publishing, 1981.

*The Holy Teaching of Vimalakīrti, a Mahāyāna Scripture*, translated by Robert A. F. Thurman. University Park and London: Pennsylvania State University Press, 1986. See also *The Teachings of Vimalakīrti*.

*Illuminations, A Guide to Essential Buddhist Practices*, by Sakya Pandita, translated by Geshe Wangyal and Brian Cutillo. Novato, CA: Lotsawa, 1988.

*The Jewel Ladder, A Preliminary Nyingma Lamrim*, by Minling Terchen Gyurmed Dorjee [Terdak Lingpa], with commentary by Garje Khamtrul Rinpoche, translated and edited by Tsepak Rigzin. Dharamsala: Library of Tibetan Works and Archives, 1990.

*The Jewel Ornament of Liberation*, by Gampopa, translated by Herbert V. Guenther. Berkeley: Shambhala, 1971.

*Joy for the World*, by Candragomin, translated by Michael Hahn. Berkeley: Dharma Publishing, 1987.

*Kindly Bent to Ease Us*, by Longchenpa, translated from the Tibetan and annotated by Herbert V. Guenther. 3 vols. Berkeley: Dharma Publishing, 1975.

*Kum Nye Relaxation, Parts I and II*, by Tarthang Tulku. 2 vols. Berkeley: Dharma Publishing, 1978.

*Kun-zang La-may Zhal-lung*, by Paltrul Rinpoche, translated by Sonam T. Kazi. 2 vols. Upper Montclair: Diamond-Lotus Publishing, 1989, 1993. See also *The Words of My Perfect Teacher*.

*A Lamp for the Path and Commentary* (Atīśa's Bodhipatha-pradīpa), translated and annotated by Richard Sherburne. London: George Allen & Unwin LTD, 1983.

*Light of Liberation, A History of Buddhism in India*, by Elizabeth Cook. Berkeley: Dharma Publishing, 1992. (Crystal Mirror Series VIII)

*Love of Knowledge,* by Tarthang Tulku. Berkeley: Dharma Publishing, 1987.

*Mahāmudrā, The Quintessence of Mind and Meditation*, by Takpo Tashi Namgyal, translated and annotated by Lobsang P. Lhalungpa. Boston: Shambhala, 1986.

*Mastering Successful Work*, by Tarthang Tulku. Berkeley: Dharma Publishing, 1994.

*The Nyingma School of Tibetan Buddhism*: *Its Fundamentals and History*, by Dudjom Rinpoche, translated and edited by Gyurme Dorje with the collaboration of Matthew Kapstein. 2 vols. Boston: Wisdom Publications, 1991.

*Openness Mind*, by Tarthang Tulku. Berkeley: Dharma Publishing, 1984.

*Perfect Wisdom: The Short Prajñāpāramitā Texts,* translated by Edward Conze. Totnes, Devon: Buddhist Publishing Group, 1993 (First published London: Luzac, 1973).

*The Perfection of Wisdom in Eight Thousand Lines & Its Verse Summary*, translated by Edward Conze. Berkeley: Four Seasons Foundation, 1975.

"Samantabhadra's Prayer for Enlightened Practice" (Samantabhadra-praṇidhāna-rāja). In *World Peace Ceremony, Bodh Gayā*. Berkeley: Dharma Publishing, 1994, 162–75.

(Samantabhadra-praṇidhāna-rāja). In *Entry into the Realm of Reality, The Text*, translated by Thomas Cleary. Boston: Shambhala, 1989, 387–94.

*Skillful Means: Patterns for Success*, by Tarthang Tulku. Second ed. Berkeley: Dharma Publishing, 1991.

*The Tantric Mysticism of Tibet; A Practical Guide,* by John Blofeld. Reprint ed., New York: Causway Books, 1974.

*Tantric Practice in Nying-ma,* by Khetsun Sangpo Rinbochay, translated and edited by Jeffrey Hopkins, co-edited by Anne Klein. Ithaca, NY: Gabriel / Snow Lion, n.d.

*The Teachings of Vimalakīrti (Vimalakīrtinirdeśa),* from the French translation with introduction and notes by Étienne Lamotte, rendered into English by Sara Boin. London: The Pali Text Society, 1962.

*Tibetan Buddhism in Western Perspective, Collected Articles of Herbert V. Guenther.* Berkeley: Dharma Publishing, 1977.

*The Torch of Certainty,* by Jamgon Kongtrul, translated from the Tibetan by Judith Hanson with foreword by Chögyam Trungpa. Boulder: Shambhala, 1977.

*The Voice of the Buddha, The Beauty of Compassion* (Lalitavistara Sūtra), translated by Gwendolyn Bays. 2 vols. Berkeley: Dharma Publishing, 1983.

*Ways of Enlightenment, Buddhist Studies at Nyingma Institute.* Berkeley: Dharma Publishing, 1993.

*Wisdom of Buddha: The Samdhinirmocana Sūtra,* translated by John Powers. Berkeley: Dharma Publishing, 1995.

*The Wish-Fulfilling Jewel, The Practice of Guru Yoga According to the Longchen Nyingthig Tradition,* by Dilgo Khyentse, translated from the Tibetan by Konchog Tenzin. Boston: Shambhala, 1988.

*The Words of My Perfect Teacher; Kunzang Lama'i Shelung,* by Paltrul Rinpoche, translated by the Padmakara Translation Group. San Francisco: HarperCollins, 1994. See also *Kun-zang La-may Zhal-lung.*

*World Peace Ceremony, Bodh Gayā. See* "Samantabhadra's Prayer for Enlightened Practice."

# Appendices

# Bibliography

*Selected Translations of Canonical Texts Cited*

Abhidharmakoṣabhāṣya, by Vasubandhu (NE 4089). *Abhidharma-kośabhāṣyam*, translated from the French translation of Louis de la Vallée Poussin by Leo M. Pruden. 4 vols. Berkeley: Asian Humanities Press, 1988–1990.

Abhidharmasamuccaya, by Asaṅga (NE 4049). *Le Compendium de la super-doctrine (Philosophie), (Abhidharmasamuccaya) d'Asaṅga*, translated by Walpola Rahula. Paris: École Française d'Éxtrême-Orient, 1971. Reprinted 1980.

Abhisamayālaṁkāra, by Maitreyanātha (NE 3786). *Abhisamayā-laṁkāra*, translated by Edward Conze. Rome: ISMEO, 1954. (Serie Orientale Roma 6)

Aṣṭādaśasāhasrikā-prajñāpāramitā (NE 10). *The Large Sūtra on Perfect Wisdom*, with the Divisions of the Abhisamayālaṅkāra, translated from the Sanskrit and edited by Edward Conze. Berkeley: University of California Press, 1975.

Avataṁsaka Sūtra (NE 44). *The Flower Ornament Scripture*, translated from the Chinese by Thomas Cleary. 3 vols. Boston: Shambhala, 1984–1989.

Bhadracaryā-praṇidhānarāja (NE 1095). "Samantabhadra's Prayer for Enlightened Practice." In *World Peace Ceremony, Bodh Gayā*. Berkeley: Dharma Publishing, 1994, 162–75.

————. Concluding verses in *Entry into the Realm of Reality: The Text, a translation of the Gandavyuha, the final book of the Avatamsaka Sutra*, by Thomas Cleary. Boston: Shambhala, 1989.

————. Concluding verses in *The Flower Ornament Scripture, A Translation of the Avatamsaka Sutra*, translated from the Chinese by Thomas Cleary. Vol. 3. Boston: Shambhala, 1989.

Bodhicittavivaraṇa (NE 1800), by Nāgārjuna. "Bodhicittavivaraṇa." In *Master of Wisdom, Writings of the Buddhist Master Nāgārjuna*, translations and studies by Chr. Lindtner. Berkeley: Dharma Publishing, 1986, 32–71.

Bodhipatha-pradīpa (NE 3947), by Atīśa. *A Lamp for the Path and Commentary*, translated and annotated by Richard Sherburne, S.J. London: George Allen & Unwin LTD, 1983.

Bodhisattvacaryāvatāra (NE 3871), by Śāntideva. *Entering the Path of Enlightenment*, translated by Marion L. Matics. New York: Macmillan, 1970.

————. *A Guide to the Bodhisattva's Way of Life*, translated by Stephen Batchelor and Sherpa Tulku. Dharamsala: Library of Tibetan Works and Archives, 1979.

————. *Bodhicharyāvatāra*, Sanskrit text with English translation and exposition based on Prajñākaramati's Pañjikā by Parmananda Sharma. 2 vols. New Delhi: Aditya Prakashan, 1990.

Bodhisattvamaṇyāvalī (NE 3951), by Atīśa. "The Jewel Rosary of an Awakening Warrior." In *Advice from a Spiritual Friend*, by Geshe Rabten and Geshe Dharghey, translated and edited by Brian Beresford. London: Wisdom Publications, 1986. Includes Tibetan text.

Bodhisattvasaṁvara-viṁśaka (NE 4081), by Candragomin. "Twenty Verses on the Bodhisattva Vow." In *Difficult Beginnings, Three Works on the Bodhisattva Path*, translated, with commentary by Mark Tatz. Boston: Shambhala, 1985, 27–29.

Caturaśīti-siddhi-pravṛtti (NE 4961), by Abhayadatta. *Buddha's Lions*, translated by James B. Robinson. Berkeley: Dharma Publishing, 1979.

Damamūka-nāma Sūtra (NE 341). *Sūtra of the Wise and the Foolish*, translated from the Mongolian by Stanley Frye. Dharamsala: Library of Tibetan Works and Archives, 1981.

Daśabhūmika Sūtra. Traditionally included in the Avataṁsaka Sūtra (NE 44:31). In *The Flower Ornament Scripture*, translated by Thomas Cleary. Vol. 2. Boston: Shambhala, 1986, 7–123.

Dhammapada (NE 4482). *The Dhammapada, Verses and Stories*, translated by Daw Mya Tin, with introduction by N. H. Samtani. Sarnath: Central Institute of Higher Tibetan Studies, 1990. (Bibliotheca Indo-Tibetica Series XX)

———. *Dhammapada, Translation of Dharma Verses with the Tibetan Text*. Berkeley: Dharma Publishing, 1985.

———. "Dhammapada." In *Buddha-Dharma*. Berkeley: Numata Center for Buddhist Translation and Research, 1984, 443–52.

Gaṇḍavyūha Sūtra (NE 44:45). *Entry into the Realm of Reality*, translated by Thomas Cleary. Boston: Shambhala, 1989.

Jātakamālā (NE 4150), by Āryaśūra. *The Marvelous Companion, Life Stories of the Buddha*. Berkeley: Dharma Publishing, 1983.

———. *The Jātakamālā of Āryaśūra*, translated by J. S. Speyer. London: Pali Text Society, 1895.

Lalitavistara Sūtra (NE 95). *The Voice of the Buddha, The Beauty of Compassion*. 2 vols. Berkeley: Dharma Publishing, 1983.

Laṅkāvatāra Sūtra (NE 107). *The Laṅkāvatāra Sūtra*, translated from the Sanskrit by Daisetz Teitaro Suzuki. Boulder: Prajñā Press, 1978.

Madhyamakāvatāra (NE 3861), by Candrakīrti. "The Entry into the Middle Way." In *The Emptiness of Emptiness, an Introduction to Early Indian Mādhyamika*, by C. W. Huntington, Jr. with Geshe Namgyal Wangchen. Honolulu: University of Hawaii Press, 1989.

Mahāratnakūṭa Sūtra (NE 45). *A Treasury of Mahāyāna Sūtras, Selections from the Mahāratnakūṭa Sūtra*, translated from the Chinese by The Buddhist Association of the United States, Garma C. C. Chang, General Editor. New York: The Pennsylvania State University Press, 1983.

Mahāyānottara Tantraśāstra (NE 4024), by Maitreyanātha and Asaṅga. *The Changeless Nature*, translated from the Tibetan by Ken and Katia Holmes. Scotland: Karma Drubgyud Darjay Ling, 1985.

Praṇidhānasaptati-nāma-gāthā (NE 4392). "A Daily Prayer." Partial translation. In *Advice from a Spiritual Friend* by Geshe Rabten and Geshe Dharghey, translated and edited by Brian Beresford. London: Wisdom Publications, 1986.

Ratnamālā (NE 4158), by Nāgārjuna. In *The Precious Garland and the Song of the Four Mindfulnesses*, translated by Jeffrey Hopkins and Lati Rinpoche. New York: Harper and Row, 1975, 17–93.

Saṁdhinirmocana Sūtra (NE 106). *Wisdom of Buddha*, translated by John Powers. Berkeley: Dharma Publishing, 1995.

Sañcayagāthā (NE 13). In *The Perfection of Wisdom in Eight Thousand Lines & Its Verse Summary*, translated by Edward Conze. Berkeley: Four Seasons Foundation, 1975.

Suhṛllekha (NE 4182), by Nāgārjuna. *Golden Zephyr*, translated from the Tibetan by Leslie S. Kawamura. Berkeley: Dharma Publishing, 1975.

Sūtrālaṁkāra (NE 4020), by Maitreyanātha. *Mahāyāna-sūtrālaṁkāra, Exposé de la doctrine du grand véhicule*, edited and translated by Sylvain Lévi. 2 vols. Paris: Champion, 1911.

Udānavarga (NE 326). *The Tibetan Dhammapada*, translated by Gareth Sparham. New Delhi: Mahayana Publications, 1983.

Vimalakīrtinirdeśa Sūtra (NE 176). *The Holy Teaching of Vimalakīrti, A Mahāyāna Scripture*, translated by Robert A. F. Thurman. University Park and London: Pennsylvania State University Press, 1986.

———. *The Teaching of Vimalakīrti* (Vimalakīrtinirdeśa) from the French translation with introduction and notes (L'Enseignement de Vimalakīrti), by Étienne Lamotte, rendered into English by Sara Boin. London: The Pali Text Society, 1976.

Visuddhimagga, by Buddhaghosa. *The Path of Purification*, translated from the Pali by Bhikkhu Ñyāṇamoli. Kandi: Buddhist Publication Society, 1991.

## Collections of Canonical Works

*Buddha-Dharma*. Berkeley: Numata Center for Buddhist Translation and Research, 1984.

*Buddhist Mahāyāna Texts*, translated by various Oriental scholars and edited by F. Max Müller. New York: Dover Publications, 1969.

## Selected Translations of Tibetan Texts Cited

### Padmasambhava

*Advice from the Lotus Born, A Collection of Padmasambhava's Advice to the Dakini Yeshe Tsogyal and Other Close Disciples from the Terma Treasure Revelations of Nyang Ral Nyima Oser, Guru Chowang, Pema Ledrel Tsal, Sangye Lingpa, Rigzin Godem, & Chokgyur Lingpa*, translated from the Tibetan by Erik Pema Kunsang. Hong Kong: Rangjung Yeshe Publications, 1994.

*Dakini Teachings, Padmasambhava's Oral Instructions to Lady Tsogyal, Revealed by Nyang Ral Nyima Oser and Sangye Lingpa*, translated by Eric Pema Kunsang. Boston: Shambala, 1990.

### Dharmarakṣita

*The Wheel of Sharp Weapons* (Blo-sbyong-mtshon-cha-'khor-lo), translated from the Tibetan by Geshe Ngawang Dhargyey. Dharamsala: Library of Tibetan Works and Archives, 1976.

### Dromton (1003 or 1004–1064)

bKa'-gdams-thor-bu. "Kadampa Precepts." Selections in *The Door of Liberation, Essential Teachings of the Tibetan Buddhist Tradition*, by Geshe Wangyal. Boston: Wisdom Publications, 1995, 83–122.

### Lang Tangpa (1054–1123)

Eight Verses on the Training of the Mind (Blo-sbyong-tshig-brgyad-ma). In *Four Essential Buddhist Commentaries* by His Holiness the XIV Dalai Lama. Dharamsala: Library of Tibetan Works and Archives, 1982, 89.

Gampopa (1079–1153)

*The Jewel Ornament of Liberation* (Dam-chos-yid-bzhin-gyi-nor-bu-thar-pa-rin-po-che'i-rgyan), translated by Herbert V. Guenther. Berkeley: Shambhala, 1971.

Sakya Paṇḍita (1127–1225)

*Illuminations, A Guide to Essential Buddhist Practices* (Thub-pa'i-dgongs-pa-rab-tu-gsal-ba), translated by Geshe Wangyal and Brian Cutillo. Novato, CA: Lotsawa, 1988.

Gyalsay Togmed (1295–1369)

The Thirty-Seven Bodhisattva Practices (rGyal-sras-lag-len-so-bdun-ma), translated by Ngawang Dhargyey. In *Four Essential Buddhist Commentaries*, by His Holiness the XIV Dalai Lama. Dharamsala: Library of Tibetan Works and Archives, 1982, 3–16.

Longchenpa (1308–1364)

*Kindly Bent to Ease Us* (Ngal-gso-skor-gsum), translated from the Tibetan and annotated by Herbert V. Guenther. 3 vols. Berkeley: Dharma Publishing, 1975–1976.

Tsongkhapa (1357–1419)

Three Principles of the Path (Lam-gyi-gtso-bo-rnam-gsum) in *The Door of Liberation, Essential Teachings of the Tibetan Buddhist Tradition,* by Geshe Wangyal. Boston: Wisdom Publications, 1995, 135–37.

Go Lotsawa Zhonu Pal (1392–1481)

*The Blue Annals* (Deb-ther-sngon-po), translated by George N. Roerich. Second edition. Delhi: Motilal Banarsidass, 1976.

Tashi Namgyal (1512–1587)

*Mahāmudrā, The Quintessence of Mind and Meditation* (Phyag-chen-zla-ba'i-'od-zer), translated and annotated by Lobsang P. Lhalungpa. Boston: Shambhala, 1986.

Minling Terchen Gyurmed Dorje (1643–1714)

*The Jewel Ladder* (Rin-chen-them-skas), translated and edited by Tsepak Rigzin. Dharamsala: Library of Tibetan Works and Archives, 1990.

Jigmed Lingpa (1729–1798)

The Analysis of the Three Essential Points in the Absolute-Perfection Doctrine (rDzogs-pa-chen-po'i-gnad-gsum-shan-'byed, 142-47) and The Tantra of the Reality of Transcendent Awareness as Kun-tu-bzang-po, the Quintessence of Fulfillment and Completion (rDzogs-pa-chen-po-kun-tu-bzang-po, 115-30). In *Tibetan Buddhism in Western Perspective, Collected Articles of Herbert V. Guenther*. Berkeley: Dharma Publishing, 1989.

*The Wish-Fulfilling Jewel, The Practice of Guru Yoga According to the Longchen Nyingthig Tradition*, by Dilgo Khyentse, translated from the Tibetan by Konchog Tenzin. Boston: Shambhala, 1988.

Patrul Rinpoche (1808–1888)

*The Heart Treasure of the Enlightened Ones, The Practice of View, Meditation, and Action* (Thog-mtha'-bar-gsum-du-dge-ba'i-gtam), with commentary by Dilgo Khyentse. Translated from the Tibetan by the Padmakara Translation Group. Boston: Shambhala, 1992.

*Kun-zang La-may Zhal-lung* (Kun-bzang-bla-ma'i-zhal-lung), translated by Sonam T. Kazi. 2 vols. Upper Montclair: Diamond-Lotus Publishing, 1989, 1993.

*The Words of My Perfect Teacher* (Kun-bzang-bla-ma'i-zhal-lung), translated by the Padmakara Translation Group. San Francisco: HarperCollins, 1994.

Kongtrul Lodro Tayay (1813–1899)

*The Torch of Certainty* (Nges-don-sgron-me), translated from the Tibetan by Judith Hanson, with foreword by Chögyam Trungpa. Boulder: Shambhala, 1977.

Dudjom Rinpoche (1904–1987)

Fundamentals of the Nyingma School (bsTan-pa'i-rnam-gzhag) and History of the Nyingma School (rNying-ma'i-chos-'byung). *The Nyingma School of Tibetan Buddhism*, translated and edited by Gyurme Dorje with the collaboration of Matthew Kapstein. 2 vols. Boston: Wisdom Publications, 1991.

## Texts on the Seven Essentials of Self-Mastery, the Blo-sbyong-don-'dun-ma of Chekhawa Yeshe Dorje

*Advice from a Spiritual Friend,* by Geshe Rabten and Geshe Dhargyey, translated and edited by Brian Beresford. London: Wisdom Publications, 1986. Includes Tibetan text.

*Enlightened Courage, An Explanation of Atisha's Seven Point Mind Training,* by Dilgo Khyentse. Payzac-le-Moustier: Editions Padmakara, 1992.

*The Great Path of Awakening, a Commentary on the Mahayana Teaching of the Seven Points of Mind Training,* by Jamgon Kongtrul, translated by Ken McLeod. Boston London: Shambhala, 1987.

*Start Where You Are: A Guide to Compassionate Living,* by Pema Chodron. Boston: Shambhala Publications, 1994.

*Training the Mind and Cultivating Loving-Kindness,* by Chogyam Trungpa, edited by Judith L. Lief. Boston: Shambhala Publications, 1993.

*Universal Compassion, A Commentary to Chekhawa's Training the Mind in Seven Points,* by Geshe Kelsang Gyatso. London: Tharpa Publications, 1988. Includes Tibetan text.

## Miscellaneous

*Atīśa and Tibet,* by Alaka Chattopadhyaya. Delhi: Motilal Banarsidass, 1981.

*Compassion in Tibetan Buddhism, by Tsong-ka-pa, with Kensur Lekden's Meditations of a Tantric Abbot,* edited and translated by Jeffrey Hopkins. Valois, NY: Gabriel / Snow Lion, 1980.

*Mind in Tibetan Buddhism,* by Lati Rinbochay and Elizabeth Napper. Ithaca: Snow Lion Publications, 1986.

# Index of Texts Cited

*Tibetan, Sanskrit, English Text Titles*

*Sūtra Tradition*

---

NE = *Nyingma Edition of the bKa'-'gyur and bsTan-'gyur* (Berkeley: Dharma Publishing, 1981). Referenced where citation has been confirmed.

mDo-rgyal-mtshan-dam-pa, Dhvajāgra, Sacred Victory Banner of the Dharma (NE 293), 185

mDo-sde-dkon-mchog-sprin. *See* dKon-mchog-sprin

mDo-sde-las-brgya-pa, Karmaśataka (NE 340), 112, 116, 130

'Da'-ka-ye-shes, Ārya-atyayajñāna, Sūtra of Pristine Awareness (NE 122), 32, 122, 275

'Dul-ba, Vinaya, 231

'Dul-ba-rnam-'byed, Vinaya-vibhaṅga (NE 3), 64

'Dul-ba-lung, Vinayāgama, 63, 98, 105, 140

'Dus-pa-rin-po-che'i-tog, Mahāsannipāta-ratnaketu, Precious Collection, 85

sDud-pa, Saṁcayagāthā, Verse Summary of the Prajñāpāramitā (NE 13), 38:15.1, 62:32.2, 232:21.4–6, 237:16.5, 240:31.5, 261:5.5, 276:1.26, 277:1.9, 277–78:12.9–10, 278:5.2, 282:2.11, 286:11.7, 292:10.2, 294:18.5, 319:16.6, 401:20.24, 414:27.2–3, 414–15:3.1, 446:20.10, 475, 490:6.7, 496:21.1, 491:15.2, 513:1.21

sDong-po-bkod-pa, Gaṇḍavyūha, Sūtra of the Ornamental Array (NE 44), 39–40, 43, 65–66, 68, 116, 222–23, 246, 319, 521–22

Nam-mkha'-dri-ma-med-pa'i-mdo, Sūtra of the Stainless Sky, 44

rNam-snang-mngon-byang, Mahāvairocanābhisambodhi, The Manifestation of Vairocana (NE 494), 121, 240

dPal-'byung-gi-rnam-thar, Śrīsambhavavimokṣa, The Story of Śrīsambhava, 43, 45. *See also* Gaṇḍavyūha

dPal-sbas-kyis-zhus-pa'i-mdo, Āryagupta-sūtra, Sūtra Requested by Śrīgupta, 72–73

dPas-byin-zhus-pa'i-mdo, Vīradatta-paripṛcchā-sūtra, Sūtra of the Questions of Vīradatta, 90, 246, 309

dPung-bzang-gi-zhus-pa, Subāhuparipṛcchā, Sūtra of the Questions of Subāhu (NE 805), 136

sPyod-yul-yongs-su-dag-pa'i-mdo, Sūtra on the Purification of Activity, 426–28

## Śāstra Tradition

b**Sh**es-spring, Suhṛllekha, Instructions from a Spiritual Friend, by Nāgārjuna (NE 4182), 59:63–64, 65:59, 71:60, 87:57, 89:56, 95:55, 122:8, 129:31, 129:42, 130:30, 136:66, 138:68, 139:68, 139:69–70, 152:77–78, 152:83–86, 154:87, 160:88, 160:91, 162:93–94, 162:95, 162:96, 163:97, 164:89–90, 173:102, 174:98–101, 175:74, 179:104–5, 188:52–53, 204:35, 224:34, 283:117, 316:68, 317:91–93, 424:14, 466:29, 475:7, 491:17, 507:13, 510:28, 511:117

**S**ems-'brel. *See* Byang-chub-sems-'grel

Slob-spring, Śiṣyalekha, Letter to a Disciple, by Candragomin (NE 4183), 66–67:63, 69:9, 70:64, 136–37:91, 137:93, 152–53:54–55, 153:55, 156–57:41–44, 159:52–53, 161:35, 161:40, 162:39, 169:19–20, 199:74–76, 240:96, 316:97–98, 510:15

b**S**am-gtan-gyi-chos-drug-rnam-par-bzhag-pa, Dhyānaṣaḍdharma-vyavasthāna, Presentation of Six Objects of Meditation, by Avadhūtipa (NE 3926), 228-31

b**S**lab-btus, Śikṣāsamuccaya-kārikā, Compendium of Training, by Śāntideva (NE 3939), 217, 232

## Texts of the Tibetan Tradition

**K**un-spang-lha-btsun-chen-po-mgur, 479

**Kh**a-rag-sgom-chung-gi-tho-yig, 103

Khyad-par-blo-sbyong-mtshon-cha'i-'khor-lo, The Wheel-Weapon of Self-Mastery, by Dharmarakṣita, 331:96–98, 371–76:9–48, 376:56–91

**G**u-ru'i-gter-lung, 203

Gyer-sgom-rdo-rje'i-glu, Song of Adamantine Meditation, by Maitriyogin, 332

m**Ng**a'-bdag-rgyal-po-la-gdams-pa-nyang-gter-smar-khrid, Advice to the King, by Orgyan Dusum Khyenpa, 361–64

mNga'-bdag-khri-srong-la-gdams-pa, Advice to King Trisong, 215–17

## *Sanskrit/Tibetan/English Title List*

**A**kṣayamati-paripṛcchā, Blo-gros-mi-zad-pas-zhus-pa'i-mdo, Sūtra Requested by Akṣayamati

Ajātaśatru-kaukṛttyavinodana, 'Gyod-bsal, Sūtra Dispelling the Grief of Ajātaśatru

Atyayajñāna, 'Da'-ka-ye-shes, Sūtra of Pristine Awareness

Adhyāśayasañcodana, lHag-pa'i-bsam-pa-bskul-ba, Appeal for Open-Minded Caring

Anityārtha-parikathā, Mi-rtag-pa'i-gtam, Teachings on Impermanence

Anantamukha, sGo-mtha'-yas-pa-sgrub-pa'i-gzungs, Dhāraṇī of Attaining Limitless Access

Abhidharmakoṣa, Chos-mngon-pa-mdzod, Treasury of Abhidharma

Abhidharmasamuccaya, Kun-btus, Compendium of Abhidharma

Abhisamayālaṁkāra, mNgon-rtogs-rgyan, Jewel of Realizations

Avataṁsaka, Phal-po-che, Flower Ornament Sūtra

Aṣṭasāhasrikā-prajñāpāramitā, 'Phags-pa-brgyad-stong-pa, Perfection of Wisdom in Eight Thousand Lines

**Ā**ryagupta-sūtra, dPal-sbas-kyis-zhus-pa'i-mdo, Sūtra Requested by Āryagupta

**U**dānavarga, Ched-du-brjod-pa'i-tshom, Udānavarga

**K**aruṇāpuṇḍarīka, sNying-rje-pad-dkar, The White Lotus

Karmavibhaṅga, Las-rnam-'byed, Classification of Karma

Karmaśataka, mDo-sde-las-brgya-pa, Karmaśataka

Kāśyapaparivarta, 'Od-srung-gi-le'u, Chapter of Kāśyapa

**G**aṇḍavyūha, sDong-pos-bkod-pa, Sūtra of the Ornamental Array

Garbhāvakrāntisūtra, mNgal-'jug-gi-mdo, Sūtra of Entering the Womb

Gurupañcāśikā, Bla-ma-lnga-bcu-pa, Fifty Verses on Devotion to the Lama

Gṛhapati-ugra-paripṛcchāsūtra, Khyim-bdag-drag-shul-can-gyis-zhus-pa'i-mdo, Sūtra Requested by the Householder Ugra

**Gh**anavyūha, rGyan-stug-po-bkod-pa'i-mdo, Sūtra of Majestic Adornment

**C**aturdharma-nirdeśa, Chos-bzhi-bstan-pa'i-mdo, Teaching of the Four Dharmas

Caturviparyayaparihāra-kathā, Phyin-ci-log-bzhi-spang-ba'i-gtam, Verses of the Four Abandonments

Catuḥśataka, bZhi-brgya-pa, The Four Hundred

Candrapradīpasūtra, Zla-ba-sgron-me'i-mdo, Lantern of the Moon Sūtra

Candrarāja-lekha, rGyal-po-zla-ba-la-spring-yig, Letter to King Candra

**T**athāgatagarbhasūtra, De-bzhin-gshegs-pa, The Tathāgata Sūtra

Tathāgathācintyaguhyanirdeśa, De-bzhin-gshegs-pa'i-gsang-ba'i-mdo, Secret Teaching of the Inconceivable Tathāgatha

Triśaraṇasaptati, sKyabs-'gro-bdun-cu-pa, Seventy Verses of Refuge

**D**amamūka, mDzangs-blun, Sūtra of the Wise and Foolish

Daśadharmaka-sūtra, Chos-bcu-pa'i-mdo, Sūtra of Ten Dharmas

Daśabhūmika, Sa-bcu-pa, Sūtra on the Ten Stages

**Dh**armadhātu-darśanagīti, Chos-kyi-dbyings-la-lta-ba'i-glu, Song of the Vision of Dharmadhātu

Dharmadhātu-stava, dBu-ma-chos-dbyings-bstod-pa, Praise of the Dharmadhātu

Dharmasaṁgītisūtra, Chos-yang-dag-par-sdud-pa'i-mdo, Sūtra Assembling the Dharmas

Dhāraṇī of Attaining Limitless Access, sGo-mtha'-yas-pa-sgrub-pa'i-gzungs

Dhyānaṣaddharma-vyavasthāna, bSam-gtan-gyi-chos-drug-rnam-par-bzhag-pa, Presentation of Six Objects of Meditation

Dhvajāgra, mDo-rgyal-mtshan-dam-pa, Sacred Victory Banner of the Dharma

Nītiśāstra, Lugs-kyi-bstan-bcos, Treatise on Wise Conduct

Pitāputra-samāgamana, Yab-sras-mjal-ba'i-mdo, Sūtra of the Meeting of Father and Son

Praṇidhānasaptati, sMon-lam-bdun-cu-pa, The Seventy Resolves

Pradarśanānumatoddeśaparīkṣā, 'Jam-dpal-gyi-lta-'dod-mdor-bstan

Pramāṇavārttika, rNam-'grel, Treatise on Logic

Bodhicaryāvatāra, Byang-chub-sems-dpa'i-spyod-pa-la-'jug-pa, Entering the Bodhisattva Path

Bodhicitta-vivaraṇa, Byang-chub-sems-'grel, Exposition of Bodhicitta

Bodhipathapradīpa, Byang-chub-lam-sgron, Lamp of the Path of Enlightenment

Bodhisattvapiṭaka, Byang-chub-sems-dpa'i-sde-snod

Bodhisattvabhūmi, Byang-chub-sems-dpa'i-sa, Stages of the Bodhisattva

Bodhisattvamaṇyāvalī, Byang-chub-sems-dpa'i-nor-bu'i-phreng-ba, Jewel-Garland of Bodhisattvas

Bhadracaryā-praṇidhāna-rāja, bZang-po-spyod-pa'i-smon-lam, Aspirations for Proceeding in Goodness

Mañjuśrīvikrīḍitasūtra, 'Jam-dpal-rnam-par-rol-pa, The Celebrations of Mañjuśrī

Madhyamakāvatāra, dBu-ma-la-'jug-pa, Entrance to the Middle Way

Madhyāntavibhaṅga, dBu-mtha', Madhyāntavibhaṅga

Mahāmāyātantrarāja, sGyu-'phrul-rtsa-rgyud, Mahāmāyā Tantra

Mahāyānasaṁgraha, Theg-bsdus, Review of the Great Vehicle

Mahāyāna-saṁgrahopanibandhana, Theg-bsdus-bshad-sbyar, Clarification of the Review of the Great Vehicle

Mahāyānottaratantra, Theg-pa-chen-po-rgyud-bla-ma, Commentary on the Uttaratantra

Mahārājakaniṣka-lekha, rGyal-po-ka-ni-ka-yi-sprin-yig, Letter to King Kaniṣka

Mahāvairocanābhisambodhi, rNam-snang-mngon-byang, Manifestation of Vairocana

Mahāsannipāta-ratnaketu,'Dus-pa-rin-po-che'i-tog, Precious Collection

Mahoṣṇīṣa, gTsug-tor-chen-po'i-mdo, Sūtra of the Magnificent Crown

Maitreya-paripṛcchā, Byams-pas-zhus-pa, Sūtra Requested by Ārya Maitreya

Maitreya-praṇidhāna, Byams-smon, Aspirations of Maitreya

Ratnakūṭa, dKon-brtsegs, Heap of Jewels

Ratnacūḍa-paripṛcchā, gTsug-na-rin-chen-gyi-zhus-pa'i-mdo, The Questions of Ratnacūḍa

Ratnamālā, Rin-chen-phreng-ba, The Precious Garland

Ratnamegha, dKon-mchog-sprin, Cloud of Jewels

Ratnarāśi, Rin-chen-phung-po'i-mdo, The Mound of Jewels

Ratnolkā, dKon-mchog-ta-la-la, Flaming Jewel Sūtra

Rājādeśa, rGyal-po-la-gdams-pa'i-mdo, Instructions to the King

Laṅkāvatāra, Lang-kar-gshegs-pa, Laṅkāvatāra

Lalitavistara, rGya-che-rol-pa, The Voice of the Buddha

Vinayāgama, 'Dul-ba-lung

Vinaya-vibhaṅga, 'Dul-ba-rnam-'byed

Vimalakīrtinirdeśa, Dri-ma-med-par-grags-pas-bstan-pa'i-mdo, The Teachings of Vimalakīrti

Vīradatta-gṛhapati-paripṛcchā-sūtra, dPas-byin-zhus-pa'i-mdo, Sūtra of the Questions of Vīradatta

Śikṣāsamuccaya-kārikā, bSlab-btus, Compendium of Training

Śiṣyalekha, Slob-spring, Letter to a Disciple

Śīlasaṁyukta-sūtra, Tshul-khrims-dang-ldan-pa'i-mdo, Sūtra Concerned with Moral Practice

Śokavinodana, Mya-ngan-bsal-ba, Opening the Hell Realms

Śrīsambhavavimokṣa, dPal-'byung-gi-rnam-thar, The Story of Śrīsambhava

Ṣaḍaṅgaśaraṇa, sKyabs-'gro-yan-lag-drug-pa, Six Branches of Refuge

Saṃcayagāthā, sDud-pa, Verse Summary of the Prajñāpāramitā

Saṃdhinirmocana-sūtra, mDo-dgongs-'grel, Sūtra of Pure Intent

Sambhāra-parikathā, Tshogs-kyi-gtam, Various Counsels

Saṃvara-viṃśaka, sDom-pa-nyi-shu-pa, Twenty Verses on the Vow

Saddharma-smṛty-upasthāna-kārikā, Dam-pa'i-chos-dran-pa-nye-bar-bzhag-pa-tshig-le'ur-byas-pa, Verses of Mindfulness of the Holy Dharma

Samādhirāja, Ting-nge-'dzin-rgyal-po, King of Samādhis

Samādhyagrottama, Ting-'dzin-mchog-dam-pa'i-mdo, Sūtra of Supreme Meditation

Sāgara-paripṛcchā, rGya-mtshos-zhus-pa'i-mdo, The Questions of Sāgara

Sāgaramati-paripṛcchāsūtra, Blo-gros-rgya-mtsho'i-zhus-pa'i-mdo, The Sūtra of the Questions of Sāgaramati

Siṃhaparipṛcchā, Seng-ges-zhus-pa, The Questions of Siṃha

Subāhuparipṛcchā, dPung-bzang-gi-zhus-pa, Sūtra of the Questions of Subāhu

Subhāṣita-ratnakaraṇḍaka-kathā, Legs-par-bshad-pa-rin-po-che-za-ma-tog-lta-bu'i-gtam, Precious Teaching Like a Jeweled Casket

Surata-paripṛcchā, Des-pas-zhus-pa, Questions of Surata

Suvarṇaprabhāsa, gSer-'od-dam-pa'i-mdo, Sūtra of Golden Light

Suhṛllekha, bShes-spring, Instructions from a Spiritual Friend

Sūtrālaṃkāra, mDo-sde-rgyan, Crown of Sūtras

Svapnacintāmaṇi-parikathā, rMi-lam-yi-bzhin-nor-bu'i-gtams, The Wish-granting Gem of Dreams

Hevajratantrarāja, brTag-gnyis, Hevajra Tantra

## *English\*/Tibetan Title List*

**A**bhidharma, Chos-mngon-pa

Advice to King Trisong, mNga'-bdag-khri-srong-la-gdams-pa

Advice to the King, mNga'-bdag-rgyal-po-la-gdams-pa

Appeal for Open-Minded Caring, lHag-pa'i-bsam-pa-bskul-ba

Aspirations for Proceeding in Goodness, bZang-po-spyod-pa'i-smon-lam

Aspirations of Maitreya, Byams-smon

Attainment of Pristine Awareness, Ye-shes-grub-pa

**B**odhisattvapiṭaka, Byang-chub-sems-dpa'i-sde-snod

**C**elebrations of Mañjuśrī, 'Jam-dpal-rnam-par-rol-pa

Chapter of Kāśyapa, 'Od-srung-gi-le'u

Clarification of the Review of the Great Vehicle, Theg-bsdus-bshad-sbyar

Classification of Karma, Las-rnam-'byed

Cloud of Jewels, dKon-mchog-sprin

Compendium of Abhidharma, Kun-btus

Compendium of Training, bSlab-btus

Crown of Realizations, mNgon-rtogs-rgyan

**D**hāraṇī of Attaining Limitless Access, sGo-mtha'-yas-pa-sgrub-pa'i-gzungs

**E**ntering the Bodhisattva Path, Byang-chub-sems-dpa'i-spyod-pa-la-'jug-pa

Entrance to the Middle Way, dBu-ma-la-'jug-pa

Exposition of Bodhicitta, Byang-chub-sems-'grel

---

\*English = English or Sanskrit, as cited in the text

**F**ifty Verses on Devotion to the Lama, Bla-ma-nga-bcu-pa

Flaming Jewel Sūtra, dKon-mchog-ta-la-la

Flower Ornament Sūtra, Phal-po-che

Four Hundred, bZhi-brgya-pa

**G**lorious Acts, Phag-gi-rtog-pa-brjod-pa

**H**eap of Jewels, dKon-brtsegs

Hevajra Tantra, brTag-gnyis

**I**nstructions from a Spiritual Friend, bShes-spring

Instructions to King Prasenajit, rGyal-po-gsal-rgyal-la-gdams-pa

Instructions to the King, rGyal-po-la-gdams-pa'i-mdo

**J**ātaka, sKyes-rabs

Jewel-Garland of Bodhisattvas, Byang-chub-sems-dpa'i-nor-bu'i-phreng-ba

Jewel of Realization, mNgon-rtogs-rgyan

Jewel Ornament of Liberation, Dam-chos-yid-bzhin-gyi-nor-bu-thar-pa-rin-po-che'i-rgyan

**K**armaśataka, mDo-sde-las-brgya-pa

King of Samādhis, Ting-nge-'dzin-rgyal-po

**L**amp of the Path of Enlightenment, Byang-chub-lam-sgron

Laṅkāvatāra, Lang-kar-gshegs-pa

Lantern of the Moon Sūtra, Zla-ba-sgron-me'i-mdo

Letter to a Disciple, Slob-spring

Letter to King Candra, rGyal-po-zla-ba-la-spring-yig

Letter to King Kaniṣka, rGyal-po-ka-ni-ka-yi-sprin-yig

**M**adhyāntavibhaṅga, dBu-mtha'

# Glossary/Index

**A**bhidharma, 61, 523–24

accumulation, 30, 39, 239, 241, 419ff. *See also* merit and wisdom.

addiction, 196ff

Ajātaśatru *Ma-bskyes-dgra* Son of King Bimbisāra, a devoted disciple of the Buddha and King of Magadha during the last years of the Buddha's life. While Ajātaśatru assumed the throne by trickery, causing his father's death, he later repented and became the Buddha's disciple. 291, 202–3

alcohol, 200, 202–3. *See also* intoxication

All-Knowing Lama *Kun-mkhyen-bla-ma*, 65, 98, 180, 190, 204, 242, 332, 480, 519. *See also* Longchenpa.

All-Knowing Lord of Dharma *Kun-mkhyen-chos-rje*, 65, 74, 488

Amitābha *sNang-ba-mtha'-yas* The Buddha of Boundless Light. One of the five dhyāni Buddhas; the head of the lotus family. 8, 11

Ānanda *Kun-dga'-bo* The Buddha's cousin and attendant. 62

anger, 144, 206, 481

Aṅgulimāla *Sor-'phreng* Promised enlightenment by an unscrupulous teacher if he killed one hundred people and made a rosary of

their fingers, Aṅgulimāla was finally saved by the Buddha and became a famous and holy disciple. His story is told in the Sūtra of the Wise and Foolish. 424–25

animals, 57, 59, 64, 116, 144–45, 147, 482, 510, 526, 529–32; as object of meditation, 311

antidotes, 31, 118–19, 129, 178, 23,199–200, 221, 231, 239, 245, 271, 276ff, 284, 361, 370; activating the, 371ff, 384, 423–24, 434, 495, 499, 529–30, 536; depending on the, 385ff, 510

Aparāntaka, 128

aperture of Brahma *Tshangs-bug*   The opening at the top of the head, approximately eight finger-widths above the hairline. 50, 406

appearances, 273–74, 289ff, 351, 362; as mind, 513

Arhat *dGra-bcom-pa*   In the system of the Lower Vehicle, Arhatship is the highest attainment, the culmination of the four states of perfections: stream-winner, once-returner, non-returner, and Arhat. In the system of the Great Vehicle, Śrāvakas and Pratyekabuddhas attain Arhatship when they reach the fifth of the five paths, the path of no-more-to-learn. Bodhisattvas who attain this path become Buddhas. 114–15, 127, 131, 233, 236, 239, 425, 432

Aro Yeshe Jungnay *A-ro Ye-shes-'byung-gnas* (10th c.)   Progenitor of the Dzogchen lineage according to the Khams method. Atīśa, when shown Aro's Theg-chen-rnal-'byor, praised it greatly. 72–73, 91

Ārya *'Phags-pa*   Exalted or saintly being, epitaph used for one who has attained the third of the Five Paths, the Path of Seeing. 142, 228, 324, 427

Āryadeva *'Phags-pa'i-lha*   Disciple of Nāgārjuna. 414

Asaṅga *Thogs-med* (4th c. C.E.)   Great Mahāyāna master whose works were the foundation of the Yogācāra school. 7, 342, 542

asceticism, 81, 215, 283, 436, 492, 540

aspirations for enlightenment, 40, 62, 269, 338, 448, 476

Aśvaghoṣa *rTa-dbyangs* (1st c. C.E.?)   Buddhist master and one of India's greatest poets. 83, 87, 113, 300, 316

Atīśa (982–1054 C.E.)   Also known as Dīpaṃkara or Jowojay (Jo-bo-rje). Invited to Tibet in 1042, he taught there until his death, found-

ing the spiritual lineage which was to become the Kadampa school. His teachings on self-mastery inspired all later works on this subject. 3, 7, 11–13, 43, 51, 60, 67, 104, 121, 250, 278, 300, 321, 323, 349, 417, 486–90, 495, 511, 515, 523, 539

Avadhūtipa (10th c.)   Also known as Maitriyogin or Maitripa, he was a student of the Mahāsiddha Virūpa and one of Atīśa's three main teachers. 228–29

Avalokiteśvara *sPyan-ras-gzigs*   One of the eight foremost Bodhisattvas; embodiment of enlightened compassion. 3, 319, 323, 344

**B**en Gung Gyal *'Ban Gung-rgyal* (11th c.)   A great lama who received the tradition of Saṁvara and the Kālacakra teachings from Padampa Sangyay. 131, 391

bardo *bar-do*   The period after death—anywhere from a moment to forty-nine days—before rebirth in one of the six realms. 97–98, 102, 149

basis-of-all *kun-gzhi*, 281. *See also* ground of being.

beliefs, 479, 487

Bhadra, story of, 289ff

bhikṣu *dge-slong*   Buddhist monk, a member of the Sangha. 80, 127, 134, 159, 232, 274, 290, 378, 452

birth, suffering of, 69, 141, 168–69

birthlessness, 264, 413

blame, accepting, 403–4

blo-rigs, 285, 548

Bodhi tree, 64

Bodhicitta, 7, 10ff, 217, 534; increasing, 260; practice of, 8–9, 48, 255ff, 295ff, 454ff; relative, 7, 266; two aspects of, 255ff, 334, 466, 498, 523, 535; ultimate, 7ff, 266–67

Bodhisattva *Byang-chub-sems-dpa'*   Lit: Hero of Enlightenment. Through great compassion and the practice of the six pāramitās, the Bodhisattva seeks to liberate all beings from samsara. 39; path of, 45, 73, 77, 115, 121, 213, 214; vehicle, 3, 228, 512–13

eighteen free and fortunate conditions, 62

elements *khams*    The elements (Skt: dhātu) are related to the senses and their relationship with both subject and object. Thus the eighteen dhātu: Eye, forms, eye-consciousness; ear, sounds, ear-consciousness; nose, smells, nose-consciousness; tongue, tastes, tongue-consciousness; body, tangibles, body-consciousness; mind, mental objects, and mind-consciousness.

emotional afflictions *nyon-mongs*, 26, 28ff, 119, 144, 146, 163–66, 172, 176, 178–79, 197, 385, 391, 491, 529; as manifestations of the Buddha, 415; transforming the, 343ff. *See also* kleśas.

enlightenment, 6, 26, 67, 167; and non-conceptual meditation, 322; path of, 39; seeds of, 33. *See also* Bodhicitta.

eternalism, 247, 385, 495, 539

environment, 118, 272

equanimity, 284, 310

exchanging self for other, 298ff, 359, 529

existence, nature of, 55, 56, 121, 133, 182, 257, 268, 270ff, 281, 293


**F**aith, 55–56, 59–62, 103, 107, 188, 249, 291, 364, 460, 511, 533

famine, 117

farming, 223, 227–28, 251, 497

Field of the Assembly *Tshogs-zhing*    A pure realm including your root lama and all the lamas of the lineage as visualized in Guru Yoga. 15

Five Degenerations *sNyigs-ma-lnga*, 539

five fortunate conditions; relating to own state of being, 59; relating to outside circumstances, 59–60

five obscurations, 29

Five Paths *Lam-lnga*    Path of preparation, path of linking, path of seeing, path of meditation, path of no-more-to-learn. 251, 341, 550

five poisons, 29, 193, 361, 384, 434, 465, 529–30, 533

Five Powers *sTobs-lnga*   Projecting resolve, familiarity, seeds of goodness, renunciation, and aspiration. 443ff, 451ff

five senses, 138, 169

five skandhas *phung-po-lnga*   Form, feeling, perception, motivational factors, and consciousness. 172

Five Treasures   Vast collections of the teachings compiled by the great Master Kongtrul: Shes-bya-kun-khyab; gDams-ngag-mdzod; bKa'-brgyud-sngags-mdzod; Rin-chen-gter-mdzod; and Thun-mong-ma-yin-pa'i-mdzod. 13

form, 273ff

form realm, 126, 174–75

formless realm, 174–75

fortunetelling, 361, 389, 423

four applications, 421ff, 437

Four Bases for Supernatural Power *rDzu-'phrul-gyi-rkang-pa-bzhi*   The sāmadhis based on willingness, mind, effort, and analysis. 251

four demons *bdud-bzhi*   The demons of the emotions, the aggregates, death, and divine delights. 214, 414

four dharmas, 225, 291

four dharmas of pure virtue   Although abused, you do not return abuse. Although made angry, you do not respond with anger. Although censured, you do not respond with criticism. Although struck, you never strike back. 444

Four Forces, 423–24

Four Foundations of Mindfulness *Dran-pa-nye-bar-bzhag-pa-bzhi*   Mindfulness of body, feelings, mind, and dharmas. 251

Four Immeasurables *Tshad-med-bzhi*   Love, compassion, joy, and equanimity. 225, 333, 362, 395

four joys of the mendicant, 211

Four Kāya *sKu-bzhi*, 411, 413–14, 436; as illusory appearance, 414. See *also* Kāya.

four liberating techniques, 401, 414

four limits *mu-bzhi*  These can refer to the four pairs of the Eight Extremes: production and cessation, eternalism and nihilism, coming and going, diversity and singularity, or to the set made up of production and cessation, eternalism and nihilism, existence and nonexistence, and appearance and emptiness. 122

Four Noble Truths *bDen-pa-bzhi*  These are the truths of suffering, the origin of suffering, the cessation of suffering, and the path. xvi-xvii, 61

four sessions of practice  Dawn, morning, afternoon, and evening.

freedom, 179, 187, 196

freedom and good fortune *dal-'byor*, 54ff, 221, 519; four aspects of, 58; waste of, 71

Gain and admiration, evils of, 225ff, 229

Gampopa *sGam-po-pa* (1079–1153)  Also known as Dwags-po lHa-rje (the Physician of Dwags-po). He was the main disciple of the great Yogin Milarepa. 13, 27, 107, 246, 251, 526

gandharva *dri-za*  Lit: eater of smells. A class of demigods. 214

garuda *mkha'-lding*  A huge eagle-like bird considered to be the natural enemy of snakes and snake-like creatures. Symbolically, enemy of the 'snake' of hatred. 175

geshe *dge-bshes*  Lit: friend of virtue. Term of respect given to those who have undergone rigorous scholastic training in the Kadampa or Gelugpa monastic order.

Geshe Tonpa. *See* Dromton.

giving, 237, 291, 336, 387, 475; unconditional, 339ff, 391, 451, 495, 533. *See also* Three Spheres of Action and Six Perfections.

Glang-thang-pa. *See* Lang Tangpa.

God, 472, 496

gods, 58–59, 64, 68, 81, 84, 167, 173–75, 214

Godtsangpa *rGod-tshang-pa* (1189–1258)  Master of the Drugpa Kargyud lineage. 51, 401, 513

Jātaka *sKyes-rabs*   Stories of the Buddha's previous lives as a Bodhisattva. 251, 298, 300, 330–31, 453, 454, 489, 549

jealousy, 123, 167, 172, 530–31

Jigmed Lingpa *'Jigs-med-gling-pa* (1729–1798)   Great Nyingma master who was instrumental in compiling the definitive Nyingma Gyudbum, or Collection of Nyingma Tantras. He catalogued the texts and wrote a definitive history of the Nyingma lineage. 45

Jina *rGyal-ba*   Lit: Victorious One. Epithet of the Buddha.

Jonangpa *Jo-nang-pa*   Tibetan Buddhist sect now subsumed under other traditions, founded at Jonang by Kunpang Thugjay Tsondru (Kun-spang Thugs-rje-brtson-'grus) (b.1243). Associated with the practice of the Kālacakra-tantra, the Jonangpas formulated a unique system of yoga following the Five Treatises of Maitreya. 444


**K**adampa *bKa'-gdams-pa*   Lineage of Tibetan Buddhism originating in the eleventh century with the teachings of Atīśa, emphasizing moral discipline and the practice of compassion. While the Kadampa School itself was subsumed under the Gelugpas, its influence has been felt in all the schools of Tibetan Buddhism. 3, 13, 43, 64, 347, 463, 479

bKa'-babs-bdun. *See* Seven Streams of Transmission.

Kaliyuga, 8, 36, 287, 357, 359ff, 509, 539

kalpas, dark, 58, 259

Kapilavastu   Capital of the Śākya clan; the Buddha's early home. 68

Kargyudpa *bKa'-brgyud-pa*   Founded by Marpa Chogyi Lodro (Mar-pa Chos-kyi-blo-gros 1012–1097), who began his studies with Drogmi ('Brog-mi) in Tibet and received the lineages of Maitripa and Nāropa in India. There are four great and eight minor sub-sects.

karma, 55, 58, 61, 69–70, 74, 92, 96, 98, 103, 109ff, 145–46, 149, 167, 170–74, 176, 201, 215, 238, 248–49, 268, 272, 279, 288, 298ff, 313–15, 318, 331, 334, 338–39, 346, 348, 367, 371ff, 383, 388, 400, 509, 539, 540; accumulated, 124, 128, 130; completion, 125–26; force of, 423; four alternatives, 126; intention and field, 127; maturation of, 116ff, 130, 299ff, 493–94; projecting, 125–26; ripening of, 130; special features of, 127; three types of virtuous, 128; unpolluted, 126

**M**ādhyamika *dBu-ma* Lit: Middle Way, the highest Mahāyāna school of philosophy, propounded by the great master Nāgārjuna. 13, 157, 293

magic, 361, 380, 494

Mahākāla *Nag-po-chen-po* Wrathful deity and protector. 404

Mahāmudrā *Phyag-rgya-chen-po* Lit: Great Seal. One of the main Vajrayāna practices of the Sarma schools. 51, 485

Mahāyāna *Theg-pa-chen-po* Lit: Great Vehicle. *See* Vehicle. 7, 38, 235–36, 240, 249, 260, 430, 476

Maitreya *Byams-pa* Lit. Loving Kindness. Maitreya is considered a Tenth-Stage Bodhisattva and the coming Buddha. 3, 7, 11, 225–26, 228, 246, 286, 324

Maitreyanātha Lit: Protector Maitreya. Author, through Asaṅga, of the works known as the Five Treatises of Maitreya: the Abhi-samayālaṃkāra, Sūtrālaṃkāra, Madhyāntavibhaṅga, the Dharma-dharmatāvibhaṅga, and the Uttaratantra. 175, 293

Maitriyogin *Byams-pa'i-rnal-'byor* A master of the Vajrayāna, he was one of Atīśa's three main teachers. 11, 300, 332. *See also* Avadhūtipa.

mandala, 15, 44, 116, 293, 349, 416, 422–23, 446

Mañjuśrī *'Jam-pa'i-dbyangs* Lit: Sweet Melody. One of the eight great Bodhisattvas. Mañjuśrī embodies wisdom and is usually de-picted holding a book and a sword. 3, 7, 12, 25, 273

Mantra, 51, 84, 199, 260, 263, 389, 424, 431, 484, 492, 498

Mantrayāna, 47, 431, 472–73, 477

Māra *bdud* Chief of the gods of the highest heaven in the desire realm, and so lord of the whole realm of desire; also known as the demon Māra, the tempter of the Buddha. 3

Marpa Chogyi Lodro *Mar-pa-chos-kyi-blo-gros* (1012–1097) Great translator and founder of the Kargyudpas. 46, 480

Mātṛceṭa Great Buddhist poet and disciple of the Master Āryadeva. 359

motivated application, 368ff; concentration, 358, 401ff; on relative Bodhicitta, 368ff; on ultimate Bodhicitta, 413ff

motivation, 114, 116, 125, 214, 234, 237, 269, 305, 333

Mount Meru *lHun-po*   The highest mountain in the world, considered the center of the world. 137–38, 161, 177, 265, 315, 370

mudrā *phyag-rgya*   Lit: hand gesture. Mudrās are different placements or gestures of the hands employed while teaching or in meditation.

Muni *Thub-pa*   Lit. Sage. An epithet for the Buddha.


**N**āga *klu*   Snake-like beings who generally reside in oceans or lakes. While some are destructive and cause illnesses, others are great Dharma Protectors. 70, 204, 214, 505

Nāgārjuna, 7, 28, 59, 87, 187, 245, 265, 316, 323, 329, 347, 370–71, 393–95, 466, 482, 550

Naljorpa, 75, 104. *See also* Khyungpo.

Namkay Nyingpo *Nam-mkha'i-snying-po*, 300

Nanda *dGa'-bo*   The Buddha's cousin who became the Buddha's disciple and gained Arhatship after conquering his feelings of attachment. 331, 424

Nārāyana *Sred-med-bu*   God known for great strength.

natural mode of abiding, 29, 281, 520

Ngawang Dragpa *Ngag-dbang-grags-pa*, 221

Ngog, 12

nihilistic views, 151, 159, 351, 539

Nine Vehicles (yāna).   In the Mantrayāna traditions, the path of the Bodhisattva is closely related to the classification of the Buddha's teachings into three broad categories: the External Teachings and the Outer and Inner Tantras. The External Teachings correspond to the Śrāvaka, Pratyekabuddha, and Bodhisattva yānas; the Outer Tantras correspond to the Kriyā, Caryā, and Yoga yānas; and the three classifications of the Inner Tantras correspond to the Mahāyoga, Anuyoga, and Atiyoga yānas. 215, 216, 263

Nirmāṇakāya *sPrul-sku*   The Manifestation Body through which a Buddha appears in the world to work for the welfare of all beings. 414. *See also* Kāya.

nirvana *myang-ngan-las-'das-pa*   The profound peace gained once self-grasping comes to an end. While the followers of the Lower Vehicles can gain a form of nirvana, because they do not destroy certain subtle impediments to understanding, they later must return to the world to obtain the complete nirvana of the Buddha. 31; non-abiding, 31, 38, 67, 122, 143, 213, 217, 275, 351, 363

non-abiding, 275, 436

non-arising, 275, 277, 306, 351, 413, 436

non-cessation, 275, 436

non-conceptual, 271, 294, 307

non-dual pristine awareness, 30

non-virtue; consequences of, 63ff, 132ff

Nyingma *rNying-ma*   Generally referring to the Buddhist lineages that came to Tibet before the time of Atīśa. The foremost Nyingma master is considered to be Padmasambhava.

Objects of desire, 137, 197ff, 222, 229, 235, 415, 534

obstacles, 361, 417, 425; clearing away, 231–32

Oḍḍiyāna   A land located in Northwest India, Oḍḍiyāna was Padmasambhava's birthplace and the focal point of many of the Vajrayāna teachings.

offerings, 419ff, 476, 527

old age, 69, 86, 87, 90, 91, 100, 101, 139, 141, 143, 169, 221

omniscience, 44, 352

open-minded caring, 40, 190

openness *stong-pa-nyid*, 29–30, 33, 180, 266ff, 286, 293, 296, 349, 357, 399, 437, 446–47; of appearance, 258–59, 264–65, 411, 413, 429–30; as compassion, 350, 447; of openness, 277

Orgyan Dusum Khyenpa  *O-rgyan Dus-gsum-mkhyen-pa* (1110–1193)
Founder of the Karma Kargyud school and a disciple of Gampopa.
121, 143, 262, 322, 361, 423, 426

Orgyanpa  *O-rgyan-pa*  (1229–1309)  Also  known  as  Drubchen
Orgyanpa (Grub-chen O-rgyan-pa). Master of the lineages of both
Drugpa and Karma Kargyud schools, he was a direct disciple of
Dusum Khyenpa, the first Karmapa lama. The Orgyanpa school is
based on his teachings. 433

**P**adampa *Pha-dam-pa*  Also known as Padampa Sangyay (Pha-
dam-pa Sangs-rgyas). A Mahāsiddha who, in the eleventh century,
popularized the Zhijed (zhi-byed) and Chod (gcod) teachings in
Tibet. 73, 101, 104, 176, 397, 432–33, 446–47, 485

Padma Laydreltsal  *Padma Las-'grel-ltsal*, 98

Padmasambhava *Padma-'byung-gnas*  Lit: Lotus Born, considered
by many the second Buddha. Born in Oḍḍiyāna, he was invited to
Tibet by King Trisong Detsen at the behest of the Abbot Śāntarakṣita.
3, 11, 36, 46, 215–16, 258, 428, 464, 479, 484–86, 513, 527–30, 533. *See
also* Great One of Oḍḍiyāna.

Pagmo Drupa *Phag-mo-gru-pa* (1110–1170)  Disciple of Gampopa
and founder of the Pagdru Kargyud, one of four main Kargyud sub-
schools. 107

Paltrul Rinpoche  *dPal-sprul Rinpoche*  (1808–1888)   Also known as
Shri Gyalpo (Śrī rGyal-po) or Paltrul Orgyan Jigmed Chogyi Wangpo
(dPal-sprul O-rgyan 'Jigs-med-chos-kyi-dbang-po). He is the inspired
author of the Kun-bzang-bla-med-zhal-lung, an important work on
preliminary practices. 250, 432

pāramitās. *See* perfections and six pāramitās.

pāramitā of wisdom, 276–77, 286

Parinirvāṇa   Complete and perfect nirvana.

path *lam*  For those of the Lower Vehicle there are four: Stream-
winner, Once-Returner, Non-Returner, and Arhat. 30, 35, 57. *See also*
Five Paths.

path of aspiration, 237

residual patterns, 272, 336

responsibility, 296, 352, 493

result, 125ff; fourfold, 116, 122, 127; corresponding to cause, 116–17, 123; fully matured, 116, 122; magnified, 118, 123–24; of ownership, 117–18, 123

retaliation, 491–93, 499

retreat, 64, 230, 233, 386

retribution, 129, 313ff, 405ff, 416, 447

right and wrong, 490

Rinpoche *Rin-po-che*   Lit: Precious One, a title given to incarnate Lamas or great teachers.

rishi   Adept of great wisdom and long life. 81, 83, 333, 360

ritual, 231


Sakya Paṇḍita (1187–1251)   Also known as Kunga Gyaltsen (Kun-dga'-rgyal-mtshan), he was a great master of the Sakya school. 46, 139, 172

Śākyamuni, 46. *See also* Buddha.

Sakyapa *Sa-skya-pa*   The tradition founded at Sakya by Khon Konchog Gyalpo (Khon dKon-mchog-rgyal-po) that emphasizes teachings of the Path and Result.

Śākyas   The Buddha's countrymen. 68

Śākyaśrī (1127–1225), 347, 401, 486

samādhi, 81, 98, 175, 230, 268, 283, 285, 325, 395, 476, 504, 513

Samantabhadra *Kun-tu-bzang-po*   Lit: All-Good. The primordial Buddha of the Dharmakāya. 44

Sambhogakāya *Longs-spyod-sku*   Manner in which a Buddha manifests to highly realized beings. 414

sameness, 44

Samling, 514

samsara *'khor-ba*　Lit: wheel. The 'wheel' of existence character-ized by the suffering beings must go through in life after life. 7, 219, 234–35; degeneration of, 190ff; great power of, 460ff; identity with nir-vana, 236; suffering of, 134ff; uprooting, 367

Sangha *dGe-'dun*　Lit: Community of Virtue. A Sangha is com-posed of practitioners of the Buddha's teachings who uphold the model of mindful and virtuous action and a harmonious way of life. 3, 115, 118, 186, 312, 422

Śāntarakṣita *Zhi-ba-'tsho* (fl. 8th c.)　Indian master invited to Tibet by King Trisong Detsen to create a Tibetan Sangha. He was also known as the Great Abbot Bodhisattva. 3, 11, 250, 482

Śāntideva *Zhi-ba'i-lha* (8th c.)　Foremost scholar and siddha whose teachings on the path of enlightenment are unexcelled. 80, 95, 111, 119, 121, 197, 208, 218, 224, 272, 275, 277, 283, 292, 300, 312, 314, 328, 340, 391, 394, 417, 445, 447, 477, 489, 507, 515, 517, 531–33

Śāriputra　Disciple of the Buddha. 261–62, 274

Sarma *gSar-ma*　Lit: new. Refers to Tibetan Buddhism after the time of Atīśa. The main Sarma, or New Schools, are the Kargyud, Sakya, and Gelug.

Sautrāntika *mDo-sde*　One of the four great philosophical schools, known for being based solely on the teachings propounded in the Sūtras. 157, 300

Scriptures, 81, 83

Se Chilbupa, 51

self, 29, 132, 177, 197, 219, 258–59, 269, 386, 390, 435; conquering of, 406; grasping, 176, 301, 329, 368–70, 376ff, 388–89, 392, 462, 465, 467, 529–32, 540; identity, 218, 234, 300, 461; lack of, 265

self-destruction, 382ff

self-mastery, 3, 19, 26–27, 257, 260, 178ff, 231, 266, 269, 329, 341, 402, 463, 466–67, 484, 489, 494–95, 501ff, 528, 535, 539–40; five motivating factors, 93ff; guidelines for, 505ff; measuring progress, 457ff; as way of life, 439ff

self-nature, no, 49, 237–38

self-sacrifice, 121, 326, 337, 534

selfless love, 234ff

selflessness, 237–38, 369; of person, 238–39, 293; of phenomena, 238–39, 293

sense-fields *skye-mched* The six sense organs and six sense objects. 141

senses, 55, 179, 199ff, 235, 273ff, 303, 426, 529

Serlingpa, 12, 51, 300, 329, 539

Seven Essentials, 7, 15, 18–19, 47, 51

seven fires of sandalwood, 149

seven forms of consciousness The five sense consciousnesses, a mental consciousness, and the ālayavijñāna (kun-gzhi-rnam-shes), or mind-basis-of-all. Some schools of Buddhism accept only the first six, while other schools accept an eighth, the kliṣṭamanas (nyon-yid), or emotionally afflicted mind. 281

Seven Gestures, 453, 548

Seven Greatnesses of the Mahāyāna Seven things are greater for a follower of the Great Vehicle than for a follower of the Lesser Vehicle: great thought and aim (dmigs-pa-chen-po), great attainment of the purpose of self and others (sgrub-pa-chen-po), great awareness (ye-shes-chen-po), great effort (brtson-'grus-chen-po), great skillful means (thabs-mkhas-chen-po), great achievement (yag-dag-'grub-pa-chen-po), and great charismatic activity (sangs-rgyas-'phrin-las-chen-po).

Seven-Limbed Practice *Yan-lag-bdun* Homage, presenting offerings, confessing harmful actions, delighting in wholesome actions, urging teachers to preach the Dharma, urging enlightened ones not to pass into nirvana, and dedicating all merit earned to the enlightenment of all beings. 16, 18, 49, 422

seven precious gems *rin-chen-sna-bdun* Gold, silver, turquoise, coral, pearl, and sapphire. 340

Seven Streams of Transmission *bKa'-babs-bdun* These consist of transmitted precepts (bka'-brgyud), earth treasures (sa-gter), reconcealed treasures (yang-gter), mind treasures (dgongs-gter), recollected treasures (rjes-su-dran-pa'i-gter), pure vision (dag-snang), and hearing lineage of realization (snyan-brgyud). 13

Three Vows   The Prātimokṣa vows of the Lower Vehicle, the Mahāyāna vows of a Bodhisattva, and the Vajrayāna vows of a vidyādhara. 477ff, 495, 509, 537. See also vows.

Three World Realms   *Khams-gsum*   The samsaric realms of desire, form, and formlessness. 79

Tilopa (988–1069)   Also known as Telopa. An Indian Mahāsiddha, guru of Nāropa, and father of the Kargyud lineage. 486

time, 76; beginningless, 519

Tīrthika   *mu-stegs-pa*   A person who holds heretical views. 186, 300

tobacco, evils of, 203

Togmed   *Thog-med* (1295–1369)   Also known as Gyalsay Togmed (rGyal-sras Thog-med) or Togmed Zangpo (Thog-med-bzang-po). Gyalsay Rinpoche was trained mostly in the Sakya tradition and became known for his manifestation of Bodhicitta. 318

Tong Len   *gTong-len*   Lit: giving and taking. Unconditional giving and taking on all suffering. 391, 402ff

torma   *gtor-ma*   Offerings, often in the shape of stupas, made out of barley and butter. 421–22, 425, 448

tranquility   *zhi-gnas*   Śamatha meditation. 271, 279ff, 350. *See also* meditation.

transfer of consciousness, 50, 451ff. *See also* Phowa.

transforming adversity, 355ff, 368, 508

trichiliocosm   A universe comprising 1,000 million world-systems, with suns and moons, heavens and hells and the like. 64

Trisong Detsen   *Khri-srong-lde-btsan*   Eighth-century king of Tibet who invited the Indian masters Śāntarakṣita and Padmasambhava to the Land of Snow. 3, 215–17, 250, 258

truth, 106; nature of, 30, 110, 499, 510

rtsa   Lit. vein, the 'channels' through which the 'rlung' or life-force flows through the body. 273

tsa-tsa   Small clay images of Buddhas and Bodhisattvas and the like. 422

witness, 110, 463–64

worldliness, 8, 68, 69, 81, 219, 226–31, 249, 312–13, 317, 430, 463, 466, 482, 519

wrong views, 114, 117–18, 123, 381


**Y**akṣas, 214, 405

Yamarāja *gShin-rje*   Personification of impermanence and death. 97, 153, 225

Yang Gonpa *Yang-dgon-pa* (1213–1258)   Great Kargyud practitioner and teacher. 526

Yaśas   A noble youth who, after a night of debauchery, came upon the Buddha and became one of the Buddha's earliest and most devoted disciples.

Yerpa Zhangtsun *Yer-pa'i-zhang-btsun* (11th c.)   A disciple of Atīśa. 107

Yeshe Od *Ye-shes-'od* (10th c.)   King of Gu-ge who took monastic vows. At the time the Dharma had nearly disappeared in Western Tibet, Yeshe Od was instrumental in seeing that Tibetan monks were sent to India to be trained. His nephew, Jangchub Od (Byang-chub-'od), invited Jowo Atīśa to Tibet. 12

Yidam   A personal deity, essentially a form of the Buddha, ultimately inseparable from the mind, and employed as a support for visualization and meditation practices in the Mantrayāna. 49, 115, 425, 515

yoga, 212, 350, 479–80, 503; yogins, 201, 273, 445

Yogācāra, 13, 523


**Z**hang Gomripa, 513–14

Zhang Zhungpa, 541

Zhechen Gyaltsab, x–xv, 7, 15, 26, 55, 208, 269

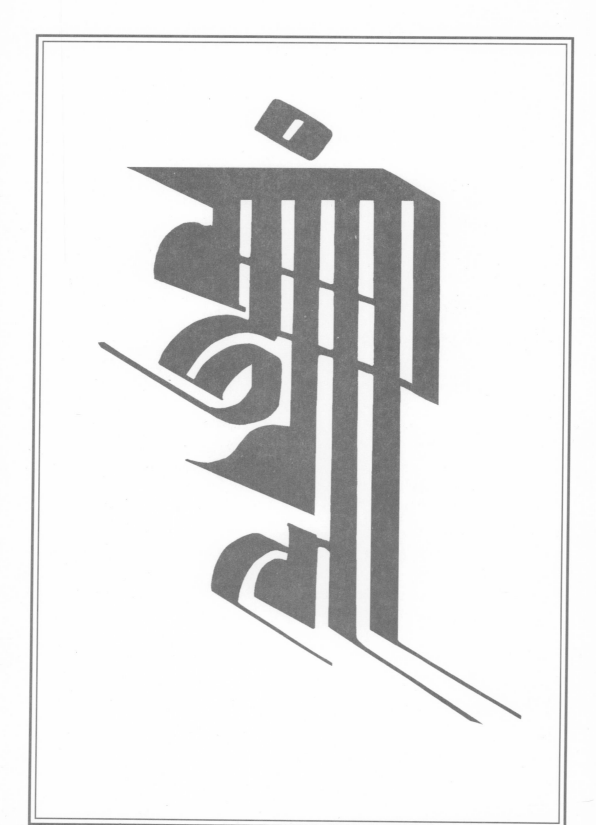

Śrī Vaiśravaṇa